W9-AOY-586

POPE JOHN XXIII

BY THE REV. PAUL C. PERROTTA

The Life of Blessed John of Vercelli

Catechism on the Religious State

POPE JOHN XXIII

His Life and Character

BY

Reverend Paul C. Perrotta, O.P.

THOMAS NELSON & SONS

Edinburgh NEW YORK *Toronto*

Nihil Obstat:
Dennis Bernardine McCarthy, O.P., S.T.Lr., Ph.D.
Edward Raymond Daley, O.P., S.T.Lr., J.C.D.

Imprimi Potest:
William Dalmatius Marrin, O.P., P.G., S.T.D.,
Prior Provincial of St. Joseph's Province

Nihil Obstat:
Right Reverend Monsignor,
Peter B. O'Connor
Censor Librorum

Imprimatur:
The Most Reverend
✠Thomas A. Boland,
Archbishop of Newark

 Published in New York by Thomas Nelson & Sons and simultaneously in Toronto, Canada by Thomas Nelson & Sons (Canada) Ltd.

Library of Congress Catalog Card No.: 59-9189

MANUFACTURED IN THE UNITED STATES OF AMERICA

Contents

Preface

ONE of the most extraordinary events of our time has been the universal and genuine homage paid to one man, Pope Pius XII, in his life and death.

The industry with which reporters gathered every scrap of news about him, and the avidity with which the reporting was read by the public bespeak the deep impression he made on the world. Catholic and non-Catholic, alike, recognized in him an exceptional man of our age, a man who had singularly devoted himself to the task of making men good, of safeguarding peace, and of bringing humanity to a greater consciousness of its dignity as made in God's image. He held an office unique in the world, and the most exalted possible: he was the Vicar of Christ. He was a prophet, priest and king; he was Bishop of Rome, the spiritual head of all humans baptized in the name of Christ. Some of them denied him obedience, but no one could deny him respect. Combining with his exalted office an exceptional intellect and warmth of person, he achieved one great objective in life: he brought the papacy to the highest position of honor it had ever enjoyed from the non-Catholic world. Men saw in him the strongest force working for the peace of the world and for the forging of a better bond of human brotherhood. He enriched his time, and as President Eisenhower put it in his cable of condolence, "the world is poorer now for his passing."

In an atmosphere of great sadness over his death, the deathless Church proceeded to the task of choosing a new shepherd of Christ's flock. In canonical procedure, eighteen days after the death, which had occurred on October 9, 1958, the Sacred College of Cardinals met in conclave on October 26, the feast of Christ the King, to choose the successor of Pius XII. Fifty-one cardinals participated. Two of them, Cardinals Costantini, Chancellor, and Mooney of Detroit, died in the interval between the death of Pius and the opening of the conclave.

After three days of balloting, on the twelfth ballot, taken Tuesday, October 28, the feast of Saints Simon and Jude, Apostles, the world learned that a successor had been chosen. A new Peter had been called to the supreme pontificate in the person of Angelo Joseph Cardinal Roncalli, who took the name of John XXIII.

This book is about this New Peter. The world, grown fond of news from the Vatican, wants to know as much as possible about the man chosen to fill the office vacated by the colossus, Pius. The world, worried about dark clouds in the horizon of peace, wishes to know what to expect from this new universal shepherd. Any man's life is interesting. The life of a new Pope should be highly interesting. "This is Your Life" may concern only the individual whose life is portrayed on television, but in the case of the Pope, his life becomes the life as well of all humans, for he holds in his hands a good bit of the destiny of the human race.

This book is not intended as an exhaustive, completely documented life of the new pontiff. Rather, it is written to appeal to the common man and to afford him an easy-to-read, popular life of the new occupant of Peter's throne. Neither is it intended to be controversial. It is simply a biography of the new Pope, with a description and explanation of the several bits of historical background and ceremonial ritual pertinent to his office. The Catholic will find in it an exposition of his Church's doctrine on the papacy, while the non-Catholic will be helped to understand better the part which a pope plays in the workings of the Church. Animosities largely spring from misinformation. It is hoped that the information contained in this book will bring about a more friendly relationship among all Christians.

The popular interest in the papacy today demands a popular history. It is good journalism to supply the demand of an eager public. The great biographies will appear in due time.

I want to acknowledge gratefully the help which the seniors of Caldwell College have given me in the marshalling of certain data and in typing. I include as well the librarian of Caldwell College and the librarian of Lacordaire School.

Particularly I wish to thank Father Benedict Joseph, O.P., who sent me from Rome the best journalistic accounts of the current papal events.

THE AUTHOR

pertinent to his office. The Catholic will find in it an exposition of his Church's doctrine on the papacy, while the non-Catholic will be helped to understand better the part which a pope plays in the workings of the Church. Animosities largely spring from misinformation: it is hoped that the information contained in this book will bring about a more friendly relationship among all Christians.

The popular interest in the papacy today demands a popular history. It is good journalism to supply the demand of an eager public. The great biographies will appear in due time.

I want to acknowledge gratefully the help which the seniors of Caldwell College have given me in the marshalling of certain data and in typing. I include as well the librarian of Caldwell College and the librarian of Immaculate School.

Particularly I wish to thank Father Benedict Joseph, O.P., who sent me from Rome the best journalistic accounts of the current papal events.

THE AUTHOR

POPE JOHN XXIII

❀ 1 ❀

Origination of the Papacy

PASTOR ET NAUTA! Shepherd and Sailor! This is the title given to the new Pope by Malachy, the Irish monk, whose remarkable prophecies on the Popes have claimed the attention and respect of papal historians. The prophecies have been fairly true in hitting the mark. Malachy wrote them about a thousand years ago, midway, as it were, between the origination of the papacy and its present incumbent. We shall see later how true the prophecy is of John XXIII, but what intrigues us at the start of his biography is the actual link his title has with the first Peter, a sailor appointed shepherd.

The Saviour of men, himself the Good Shepherd, came on earth to lay down his life for his sheep and, by his death on the cross, give them supernatural life. He came to save all men and, if they accepted him, to incorporate them by his death, into his own body, forming them into a distinct fold or body, mystical but true, of which he would be the everlasting head.

This visible body, as do all bodies, needed a head. The Saviour was that head and continues to be that head. In his plan, he was not to remain visibly on earth forever, but was to ascend corporeally into the heavens to take his rightful place at the right hand of God, his Father Almighty. From that vantage point, he would continue to direct the affairs of the Church, the spiritual kingdom he had founded. However, and this is the Catholic contention, in view of the need of the visible church for a visible head, he appointed, even before he became invisible, a visible head, a vicar, to act for him in his corporal absence over the members of the Church. Hardly anything in the New Testament is clearer than this definite appointment of a vicar. The Church of Christ's earthly days and the Church of the apostolic age clearly understood and accepted this appointment. It is a sad bit of private interpretation to choose to ignore or slight this clear action of the Master, while asserting fidelity to the written word.

Herein lies essentially the difference between Catholics and Protestants. The papacy is the rock of contradiction. All doctrinal and disciplinary differences have stemmed from and continue in this one point, while all commonness of theological tenets and moral principles dissipates itself in the refusal of the non-Catholic Christian world to recognize the action of Christ in appointing a vicar with power over his visible Church.

In order to understand to what John XXIII, the new Peter, succeeds, let us go to the first Peter. The homage which the Catholic world pays to John—a homage not merely of reverence but of submission to his authority—is not an unevangelical novelty developed by the Church, but is clearly discoverable in the gospels and in the historical evidence of the times.

John the Baptist, whose vocation it was to prepare the way of the Lord, preached to the manhood of Israel the gospel of penance. "Unless you repent you will all perish in the same manner." (Luke XIII, 5) Among those who heard these honest, vibrant words of the Precursor were the fishermen of Galilee, and among them particularly was Andrew, who became a disciple of John. Andrew had a brother named Simon. When John was asked, because of his purity of life and powerful preaching, if he were the Messias that was expected, he honestly replied: "No. I am the voice of one crying in the desert. I baptize with water, but in the midst of you there has stood one whom you do not know. He it is who is to come after me, who has been set above me, the strap of whose sandal I am not worthy to loose." The next day, John saw Jesus coming to him, and he said, "Behold the Lamb of God who takes away the sins of the world." (John I, 22-29) Upon this declaration of John, that Jesus of Nazareth was the Messias, Andrew became a disciple of Jesus. He told this to his brother Simon. "We have found the Messias," and Andrew led Simon to the Master. When Jesus saw this rugged fisherman-brother of Andrew, he said to him, "Thou art Simon, the son of John; thou shalt be called Cephas." (John I, 41-42) The name Cephas is Peter in our language. It is quite evident from this that Our Lord was already singling out Peter for a special mission, the hint of which was in the name bestowed upon him.

Whenever the list of the apostles is given in the New Testament, Peter's name is always cited first, even though Andrew became an apostle before Peter. In fact, Saint Matthew uses the word "first," referring to Peter. (Matthew X, 2) He is named first in all the gospels although he was not the oldest nor the most beloved. This is quite significant. It certainly shows that he enjoyed distinction.

Primacy can be considered in three ways: of honor, of direction, and of jurisdiction. It is quite contrary to the letter and sense of scripture to deny to Peter the primacy of honor and even of direction. Honor means to precede, direction means the right to preside, like a chairman, while jurisdiction means the right to command. Non-Catholic Christians, when pressed, will admit that Peter had the primacy of honor and of direction, but they vehemently deny that he had the primacy of jurisdiction. As said before, the heart of the whole difference between the Catholic world and the non-Catholic Christian world is this very matter: is Peter the legal superior and commander-in-chief of all the bishops, or just a *primus inter pares,* the first mentioned among equals? Because it will bring out the true nature of the office to which Cardinal Roncalli, now Pope John XXIII, has succeeded, it is advisable to discuss the question.

Truly, all partisanship aside, what other interpretation can be put on the following words of the Master? "Blessed art thou, Simon Bar-Jona, for flesh and blood has not revealed this to thee, but my Father in Heaven. And I say to thee, thou art Peter and upon this rock I will build my Church, and the gates of hell shall not prevail against it. And I will give thee the keys of the kingdom of heaven, and whatever thou shalt bind on earth shall be bound in heaven, and whatever thou shalt loose on earth, shall be loosed in heaven." (Matthew XVI, 17-19) It was a promise to confer the highest honor and the widest power as a reward for Peter's straightforward answer to the question Christ had put to his apostles: "What do men say the Son of Man is?" While some apostles had quoted others as saying that he was John the Baptist, or Elias, or Jeremias, or some other prophet, Peter forthrightly made the grand confession: "Thou art the Christ, the Son of the living God." (Matthew XVI, 13-16) Peter had commenced the role which the Popes, his successors, were to play throughout history: the ready announcers and staunch defenders of the divinity of Christ.

The promise made by the Master in the colloquy cited above in the district of Caesarea Philippi was amply fulfilled after his resurrection when, appearing to his apostles on the shore of Lake Genesareth (sometimes called Tiberias), He put to Peter a direct question: "Simon, son of John, dost thou love me more than these do?" Peter answered promptly: "Yes, Lord, thou knowest that I love thee." Christ then said to him: "Feed my lambs," and he immediately asked him again: "Simon, son of John, dost thou love me?" Peter repeated his confession: "Yes, Lord, thou knowest that I love thee." Once more Christ rewarded him with the charge: "Feed my lambs," and then for the third time he demanded to know if Peter loved him. Though disturbed by the frequency of the question, Peter again promptly answered: "Lord, thou knowest all things, thou knowest that I love thee." Peter's three-fold denial during his Lord's passion was at last atoned for by his three-fold confession. Christ was now satisfied and rewarded him with the grand commission: "Feed my sheep." (John XXI, 15-17)

Simple words indeed, "Feed my lambs, feed my sheep," but they have a profound significance. The divine shepherd is asking a man to feed his lambs, the virginal young of his mystical body, and his sheep, the mature faithful and officers of his flock. Why utter these words—Christ never uttered an idle word, and he always meant what he said—unless he meant just what they imply, namely, that Peter was to be his *alter ego* in the task of leading his flock to the green pastures of spiritual truth and grace, the only food proper for souls for whose salvation Christ had shed his blood? The citation of the rock, the conferring of the keys, the inference of the rope that binds or is to be loosened from the verse, "Whatever thou shalt bind . . . loose," are all clear indications of the will of Christ to make Peter his vicar in the government of the Church. The analogy of the rock, which had become his name, made Peter the cornerstone vicariously with Christ, the true cornerstone of the edifice which is the Church. The allusion of the keys indicates the authority with which he was invested, since keys always signify power and right to open or shut. Notice the confirmation of this grant in the words: whatever thou shalt bind, whatever thou shalt loose, shall be bound, shall be loosed in heaven. This is a clear bestowal of a primacy of jurisdiction, a personal responsibility in government.

True, as Matthew cites in XVIII, 18, Christ conferred this binding and loosening power on all the apostles, but to none except Peter did he give the designation of foundational rock or confer the keys of the kingdom of heaven.

This cardinal point of the exclusive primacy of Peter is borne out by other passages in the gospels. While all apostles were called to be fishers of men, Peter by name was told explicitly: "Henceforth, thou shalt catch men." (Luke V, 10) Christ asks Peter to pay the tribute "for me and for thee" with the coin taken from the mouth of the fish which Peter was to catch. (Matthew XVII, 26) Who is not impressed with the account of the washing of the feet at the Last Supper? Peter alone demurs: "Lord, dost thou wash my feet?" . . . "Thou shalt never wash my feet." But when Christ pointed out that if his feet were not washed he would have no part with the Master, Peter took back his protests and pleaded: "Lord, not my feet only, but also my hands and my head." (John XIII, 8-9) After his resurrection, Christ singled out Peter by appearing to him. (Luke XXIV, 33) Christ foretold the manner of Peter's death. (John XIII, 6) The crowning testimony is from the lips of the Saviour himself when he said: "Simon, Simon, behold Satan hath desired to have you that he may sift you as wheat, but I have prayed for thee, that thy faith may not fail; and do thou, when once thou hast turned again, strengthen thy brethren." (Luke XXII, 31-32)

After Our Lord ascended into heaven, Peter assumed the active government of the visible Church and no one questioned his authority to do so. He directed the election of Matthias to fill the place vacated by Judas. (Acts I, 15-26) After the Holy Spirit had descended upon the apostles, Peter preached the first sermon. (Acts II, 14) Peter sat in judgment on Ananias and Saphira. (Acts V, 4) Aided by revelation personally made to him, he received Cornelius into the Church, and thus began the expansion into the Gentile world. (Acts X and XI) It is significant that verse 48 of Chapter X says: "And he commanded them (the Gentiles) to be baptized in the name of the Lord Jesus Christ." It was he who presided at the first Council of the Church held in Jerusalem. Protestants are fond of citing that Saint Paul resisted Saint Peter. There would be no point in mentioning it by Saint Luke unless it meant that Saint Peter had the authority and it was novel for anyone to resist it. Saint Paul, upon his conversion, was anxious to meet Peter. (Galatians I, 18) This shows that Saint Paul accepted what was the common understanding in the Church: Peter was the visible head of the Church.

We have from tradition an abundance of evidence that this acknowledgment of the primacy of Peter, and of his successors after his death, was firm and universal. Surely no one can pretend that primacy in the Church was to end with Peter. The Church has a mission to minister to men to the end of time, and, as it needs a visible head armed with authority as in Peter's days, it needs equally such a head after Peter's days. Who should succeed to the primacy? Naturally, he who succeeded in Peter's post. Peter had taken as his See, first Jerusalem, then Antioch. Finally as history clearly testifies, he established his See at Rome. He was then the Bishop of Rome.

When he died, someone was elected Bishop of Rome, and thus he succeeded Peter in the primacy. It mattered not that the apostle John was still alive when Peter died in 67 A.D. The primacy did not pass to him. It passed to Linus who was elected to be the Bishop of Rome, and thus it has passed to each person elected to that particular post. A man is the Pope possessing the primacy of honor and jurisdiction precisely and primarily because he is the Bishop of Rome.

He assumes the office, the powers, and the character of Peter. He is always the Peter renewed.

Let us cite a few worthwhile, early instances of the acceptance of the Church that the Bishop of Rome was Peter renewed. In 96 A.D. Pope Clement, the second successor of Saint Peter, wrote to the Church of Corinth which was torn by schism: "But if some shall disobey the words which have been spoken by God through us, let them know that they will involve themselves in no small transgression and danger." (Patristic Writings; also in Harnack, Funk, Bardenhewer, Lightfoot, and others) Corinth did not question the authority behind the letter and the schism was composed. Saint Ignatius of Antioch, before his martyrdom in 107 A.D., wrote a letter to the Church of Rome calling it: "The President of the Bond of Love." Pope Victor I, (189-199 A.D.), in his dispute with the bishops of Asia Minor concerning the date of Easter threatened them with excommunication because they would not conform to the Roman decision of the date. Saint Irenaeus, the Bishop of Lyons, and others thought the action was too severe, and Pope Victor never did issue the decree of excommunication, while no one questioned his right to do so. This same Irenaeus in a memorable book, *Against Heretics,* calls Rome "the very great, the very ancient and universally known Church founded by and organized by the two most glorious apostles, Peter and Paul . . . and because of its pre-eminent authority, every Church . . . must agree with this Church." Saint Cyprian who differed with the Popes on several matters, nevertheless wrote glowingly of their authority. Here are a few excerpts from his letters:

"Cornelius was made bishop . . . when the place of Fabian, that is, when the place of Peter . . . was vacant."

"The African schismatics dare to set sail and bring letters to the throne of Peter and the chief Church, whence priestly unity came forth."

"One Church and one see, founded by the Lord's voice on Peter. No other altar can be set up, no new priesthood made, except the one altar and the one priesthood. Whoever gathers elsewhere scatters."

We have the case of the Patriarch of Alexandria who was denounced by his clergy to Rome. Pope Denis (259-268 A.D.) studied the protest with the Patriarch's defense and exonerated him of the charges. Socrates in his *Historia Ecclesiae,* II, 15, reported the following words concerning the illustrious Saint Anthanasius who with four other bishops had gone to Rome to seek redress against certain accusations: "When they had explained their cause to Julius, Bishop of the City of Rome, he sent them back to the East and restored each to his see, as is the prerogative of the Roman Church."

Saint Jerome, the great scripture scholar, with his usual straightforwardness, wrote these words to Pope Damasus who ruled from 366 to 384 A.D.

> I speak with the successor of the fisherman and the disciple of the cross. I, following no one as my chief but Christ, am joined in communion with thy holiness, that is, with the See of Peter. On this rock, I know that the Church is built. Whoever eats the Lamb outside this house is profane. Whoever is not in the ark of Noe will perish when the deluge comes. (Epistle XV, 2)

The provincial Council of Sardica, held in 344, formally acknowledged: "It seems best and most proper that the bishops from every province should refer to the head, that is, to the see of the Apostle Peter." (Harduin I, 653)

Although the first ecumenical Councils were held in the East attended by a majority of the bishops of that region, they all accepted the protocol that no Council was valid unless called by or approved by the Bishop of Rome, and presided over by himself or his delegate. No one objected when Philip, the papal legate to the Third General Council held at Ephesus in 431, stated:

> There is no doubt, indeed it is known to every age, that the holy and most blessed Peter, prince and head of the apostles, column of faith, and the foundation of the Catholic Church, received the keys of the kingdom from Our Lord Jesus Christ, Saviour and Redeemer of the human race; that to him was given power of forgiving and retaining sins, who to this time lives and judges in his successors. (Mansi IV, 1295)

Saint Ambrose, the great Bishop of Milan, summed it up classically and imperishably with his famous phrase: *Ubi Petrus, ibi Ecclesia,* Where Peter is, there is the Church.

To this clear and authoritative primacy, John XXIII falls heir. He is the new Peter, the shepherd and the fisherman in Christ, charged to feed the Master's lambs and the Master's sheep.

❁ 2 ❁

A Brief History of the Papacy

JOHN XXIII has fallen heir as well to almost two thousand years of memorable history. He is the two hundredth and sixty-first successor of St. Peter, a number spanning the years 29 to 1958. Every year of it has been eventful, and for more than fifteen hundred years of it, from the time in 313 when by the Edict of Milan the Church received recognition by Constantine, and Pope Sylvester I assumed politically among the nations his role as head of Christendom, world history has been inseparable from and largely influenced by the papacy.

The Acts of the Apostles, composed by St. Luke, one of the finest gems of history writing in world literature, gives us the brave beginnings of that timid flock left orphaned by the ascension of the Saviour. Christ had removed himself in visible presence, leaving his visible vicar. Ten days after his ascension, he sent the Holy Spirit to the frightened little flock huddled wonderingly in the cenacle. The fiery tongues of flame of the Holy Spirit which descended upon them changed the whole character of the band. From a cowering, fumbling, inept group of men and women it became a dynamic, fearless, eloquent and dedicated band. It announced itself openly as the flock of Christ. The Church that had been symbolized as created from the rent side of the Crucified as it gushed out blood and water, reminiscent of the manner in which Eve had been fashioned from the side of the sleeping Adam, was now officially born, and this is why Pentecost Day is regarded as the birthday of the Church.

Peter, whose previous cowardice had made him deny his Lord, now boldly faced the crowd that had poured into Jerusalem for the feast and by one simple sermon converted three thousand to the cause of Christ. Another sermon brought in five thousand, and more and more thousands by later sermons, and by sermons of the other Apostles. Jewish officialdom tried every means in the book to stop the flocking to the cross—threats, whippings, imprisonment, execution—but the newfound courage and eloquence of the apostles was irrepressible. "Their voice has gone forth into all the earth." No matter that many were put to death; ten others took the place of each one martyred. One of the great persecutors, Saul, himself became an ardent Christian, and as the Apostle Paul repaired magnificently his early damage to the Church.

After a little hesitancy, due to the tradition of his Jewish blood, Peter admitted the Gentile world into the ark of salvation, and so the Church went mightily forward in her mission of advancing the spiritual kingdom of Christ. By the time John, the last of the Apostles, died about the year 100, the Church was well-established in Asia Minor, northern Africa, the Balkan peninsula, Spain and Italy. John mentions seven dioceses of Asia in his Apocalypse, while St. Paul mentions several in Europe, chief of which was the diocese of Rome. This is suggested by his first Epistle and the noble tone in which it was written.

It is historically established that St. Peter, after having presided over the Church in Jerusalem and then at Antioch, went to Rome and officially made it his diocese. He was Bishop of Rome, and in that post and in that city he died a martyr's death on June 29, 67, a victim of Nero's wickedness.

After burying the martyred first Vicar of Christ in a recess of Vatican Hill, the Christians of Rome gathered to elect a successor. The choice fell on Linus, and Linus, as Bishop of Rome, was head of the Church, notwithstanding the fact that the great Saint John the Apostle was still alive. After eight years, Linus joined St. Peter in martyrdom, and so did twenty-two successors, Pope Denis in 268 alone dying a natural death. In the fury of the ten cruel persecutions of the Roman Emperors, the papacy went underground, but was able, nevertheless, to conduct the affairs of the universal church with amazing effectiveness. Heresies were denounced, doctrine was clarified, discipline was enforced, new bishops were consecrated and dioceses were established.

When Constantine issued in 313 his famous Milan decree granting freedom to the Church, the Pope, Melchiades, started a new era. His great successor in 314, Sylvester I, proved to be a fine type of administrator who expanded spiritually and materially the kingdom entrusted to him. The Church had emerged from the catacombs into the light of day and she was able to exercise more effectively her mission to apply the redeeming blood of Christ to all men. Sylvester started the building of some great churches: St. Peter's on Vatican Hill, St. Paul outside the walls, and his own cathedral, St. John Lateran, which he entitled: *Omnium Urbis et Orbis Ecclesiarum Mater et Caput,* the Mother and Head of all the Church of Rome and of the World.

The Christian Emperors following Constantine naturally were of great help to the papacy in its efforts to Christianize Asia, Africa, and Europe. However, they often proved a hindrance as well. One of them, Julian, apostatized and revived the old persecutions. Others of them tended to encroach on the spiritual power. The old Roman Emperors had been supreme in temporalities and spiritualities, the pontifex maximus office being a mere branch of the political power.

The Popes had to resist this tendency to make of the papacy a political branch subservient to the Emperor. Cruel conflicts ensued to the scandal and detriment of the Christian cause. At one point the Emperors actually abetted the very insidious heresy of Arius, which denied the divinity of Christ.

Slowly, however, the Emperor's power waned while the papal power strengthened. The barbarians were pressing hard on the decadent empire. People began to look for protection more to the Pope than to the Emperors whose legions were no longer able to stem the tide. Everyone remembers the story of Pope Leo going out to meet the dread Attila. In 476, the great Roman Empire fell. A barbarian made himself King of Italy, and the papacy had a new set of problems to face.

It faced them well. Calmly and persistently the Popes went about the task of making the barbarians Christian and of refining their manners and morals. They went through hard times doing it, but achieved many glorious moments as well. Out from Rome went the great missionaries, Patrick, Augustine, Boniface, and there were so many others, who, inspired by a Pope's word, went forth into infidel lands and brought so many into the Kingdom. On top of this problem of the barbarians came the cruel one of Mohammedanism, which, with savage rapacity, devastated the Church in Asia Minor, Africa, Spain and southern France. The night would have descended completely on the civilized world had it not been for the valiant effort of Popes to keep the Faith alive.

The Popes encouraged scholarship during this hard period, and while the world little appreciates what was done, calling the subsequent age a dark one, the fact is that learning did survive, thanks to the example and efforts of the Popes. Pope Gregory the Great, 590-604, himself a superb scholar, gave impetus to much literary production. It was he, incidentally, who inaugurated the phrase, thereafter employed by all Popes, to signify the true spirit of the papal office: *Servus servorum Dei,* The Servant of the Servants of God. Great schools of learning in Ireland, Switzerland, Germany, England, Scotland, France and northern Italy offset the encircling gloom. If the modern world still possesses the literary gems of classical antiquity, it has to thank the patient monks who transcribed them lovingly and thus preserved them under the encouragement of the papacy, which never forgot its mission "to teach all nations."

In between this battle of light against darkness, a Pope, Leo III, on Christmas Day of the year 800 crowned Charlemagne, a descendant of barbarians, Holy Roman Emperor. It was a most significant historic act, for it attempted to restore in Europe a strong, unifying political power, which it sadly needed to keep the wild elements that were roaming the continent in some semblance of order.

We mentioned the monks. The Popes had approved the consecration of men and women in religious living, secluded from the world. The Master had counselled the virtues of poverty, chastity and obedience. With papal approval, men and women took vows that bound them to a life of poverty, chastity and obedience. This institution of monasticism sanctified the lives of many, and brought innumerable benefits to the spiritual, intellectual and economic life of the Church. Celebrated in the early era was the Benedictine Order, founded by St. Benedict towards the beginning of the sixth century. Its chief house, Monte Cassino, became famous for its spirituality and scholarship, and it proved to be the seminary of many popes. Later, other monastic orders came into being, such as the Cistercians and Carthusians, which, while dedicating themselves primarily to personal sanctification, contributed vastly to the general welfare by achievements in letters and agriculture.

The fall of the Roman Empire in 476 had liberated the popes from being legal subjects of the crown. As we have seen, the Christian emperors, as well as the pagan ones, tended to regard the pope as a subject. It was not fitting that this should be so, since, as Vicar of Christ, he is chief in a field far more important than any temporal or political one, namely, the spiritual. If the person possessing supreme spiritual power is beholden to one possessing political power, he can be prevented from exercising his office. It was felt, then, that the pope should seek to be politically independent of any earthly sovereign, and it became the policy of the popes to achieve this independence. Charlemagne, the conqueror of France, Germany and Italy, agreeable to this plan of papal independence, deeded to the pope the territory around the City of Rome as a temporal domain. The pope thus became a temporal sovereign, and, as such, was independent of any political power. In the course of the years, the original grant of territory was enlarged. By the middle of the nineteenth century it had grown to a goodly size and separated the Kingdom of the Two Sicilies from the northern kingdoms or republics of the Italian peninsula.

The agitation for a united Italy, in the nineteenth century, era of revolutions, demanded either that the pope should become president of the whole peninsula or give up his temporal holdings. In the midst of the doubting and debating as to what should be done, the armies of Garibaldi in 1870 settled it practically by capturing Rome and taking over the papal states. The pope, Pius IX, kept maintaining his right to political sovereignty and made himself a voluntary prisoner in the Vatican in protest against the violation of his right. This unhappy situation, which hampered and embarrassed the papacy in its own home, was at last resolved when in 1929 the Lateran Treaty was signed by Premier Mussolini for Italy and Cardinal Gasparri for the papacy. By this treaty, the pope ceded to Italy all its former territorial holdings except the tiny territory of Vatican City. In this way, the pope retains his political independence, since he is sovereign of Vatican City, while the Italian people enjoy their territorial integrity.

Let us return now to the period when the nations of Europe were forming. The papacy faced very difficult times contending with distant kings on one hand, and with political factions at home on the other hand. The German Emperors were prepossessing; they wanted to dominate the papacy. In fact, it became the sport of all the kings to try to make the pope subservient. In every crisis, however, strong popes emerged like Martin I, Nicholas I, Leo IX and Gregory VII. This great pope, Gregory VII, forced the strong-willed German emperor Henry IV to kneel penitently in the snow at Canossa, and fairly settled for all time, though here and there it arose again, the vexing question of investiture of a bishop by a temporal ruler. He settled also the question of the celibacy of the clergy, remaining iron-willed, for all of his frail physique, against the forces within the Church which wanted to permit marriage or condone concubinage.

The crusades, one of the great epochs of human history, were inaugurated by the Popes. Urban II in 1095 approved and blessed the project of Christian armies marching to the Holy Land to redeem the sacred places then held in subjection and desecrated by Seljuk Turks. The first crusade succeeded and established a Christian kingdom in Palestine with Geoffrey of Bouillon as sovereign. However, it was short-lived. In 1144, the Turks overthrew the Christian kingdom and things in Palestine returned to their former wretchedness for Catholic pilgrims. The popes approved other crusades, eight in all.

Except for some sporadic victories, the eight were all miserable failures. However, they accomplished some good. The papacy, in the first place, began to be more and more recognized as the superior and unifying power in Christendom, able to command and to direct the kings to concerted action. Fine personalities emerged, such as Richard I of England,

St. Louis IX of France, Peter the Hermit, St. Bernard, Count Baldwin, and Frederick Barbarossa. Commerce was enlarged, the wisdom and fine manners of the East were brought to Europe, the knowledge of geography, of mathematics, and of many skills was increased, while a good motive of national spirit was aroused. Born, too, was a spirit of chivalry which did so much to bring grace and polish and nobility of action to peoples who were but a few generations away from crudeness and barbarism.

One thing happened before the crusades, which must be mentioned in this brief history of the papacy, because it vitally affected the papacy and has remained one of its chief sorrows. This was the withdrawal from its communion of the Greeks in 1054. The transference of the seat of empire by Constantine to Byzantium, and the growth of Constantinople with the commensurate decline of Rome, made many of the Greek bishops believe that Constantinople should hold the primacy in the Church. John the Faster, Bishop of Constantinople, in 583, had the effrontery to assume the title of universal patriarch, and despite the vehement protests of popes, the title was kept by the succeeding bishops of Constantinople. The Eastern emperors abetted the scheme of making Constantinople the chief city of Christendom.

The popes held firmly to the doctrine that the Church was founded on a stable rock and should not be subjected to the shifting sands of the political prestige of a city. Holding firm, they insisted on, and succeeded in having, the election to Eastern bishoprics confirmed by Rome. We thus come to the time of Photius, who in the pontificate of Nicholas I, 858-867, with the connivance of the Emperor, Michael III, deposed the rightful patriarch of Constantinople, Ignatius, and usurped his post. Wishing to make it "legal," he asked Nicholas I to confirm him in office. In his letter, Photius professed firm adherence to the true Faith and acknowledged the primacy of the pope. This profession of faith drew praise from Nicholas, but not confirmation. In fact, Nicholas excommunicated Photius. A weak pope, John VIII, 872-882, was prevailed upon to rescind the excommunication and grant the office to Photius. However, correcting his weakness, after seeing the true wickedness of Photius, John excommunicated him. Photius' animosity against Rome soon showed itself. He denounced the pope as an usurper of power over other bishops and as a heretic for upholding the term *filioque* in the Creed. The schism of Photius did not extend to all the Greek bishops, and after his death the breach healed.

However, in 1054, Michael Cerularius, Patriarch of Constantinople, brought about a complete break with Rome and from that year on to this, with the exception of a brief period after a reconciliation effected by the Council of Florence in 1439, during the pontificate of Eugene IV, the rift has remained. All popes have tried to bring the Greeks back to communion, but have failed.

The papacy reached the crest of its power during the reign of Innocent III, 1216-1227. The Christian kings acknowledged the pope as overlord and respected his decisions—unless they seriously interfered with their own national aspirations. It was a sort of united nations bound together by a spiritual bond. The bond was true but did not prevent wars and controversies, to the scandal of Christendom and the distress of the papacy, particularly when it involved the papacy in a war or rebellion. The feudal system provoked much unrest.

The thirteenth century has been called the greatest of the centuries. The papacy was dominant in Europe, spirituality was revived, two of the great Orders, the Dominicans and Franciscans, came into being, letters and arts flourished, and the whole Church was joyous in doing the manifold things required of a Christian civilization.

Then came a very sad period—the Babylonian captivity.

The aggressive French kings began to exercise an undue influence on the papacy and succeeded in having the popes transfer their residence to Avignon. For seventy-one years, seven months and eleven days, from the pontificate of Clement V in 1305 to that of Gregory XI in 1376, the popes lived in Avignon regrettably subservient to the French monarchs. Nor was the situation improved soon after Gregory XI courageously returned to Rome where he belonged. There started that other great distressful situation, the Western Schism, which saw Christendom divided among the claims of one anti-pope after another. For forty years, 1378 to 1417, most Catholics did not know who exactly was the legitimate pope. Modern history has cleared up the matter, although at that time it was difficult even for saints to know. The Church emerged from that awful crisis only to run into another soon after, and one of a most grievous nature, the Protestant Rebellion.

In 1517, Luther sounded the call to break away from the papal rule, and in time half of Europe obeyed that call. It was a most sorrowful time for the papacy, to see Germany, the Scandinavian countries, England, Scotland, with many in Holland, France, Switzerland and Italy recede from communion.

Valiantly, the papacy has tried its best to bring back the protesters. It convoked the great Council of Trent, 1545-63, which clarified many points of doctrine that had been at issue, and it revitalized the apostolic spirit in the Church. The Jesuit Order was approved specifically to counteract the revolt. The losses in Europe were compensated by conversions in Asia, but the secession of half of Europe from unity with Rome has continued to be a painful heartache.

There was no greater term of derision in Protestant England than that of "papist" to signify one who retained loyalty to the See of Peter. The Pope was the *bête noire,* the bugaboo, the definite objection of the reformers. Nothing he did was

Don Angelo Roncalli as he looked when he was a sergeant in the Medical Corps of the Italian Army in 1915, the only time he grew a mustache. *United Press International Photo*

The former Angelo Giuseppe Roncalli is the young priest in the center, flanked by unidentified fellow students. The picture was taken in Rome in 1901. *United Press International Photo*

Angelo Cardinal Roncalli walking in St. Mark's Square in Venice. *United Press International Photo*

Pope John XXIII served as Papal Nuncio to France. He received the traditional cardinal's red biretta from French President Vincent Auriol. *United Press International Photo*

good. He was painted as an evil tyrant intent on keeping the nations supine and enslaved. Even when he proposed so helpful a thing as the reform of the calendar, they refused for almost two hundred years to comply. We cite this not in animosity, but as a sad commentary on the fall of the papal office in the minds of many Christians from the high position it once held when all Europe was Catholic. Not even in the dark days of the tenth century when the papacy was the plaything of rival factions and disgraced by very unworthy occupants had the office dropped as low in the esteem of men as it did with the followers of Luther, Calvin, Zwingli, Knox and the other chieftains of the rebellion.

It has been the ardent aim of the post-reformation popes to win back to communion those who went away. At times a severe attitude seemed best, at times a gentle persuasion; at times mistakes were made and golden opportunities missed; but the desire has remained sincere to have them return to allegiance. This has been the chief problem of the papacy from Luther's day. Other problems came that required intense and immediate attention, such as the quarrel with Napoleon, the dispute with Bismarck, the danger from the Modernists, but the Protestant movement remains the chief concern. One fold under one shepherd is the cry of Christendom.

For the past hundred years the papacy has been graced by splendid men whose attainments in priestliness and intellectuality have largely restored the prestige the popes once enjoyed in the world. Pius IX was a model of courage; Leo XIII a brilliant luminary; St. Pius X the zealous pastor of souls awakening the Catholic world to the sweetness of the Bread of Life; Benedict XV a diplomatic genius during the horror of World War I, giving to the belligerents the acceptable bases of an honorable and permanent peace, although much of the credit for them was appropriated by Woodrow Wilson; Pius XI, the rugged Alpinist, who hammered hard against the social evils of his day; and, finally, Pius XII, universally esteemed for his spirituality and affableness. The encyclicals of these men will remain for all ages both as gems of literature and as a treasury of exalted theology, of inspiring morality, of solid economics, of splendid pedagogy and of far-sighted social science. At no time in the history of the Church has the *magisterium*, the teaching office of the papacy, been so brilliantly exercised. They wrote on an amazing variety of subjects, all pertinent to their times and all practicable for achieving the highest standard of Christian living.

Each pope is the heir of the labors of his predecessors. Pius XII added immensely to the riches he had inherited. Our present pope has had many before him in the high office he holds. It will be good to mention each of them as a natural sequence to this chapter.

❀ 3 ❀

The List of the Popes

POPE JOHN XXIII is known as the two hundredth and sixty-second Bishop of Rome. The listing of such a great number may appear to be dry and tedious, but in reality it should prove fascinating. A wealth of history surrounds each name. Each was a human being armed with great honor and power. His decisions affected the lives of many. It may be helpful to remember as we read his name in the following list that he was acclaimed by his contemporaries with the same enthusiasm with which we have greeted the person of John XXIII. Most of the names in the list are unknown to the general public, including Catholics, but each one was the focal point of the world in his day and his name will live forever in history whether he was a strong or weak pope, a holy one or a sinner, intellectual or mediocre. Each one was the Bishop of Rome, Vicar of Christ on earth for the period allotted by divine Providence, and as such is entitled to our respect.

In the majestic basilica of St. Paul outside the Walls, the portraits of all the Popes done in fine mosaic stand as colorful documents of the amazing dynasty which is the papacy. The following is the list drawn from these portraits as amended by later research. Lists of Popes differ by reason of some historians inserting the names of those who later proved to be anti-popes. There were thirty-seven anti-popes, the claims of most of them being clearly spurious, while in the case of a few it was rather difficult for the historian to determine their merit with precision. The list given below is the official one of the pontifical annuary. It may be found in our Catholic Directory and in many other directories and almanacs.

We have thought it would be of interest to add to the names not only the dates of their pontificate, but the exact length of their reign in years, months and days. These are from the best sources extant, although for the early popes it cannot be hoped that the citations are always accurate. We indicate as well if a pope achieved sainthood by the common abbreviation of St., and if he was a martyr by the letter M.

POPE	YEARS OF REIGN	DURATION IN YEARS, MONTHS AND DAYS	BIRTHPLACE
1. St. Peter (M)	29–67	38 years	Bethsaida, Galilee
2. St. Linus (M)	67–76	9– 3–11	Volterra, It.
3. St. Cletus (M) (Anacletus)	76–88	12– 1–11	Rome
4. St. Clement (M)	88–97	9– 2–10	Rome
5. St. Evaristus (M)	97–105	8– 7– 2	Antioch
6. St. Alexander I (M)	105–115	10– 7– 3	Rome
7. St. Sixtus I (M)	115–125	9– 3–21	Rome
8. St. Telesphorus (M)	125–136	11– 3–21	Greece
9. St. Hyginus (M)	136–140	4– 3– 8	Aquileia, Dalmatia
10. St. Pius I (M)	140–155	15– 3– 3	Aquileia
11. St. Anicetus (M)	155–166	8– 4–20	Syria
12. St. Soter (M)	166–175	9– 3–21	Fondi
13. St. Eleutherius (M)	175–189	14– 4– 5	Nicopolis, Epirus
14. St. Victor I (M)	189–199	10– 2–10	Africa
15. St. Zephrinus (M)	199–217	17– 2–10	Rome
16. St. Calixtus I (M)	217–222	4– 2–10	Rome

POPE	YEARS OF REIGN	DURATION IN YEARS, MONTHS AND DAYS	BIRTHPLACE
17. St. Urban I (M)	222–230	8–11–12	Rome
18. St. Pontian (M)	230–235	5– 2– 2	Rome
19. St. Anterus (M)	235–236	1– 1–10	Greece
20. St. Fabian (M)	236–250	13– 1–10	Rome
21. St. Cornelius (M)	250–253	3– 0–10	Rome
22. St. Lucius I (M)	253–254	1– 3– 3	Rome
23. St. Stephen I (M)	254–257	3– 2–15	Rome
24. St. Sixtus II (M)	257–258	1– 1– 6	Athens
25. St. Dionysius (M)	259–268	9– 3– 7	Greece
26. St. Felix I (M)	269–274	5–10–25	Rome
27. St. Eutychian (M)	275–283	8–10– 3	Tuscany
28. St. Caius (M)	283–296	13– 4– 9	Salona, Dalmatia
29. St. Marcellinus (M)	296–304	8– 4– 9	Rome
30. St. Marcellus I (M)	304–309	5– 2–25	Rome
31. St. Eusebius (M)	309	0– 7–21	Greece
32. St. Melchiades (M)	309–314	3– 7– 7	Africa
33. St. Sylvester I	314–335	21–10–27	Rome
34. St. Mark	335–340	2– 8–21	Rome
35. St. Julius I	341–352	11– 2– 6	Rome
36. St. Liberius	352–366	14– 7– 3	Rome
37. St. Damasus I	366–384	12– 2–10	Spain
38. St. Siricius	384–399	15–11–25	Rome
39. St. Anastasius I	399–401	2– 0–26	Rome
40. St. Innocent I	401–417	15– 2–20	Albano
41. St. Zosimus	417–418	1– 9– 9	Greece
42. St. Boniface I	418–422	4– 9–23	Rome
43. St. Celestine I	422–432	9–10– 9	Campania
44. St. Sixtus III	432–440	8– 0–14	Rome
45. St. Leo I	440–461	21– 1–13	Rome
46. St. Hilary	461–468	6– 3–10	Cagliari
47. St. Simplicius	468–483	15– 0– 6	Tivoli
48. St. Felix II	483–492	8–11–18	Rome
49. St. Gelasius I	492–496	4– 8–18	Africa
50. St. Anastasius II	496–498	1–11–24	Rome
51. St. Symmachus	498–514	15– 7–27	Sardinia
52. St. Hormisdas	514–523	9– 0–11	Frosinone

POPE	YEARS OF REIGN	DURATION IN YEARS, MONTHS AND DAYS	BIRTHPLACE
53. St. John I (M)	523–526	2– 9– 5	Tuscany
54. St. Felix III	526–530	4– 2–13	Benevento
55. Boniface II	530–532	2– 0–26	Rome
56. John II	533–535	2– 4–25	Rome
57. St. Agapetus I	535–536	1– 0–19	Rome
58. St. Silverius (M)	536–537	1– 0–12	Frosinone
59. Vigilius	537–555	18– 0– 0	Rome
60. Pelagius I	555–560	4–10–18	Rome
61. John III	561–574	12–11–26	Rome
62. Benedict I	575–579	4– 1–28	Rome
63. Pelagius II	579–590	11– 2–10	Rome
64. St. Gregory I the Great	590–604	13– 6–10	Rome
65. Sabinian	604–606	1– 5– 9	Volterra
66. Boniface III	607	0– 8–22	Rome
67. St. Boniface IV	607–615	8– 8–22	Valeria
68. St. Deusdedit (Adeodatus I)	615–618	3– 0–20	Rome
69. Boniface V	619–625	6– 0–10	Naples
70. Honorius I	625–638	12–11–17	Capua
71. Severinus	640	0– 2– 4	Rome
72. John IV	640–642	1– 9–18	Salona, Dalmatia
73. Theodore I	642–649	6– 5–19	Greece
74. St. Martin I (M)	649–655	6– 2–12	Todi
75. St. Eugene I	655–657	1– 7–14	Rome
76. St. Vitalian	657–672	14– 7–29	Segni
77. Adeodatus II	672–676	4– 2– 5	Rome
78. Donus I	676–678	1– 2–10	Rome
79. St. Agatho	678–681	3– 6–14	Calabria
80. St. Leo II	682–683	0–10–18	Catania
81. Benedict II	684–685	0–10–12	Rome
82. John V	685–686	1– 0–11	Antioch
83. Conon	686–687	0–11– 0	Thrace
84. St. Sergius I	687–701	13– 8–22	Palermo
85. John VI	701–705	3– 2–11	Greece
86. John VII	705–707	2– 7–17	Rossano
87. Sicinnius	708	0– 0–20	Syria

POPE	YEARS OF REIGN	DURATION IN YEARS, MONTHS AND DAYS	BIRTHPLACE
88. Constantine	708–715	7– 0–15	Syria
89. St. Gregory II	715–731	15– 8–23	Rome
90. St. Gregory III	731–741	10– 8–20	Syria
91. St. Zachary	741–752	10– 3–14	S. Severino
92. Stephen II	752	0– 0– 3	Rome
93. Stephen III	752–757	5– 0–29	Rome
94. St. Paul I	757–767	10– 0– 1	Rome
95. Stephen IV	768–772	3– 5–27	Syracuse
96. Adrian I	772–795	23–10–17	Rome
97. St. Leo III	795–816	20– 5–16	Rome
98. Stephen V	816–817	0– 7– 0	Rome
99. St. Paschal I	817–824	7– 0–17	Rome
100. Eugene II	824–827	3– 6– 0	Rome
101. Valentine	827	0– 1–10	Rome
102. Gregory IV	827–844	16– 0– 0	Rome
103. Sergius II	844–847	2–11–26	Rome
104. St. Leo IV	847–855	8– 3– 6	Rome
105. Benedict III	855–858	2– 6–10	Rome
106. St. Nicholas I	858–867	9– 6–20	Rome
107. Adrian II	867–872	4–10–16	Rome
108. John VIII	872–882	10– 0– 1	Rome
109. Marinus I	882–884	1– 5– 0	Montefiascone
110. St. Andrian III	884–885	1– 5– 0	Rome
111. Stephen VI	885–891	6– 9– 0	Rome
112. Formosus	891–896	4– 6– 0	Rome
113. Boniface VI	896	0– 0–15	Rome
114. Stephen VII	897–898	1– 2– 0	Rome
115. Romanus	898	0– 3–21	Gallese
116. Theodore II	898	0– 0–20	Rome
117. John IX	898–900	2– 0–15	Tivoli
118. Benedict IV	900–903	3– 2– 0	Rome
119. Leo V	903	0– 1–26	Ardea
120. Sergius III	904–911	7– 3– 0	Rome
121. Anastasius III	911–913	2– 2– 0	Rome
122. Lando	913–914	0– 6–10	Monterotondo

POPE	YEARS OF REIGN	DURATION IN YEARS, MONTHS AND DAYS	BIRTHPLACE
123. John X	914–928	14– 2– 3	Ravenna
124. Leo VI	928	0– 8– 5	Rome
125. Stephen VIII	928–931	2– 1–12	Rome
126. John XI	931–935	4–10– 0	Rome
127. Leo VII	936–939	3– 6–10	Rome
128. Stephen IX	939–942	3– 4– 5	Rome
129. Marinus II	942–946	3– 6–13	Rome
130. Agapetus II	946–955	10– 3– 0	Rome
131. John XII	956–964	7– 9– 0	Rome
132. Leo VIII	964–965	1– 2–25	Rome
133. Benedict V	965–966	1– 1–12	Rome
134. John XIII	966–972	6–11– 5	Rome
135. Benedict VI	973–974	1– 3– 0	Rome
136. Benedict VII	974–983	9– 5– 0	Rome
137. John XIV	983–984	0– 8–10	Pavia
138. John XV	985–996	10– 4–12	Rome
139. Gregory V	996–999	2– 8– 0	Germany
140. Sylvester II	999–1003	4– 1– 9	Aurillac, France
141. John XVII	1003	0– 4–25	Rome
142. John XVIII	1004–1009	5– 7–28	Rome
143. Sergius IV	1009–1012	2– 8–13	Rome
144. Benedict VIII	1012–1024	11–11–21	Rome
145. John XIX	1024–1033	9– 8– 8	Rome
146. Benedict IX	1033–1044	11– 0– 0	Rome
147. Sylvester III	1045	0– 0–21	Rome
148. Benedict IX	1045	0– 0–21	Rome
149. Gregory VI	1045–1046	1– 8– 0	Rome
150. Clement II	1046–1047	0– 9–15	Saxony
151. Benedict IX	1047–1048	0– 8– 9	Rome
152. Damasus II	1048	0– 0–23	Bavaria
153. St. Leo IX	1049–1054	5– 2– 7	Germany
154. Victor II	1055–1057	2– 3–15	Bavaria
155. Stephen X	1057–1058	0– 7–27	Germany
156. Nicholas II	1059–1061	2– 6–25	France
157. Alexander II	1061–1073	11– 6–21	Milan
158. St. Gregory VII	1073–1085	12– 1– 3	Tuscany

POPE	YEARS OF REIGN	DURATION IN YEARS, MONTHS AND DAYS	BIRTHPLACE
159. Victor III	1087	0– 4–26	Benevento
160. Urban II	1088–1099	11– 4–18	France
161. Paschal II	1099–1118	18– 5– 7	Bieda
162. Gelasius II	1118–1119	1– 4– 0	Italy
163. Callistus	1119–1124	5–10–12	France
164. Honorius II	1124–1130	5– 1–25	Italy
165. Innocent II	1130–1143	13– 7– 9	Rome
166. Celestine II	1143–1144	0– 5–13	Italy
167. Lucius II	1144–1145	0–11–14	Italy
168. Eugene III	1145–1153	8– 4–10	Tuscany
169. Anastasius IV	1153–1154	1– 4–24	Rome
170. Adrian IV	1154–1159	4– 8–29	Rome
171. Alexander III	1159–1181	21–11–22	Siena
172. Lucius III	1181–1185	4– 2–18	Lucca
173. Urban III	1185–1187	1–10–25	Milan
174. Gregory VIII	1187	0– 1–27	Benevento
175. Clement III	1187–1191	3– 3– 8	Rome
176. Celestine III	1191–1198	6– 9– 9	Rome
177. Innocent III	1198–1216	18– 6– 9	Italy
178. Honorius III	1216–1227	10– 8– 0	Rome
179. Gregory IX	1227–1241	14– 5– 2	Italy
180. Celestine IV	1241	0– 0–17	Milan
181. Innocent IV	1243–1254	11– 5–14	Genoa
182. Alexander IV	1254–1261	6– 5–13	Anagni, Italy
183. Urban IV	1261–1264	3– 1– 4	Troyes, France
184. Clement IV	1265–1268	3– 9–25	France
185. Gregory X	1271–1276	4– 4–10	Piacenza, Italy
186. Innocent V	1276	0– 5– 2	Savoy, Italy
187. Adrian V	1276	0– 1– 9	Genoa
188. John XXI	1276–1277	0– 8– 5	Lisbon
189. Nicholas III	1277–1280	2– 8–29	Rome
190. Martin IV	1281–1285	4– 1– 7	France
191. Honorius IV	1285–1287	2– 0– 1	Rome
192. Nicholas IV	1288–1292	4– 1–14	Italy

POPE	YEARS OF REIGN	DURATION IN YEARS, MONTHS AND DAYS	BIRTHPLACE
193. St. Celestine V	1294	0– 5– 8	Italy
194. Boniface VIII	1294–1303	8– 9–18	Anagni, Italy
195. Benedict XI	1303–1304	0– 8– 5	Treviso, Italy
196. Clement V	1305–1314	8–10–15	Villandreau, France
197. John XXII	1316–1334	18– 3–28	Cahors, France
198. Benedict XII	1335–1342	7– 4– 7	Saverdun, France
199. Clement VI	1342–1352	10– 6–29	France
200. Innocent VI	1352–1362	9– 8–25	France
201. Urban V	1362–1370	8– 1–22	France
202. Gregory XI	1370–1378	7– 2–28	France
203. Urban VI	1378–1389	11– 6– 6	Naples
204. Boniface IX	1389–1404	14–11– 1	Naples
205. Innocent VII	1404–1406	2–21– 0	Italy
206. Gregory XII	1406–1415	9– 6– 4	Venice
207. Martin V	1417–1431	13– 3–10	Rome
208. Eugene IV	1431–1447	15–11–20	Venice
209. Nicholas V	1447–1455	8– 0–19	Sarzana, Italy
210. Callistus III	1455–1458	3– 3–20	Spain
211. Pius II	1458–1464	5–11–26	Italy
212. Paul II	1464–1471	6–10–26	Venice
213. Sixtus IV	1471–1484	13– 0– 4	Italy
214. Innocent VIII	1484–1492	7–10–26	Genoa
215. Alexander VI	1492–1503	11– 0– 8	Spain
216. Pius III	1503	0– 0–26	Siena, Italy
217. Julius II	1503–1513	9– 3–21	Savona, Italy
218. Leo X	1513–1521	8– 8–20	Tuscany
219. Adrian VI	1522–1523	1– 8– 6	Utrecht, Holland
220. Clement VII	1523–1534	10–10– 5	Florence
221. Paul III	1534–1549	15– 0–28	Rome

	POPE	YEARS OF REIGN	DURATION IN YEARS, MONTHS AND DAYS	BIRTHPLACE
222.	Julius III	1550–1555	5– 1–16	Rome
223.	Marcellus II	1555	0– 0–26	Montepulciano
224.	Paul IV	1555–1559	4– 2–27	Naples
225.	Pius IV	1559–1565	5–11–15	Milan
226.	St. Pius V	1566–1572	6– 3–24	Bosco
227.	Gregory XIII	1572–1585	12–10–28	Bologna
228.	Sixtus V	1585–1590	5– 4– 3	Italy
229.	Urban VII	1590	0– 0–13	Rome
230.	Gregory XIV	1590–1591	0–10–10	Cremona
231.	Innocent IX	1591	0– 2– 0	Bologna
232.	Clement VIII	1592–1605	13– 1– 3	Fano
233.	Leo XI	1605	0– 0–27	Firenze
234.	Paul V	1605–1621	15– 8–12	Siena
235.	Gregory XV	1621–1623	2– 5– 0	Bologna
236.	Urban VIII	1623–1644	20–11–21	Florence
237.	Innocent X	1644–1655	12– 3–23	Rome
238.	Alexander VII	1655–1667	12– 1–15	Siena
239.	Clement IX	1667–1669	2– 5–19	Pistoia
240.	Clement X	1670–1676	6– 2–23	Rome
241.	Innocent XI	1676–1689	12–10–22	Como
242.	Alexander VIII	1689–1691	1– 3–27	Venice
243.	Innocent XII	1691–1700	9– 2–15	Naples
244.	Clement XI	1700–1721	20– 3–22	Urbano
245.	Innocent XIII	1721–1724	2– 9–29	Rome
246.	Benedict XIII	1724–1730	5– 9–23	Rome
247.	Clement XII	1730–1740	9– 6–25	Florence
248.	Benedict XIV	1740–1758	17– 8–16	Bologna
249.	Clement XIII	1758–1769	10– 6–27	Venice
250.	Clement XIV	1769–1774	5– 4– 3	Vado
251.	Pius VI	1775–1799	24– 6–14	Cesena
252.	Pius VII	1800–1823	23– 5– 6	Cesena
253.	Leo XII	1823–1829	5– 4–13	Genga
254.	Pius VIII	1829–1830	1– 8– 0	Cingoli
255.	Gregory XVI	1831–1846	15– 3–29	Belluno
256.	Pius IX	1846–1878	31– 7–23	Senigallia
257.	Leo XIII	1878–1903	25– 5– 0	Carpineto

POPE	YEARS OF REIGN	DURATION IN YEARS, MONTHS AND DAYS	BIRTHPLACE
258. St. Pius X	1903–1914	11– 0–16	Riese
259. Benedict XV	1914–1922	7– 4–20	Genoa
260. Pius XI	1922–1939	17– 0– 4	Desio
261. Pius XII	1939–1958	19– 7– 4	Rome
262. John XXIII	1958–		Sotto Il Monte

It is a good and glorious list including as it does eighty-two saints, thirty-two of whom were martyrs. It is impressive in its numerical total, length of years, diversity of names, and variety of national origins. While the Italian race predominates with a hundred and four Romans and a hundred from other parts of Italy, there is a fair sprinkling of Greek, German, French, Spanish, Syrian and African strains. There was one Englishman, one Hollander, and a Portuguese. St. Peter, of course, was a Jew. Furthermore, they differed sharply in individual traits. One cannot find a dynasty more varied in blood and qualities, nor one more unified and dedicated in spirit to the grand purpose of its origination. From Peter the Fisherman of Galilee to John the Farmer of Lombardy, the continuity is unbroken and the dedication is intact.

We shall be able to catch the truth of this by studying in some detail the life of the Pope who has but recently joined the papal fraternity whose two hundred and sixty-one members have had to render an account of their high stewardship before the bar of eternal justice. Pope Pius XII added immeasurably to the riches he had inherited from his two hundred and sixty predecessors. A careful review of his life should enable us to understand better the role which the present pope is expected to play as the new visible shepherd of Christ's flock.

❁ 4 ❁

The New Pope's Predecessor

THE question came to everyone's mind: can John fill the shoes of Pius? Pope Pius XII, the immediate predecessor of Pope John XXIII, grew to gigantic stature in the nineteen years of his reign. He won the admiration of the world for the spirituality that shone about him, for his exceptional talents of mind, and particularly for his warm, charming personality. The tall, thin, ascetic-looking pontiff had been piety personified, he had been the *Pastor Angelicus,* the Angelic Shepherd, as Malachy had prophesied, and he had equalled, if not surpassed, the intellectual standard of Pope Leo XIII.

For all of his gentle priestliness, he had shown great courage in guiding the flock through history's most devastating war. Despite the advice of his counselors to leave Rome when the eternal city was threatened with bombardment and when it was rumored that he would be captured and held as a hostage, he remained at his post valiantly trying to bring peace back to the world. He had helped much in bringing about this desirable state and he had done much to preserve it for the rest of his reign. The whole world hailed him as a giant in the great fields of human achievement: spirituality, statesmanship, diplomacy, letters, human relations. Men marvelled at his command of the sciences and languages; he was at home with aristocrats and with peasants, he discoursed with philosophers and was at ease with comedians. He was amazingly versatile and kept a firm grip in every phase of church government. His were big shoes, indeed, to be filled when he, the Angelic Shepherd, passed on.

How these shoes that John has to fill since 1958 grew from the baby shoes given to an infant in 1876 should prove of great interest to the world.

On March 2, 1876, a third child was born to Philip Pacelli and Donna Virginia Graziosi in an apartment house, called the Palazzo Pediconi, located at 34 Via degli Orsini, in the parish of Saints Celsus and Julianus, in the ward of Monte Giordano of the City of Rome, fairly near Saint Peter's.

The Pacelli family was noble but not rich. The father was a papal lawyer whose role it was frequently to take the cases of the poor before the Consistory. From 1886 to 1905 he served as a member of the Council of the City of Rome in which post he ably defended the rights of the Church in that period of pronounced anti-clericalism. The mother was a fine type of the Roman lady, gentle, courteous, and intensely pious. Their other children were Josephine and Francis.

The third child was baptized on March 4, two days after his birth, and given the name of Eugene Mary Joseph John by his grand-uncle, Father Joseph Pacelli.

A few years after the birth of Eugene, the family moved to a house in 19 Via Vetrina, in the same section of town. It was near the home of the famous musician, Lorenzo Perosi. His piano playing could be heard in the Pacelli household and it is surmised that Eugene's love of music was stimulated by his hearing the masterly playing of the celebrated Perosi.

The boy was thoughtful and serious from the start. He began his schooling under the Sisters of Divine Providence in the Rione Ponte section. In time he attended a sort of private junior high school in the Piazza di Santa Lucia de'Ginnasi under Professor Giuseppe Marchi. It became his custom to make a visit in the Jesuit Church nearby where there was a beautiful painting of the Madonna, the Madonna della Strada. The young boy would here pour out his heart to Mary and his deep Roman piety, the heritage of his family, thereby kept increasing. His deep devotion to the Mother of God was one of the glories of his life.

He had received the Sacrament of Confirmation at the age of five. On October 11, 1886, at the age of ten, he received his first Holy Communion in the Chapel of Saint Aloysius in the Palazzo Respighi, from the hands of the Cardinal-Vicar of Rome, Lucido Maria Parocchi. This first of Communions with the Christ whose Vicar he was to become remained a constant one and it is the sufficient explanation of the amazing force that actuated him in all his noble deeds.

The lad was very studious, his mind was keen, and he loved to delve into intellectually stimulating subjects. He needed glasses early. Though shy and reserved, he was not unsociable, and he participated somewhat in sports, loving particularly to take long walks, to hunt, swim, and ride a horse. He showed an early flair for theology, and he liked to "play the priest" before his family. He was conscious of the call of God to the altar and he planned all his studies with that grand objective in mind. He became an altar boy in the Chiesa Nuova, where Saint Philip Neri is buried, and proved punctual, circumspect and assiduous in his duties.

After finishing high school, he entered the Royal Ennio Quirino Visconti Lyceum, or college as we would call it. Like all lay schools of the period, it was anti-clerical in tone. Eugene stoutly defended the position of the Church among his freethinking comrades, kept tranquil in criticism, remained diligent in studies, and emerged a graduate *cum laude*. His first brush with the anti-Catholic world was a triumph.

At 18, in October, 1894, he began his priestly studies in the famous Capranica College. He took courses as well in the Gregorian University. He studied hard at both places, leading his class constantly, but the work proved too much for his frail physique, and he was forced to become a private student, living at home, an exceptional privilege. He studied also in the University of Rome.

On April 2, 1899, Easter Sunday, he was ordained a priest at a private ceremony in the chapel of the Patriarch of Antioch, Paul Cassetta, then Auxiliary Bishop of Rome, who ordained him. On the next day he celebrated his first Mass in the presence of distinguished prelates in the Pauline Chapel, sometimes called Borghese Chapel, because that chapel has a famous painting of Mary, the Salvation of the Roman People, likely the oldest picture of Mary and attributed to Saint Luke by tradition.

After his ordination, he attended for a while the famed seat of learning, the Apollinaris in Rome, and there received his doctorate in Canon and Civil Law. He was offered a canonry in Saint Mary Major, but he was advised by Cardinal Vanutelli to decline it. It was good advice since canons usually drop from sight of the world. At this point, Cardinal Gasparri, then Secretary of the Congregation of Extraordinary Ecclesiastical Affairs, offered the young nobleman the post of assistant in the Papal Secretariat of State. Father Pacelli mentioned to the Cardinal that his first preference was to do parish work, administering the Sacraments and having contact with the people. The Cardinal assured him that he would have a bit of time to do this along with his clerical work, and so the young priest accepted the assignment. It proved to be a momentous decision, for it made him familiar with the papal procedures and kept him under the eye of the highest officials. This was in 1901. He was a papal apprentice.

He performed his duties well. By 1904, he was officially a *minutante,* one who minutely made out a report on every document received by the papal court and who drafted a general reply. His latinity was excellent, his ideas clear and his exactitude admirable. Promotion was inevitable. He was made a papal chamberlain in 1903 and a domestic prelate in 1904.

In 1908, of special interest to us, he was offered the chair of Roman Law in the Catholic University, Washington. He wanted to accept, but again advice from high quarters made him decline. Cardinal Gasparri wanted his collaboration in the gigantic task of codifying Canon Law and this monumental work which saw the light of day in 1918 bore much of the stamp of the legal genius who was Eugene Pacelli.

On March 7, 1911, Monsignor Pacelli was appointed Assistant Secretary of the Congregation of Extraordinary Ecclesiastical Affairs. In May of 1911 he was sent to London, in company with Cardinal Pignatelli to represent the Pope at the coronation of King George V.

All the while he remained faithful to his priestly first love, the active ministry. He preached retreats to young ladies, was spiritual advisor of girls in the Cenacle in the Via della Stamperia, and was chaplain of the sisters, a post seldom desired by priests.

On June 20, 1912, Monsignor Pacelli was named pro-Secretary for Extraordinary Ecclesiastical Affairs and, by reason of that, Consultor of the Holy Office on November 25, 1912. On February 1, 1914, he became Secretary for Extraordinary Ecclesiastical Affairs. The shadows of the great war were starting to fall over Europe. On June 24, 1914, the Monsignor proved of great assistance to Pope Saint Pius X in concluding a concordat with Serbia. It was four days before the tragedy of Sarajevo which hurled the world into war.

Benedict XV became Pope on September 6, 1914, following the death of Saint Pius on August 20, the very day Monsignor Pacelli was appointed Substitute Secretary. The new

Pope bent every energy to effect a just peace among the warring nations, but no attention was paid to him until the war, after two years of copious bloodletting, reached a sort of stalemate in the trenches of France. The belligerents then began to listen to Benedict. Seeing a good opportunity to implant his ideas of peace, the Pope determined to send Pacelli to Munich as his nuncio. To this end, he himself consecrated the Monsignor as Titular Archbishop of Sardes on May 13, 1917, in the Sistine Chapel. Thus started a notable career in diplomacy.

His efforts with the King of Bavaria, Ludwig III, and with the Kaiser were promising of success, but the secret treaties which the Allied Powers had made thwarted the noble peace proposals of Benedict XV conveyed by Archbishop Pacelli. When Germany fell, the Archbishop at personal risk to his life remained at his post in Munich. He succeeded in having Rome adopt his plan to transfer the nunciature from Catholic Bavaria to Berlin, and he became the first nuncio to Germany. He worked hard to establish good relations with the Prussian government. He won the press and endeared himself to the people by his tact and gentleness. He achieved the signing of a "solemn agreement," a concordat in reality, despite Prussia's objection to the term, between Germany and the Holy See on June 14, 1929.

On December 16, 1929, the Nuncio was created a Cardinal by Pope Pius XI, and regretfully he left his foreign assignment. He left with the respect of all Germany amply expressed, and he left with a wealth of diplomatic experience that would prove invaluable later.

Nineteen-twenty-nine was the year that saw Cardinal Gasparri's greatest achievement, the reconciliation of Italy and the Holy See. Once that was accomplished, the great Cardinal desired to retire, and suggested to Pope Pius XI the naming of Cardinal Pacelli to succeed him as Secretary of State. The appointment came on February 7, 1930.

To this tremendous office, the Cardinal brought new lustre. He was indefatigable in work, astute in appraising situations, clever in his dealings with governments and sound in his counselling the chief. Throughout it all, he showed courtesy, calm, and exceptional charity. This author remembers reverently meeting Cardinal Pacelli on occasions in a quiet street of Rome as he took his walks. The Cardinal would doff his hat to me, a simple little friar, an action typical of his courtly nature.

The record of his office as Secretary of State is a splendid one. Outside of what may be classed as routine duties, whose nature despite the designation of routine is of so grave a character as to affect the welfare of all Christendom, the following are some of the special services he rendered before he became Pope.

In 1934, he went as papal legate to the Eucharistic Congress of Buenos Aires, and with his charm did much to strengthen the ties of Latin America with the Holy See. In 1935, he represented the Holy Father during the solemn Eucharistic Triduum in Lourdes which closed the Holy Year of Redemption. In 1936, he made his memorable trip to our country, still so affectionately remembered. He was hailed by popular acclaim as "The Flying Cardinal." People sensed that they were seeing the future Pope, and what they saw in him was all pleasing. In 1937, he travelled to France to inaugurate the Basilica erected in Lisieux in honor of the Little Flower, Saint Theresa.

Pope Pius XI died on February 10, 1939. It was the popular consensus that he would be succeeded by Cardinal Pacelli. The popular wish was realized when on March 2, the Cardinal's birthday, he was chosen by the Sacred College of Cardinals to be the new Bishop of Rome, taking the name of Pius XII.

This man whose name was peace, whose coat of arms bore the legend, *Opus Justitiae Pax,* Peace the Work of Justice, who spoke, prayed and planned constantly for peace, was destined to be Pope as the nations of the earth were girding for the most terrible war in human history. He faced the enmity of clever, powerful atheists, the ruthlessness of fallen-away Christian dictators, and the mania of war that had seized otherwise civilized peoples. He faced a Stalin, a Hitler, distinctly hostile; a Churchill and a Reynaud sneering and cynical; while at home in his own Italy he faced a disaster-fomenting Mussolini.

Still, calmly and patiently, he went about the task of alleviating the sorrows of war and of encouraging the efforts for peace. In his encyclical, "Summi Pontificatus," he lucidly indicated the Church's position—ally of no worldly power, but aid to all suffering humanity. He organized the Vatican as headquarters of active charity for all in the tradition of Benedict XV. The Holy See became the seat of sanity of the world amid the awful insanity of that disastrous war. We remember that our own American government recognized the power for good which the papal court represented, the vast extent and accuracy of the information it could gather, and so sent to it as special ambassador Myron C. Taylor. This eminent Episcopalian thereafter spoke glowingly of the manner in which he was received and of the help he secured in furthering American ideals.

The cessation of hostilities in 1945 did not free the Church from equally grave problems. Communism became strong, militant and overbearing. It ruthlessly took over several Catholic countries and began a cruel persecution of Catholic leaders both civil and religious. With great sadness, Pope Pius saw the harsh treatment meted out to Archbishops Stepinac and Beran and to Cardinal Mindszenty; distressfully he heard of the beatings, the imprisonment and the execution of so many of the faithful in the lands under the domination of the Hammer and Sickle. He strove manfully to arouse world opinion against the atrocities, but with little success since the democracies had no stomach to offend the Rampant Bear which is Russia.

Pius showed his far-sighted statesmanship and magnanimity of character by supporting the organization of the United Nations though this world body had rudely ignored his right to be represented in it. As we mentioned once before, the papacy in the Middle Ages had been the heart of the United Nations of Europe and had done fairly well in keeping the peace through the exercise of its spiritual authority. Although not a member, the papacy under Pope Pius XII has been a powerful friend of the United Nations and supports it in all the good it proposes for man.

In the primary concerns of the Church, the preservation and expansion of the Faith, Pius proved to be an inspired leader. His encyclical, "Humani Generis," in 1950, was a masterly exposé and defence of fundamental and pure Christian doctrine. He had proclaimed 1950 as a holy year and made it an instrument truly of enlarging the spirit of holiness in the Church. The millions who flocked to Rome during that year brought back with them a spark of his fine holiness. He proclaimed the doctrine of the Assumption of the Blessed Virgin, he proclaimed in her honor the Marian Year in 1954, he reminded the world of Lourdes and Fatima, and he dedicated the world to sanctification through the Immaculate Heart of the Mother of God. The greater devotion he inspired for Mary resulted in achieving its very purpose—to bring more to the love and service of Christ. He made clearer the ancient Catholic theory that devotion to Mary far from sidetracking the cult due to Christ actually increases it.

He concerned himself with foreign missions, and to his joy saw Africa making great strides in religion while notable gains were reported in Australia and Asia.

He canonized many, among them, very pleasing to us Americans, Mother Cabrini, an American citizen. He created cardinals in countries that had never been so privileged, and maintained the friendliest of relations in many non-Catholic countries. Our own Presidents knew they could rely on the word and friendly cooperation of Pius XII.

He was alert to the needs of education, the problems of economics, and the scope of science. He wrote and spoke learnedly on so many fields of human endeavor, secular as well as spiritual. He was aware of modern needs. His 1953 Constitution relaxing the ancient, rigid laws governing the Eucharistic fast will be remembered gratefully by the faithful who through it find easier access to the Bread of Life.

Likely, he will be remembered best for the audiences he gave. This author attended several. It is not easy to describe the respect and enthusiasm he engendered when he appeared on a balcony or was borne through Saint Peter's. All sensed that they were in the presence of a saint and his soft, gentle words made it easy for them to remember that he was the Vicar of the Good Shepherd.

He lived an austere life in the midst of papal pomp. The protocol of his high office demanded richness of apparel, an imposing residence, the luxury of richly-liveried attendants, but when he retired after all ceremonies and audiences with the great of earth, he retired to a simple study and simpler bed-room, the main feature of both being a prie-dieu. Here on his knees as a man before his God, with no flattery, or clapping, or vivas to be heard, he poured out his heart and begged for forgiveness for any fault he might have committed. Ancient popes had someone to go before them with smoking flax to remind them that all is vanity in the world. Pius needed not the flax to remind him that he was mortal. He had the deep humility of the saints from earliest days and he never forgot to be humble. The pomp of the papacy can be a powerful incentive to make a man forget his common mortality, and in weak persons it can make them feel personally superior to the common lot, but in Pius the grandiose externals never distracted him. He complied with the rugged ritual of tiara, heavy copes, incensations, bowing and scraping before him, but when he was alone, he was simple and humble.

When the news broke on October 4 of his sickness, not just because he was the Pope, but because he was a genius and a saint, the whole world stopped in its tracks and breathlessly followed every medical bulletin that was issued. When the sad news came on October 9—October 8 in the United States—that he had died, something died as well in every Catholic and friendly non-Catholic. There died the hope that they would ever see again the likes of him on this earth.

These are the big shoes that John XXIII has to fill.

❀ 5 ❀

Details of the Death of Pius XII and the Legacy He Left

THE death of a Pope is a momentous event which plunges the Church into an imposing round of ritual. It should prove interesting to narrate the details both of the death of the recent Pope and the duties that devolved thereby on the papal officials.

With the coming of October, the month of the Holy Rosary, Pope Pius began having a recurrence of hiccups which had almost taken his life four years ago. The best doctors were called in and they set about trying to correct or lessen the nervous disorder. However, early on Monday, October 6, he suffered a stroke which was medically described as a cerebral circulatory disturbance. He was partially paralyzed and incapable of speech. He was 82 years of age and his frail physique had been much weakened by days of hiccupping. The Vatican officials were greatly alarmed at his condition and saw to it that he was anointed immediately. This was done by a Jesuit. To the surprise of all, the Pope seemed to recover the next day. He could move his limbs and speak. He even took nourishment and discussed a few Church problems with his attendants.

However, a second stroke seized him at 7 A.M. on Wednesday, October 8, and his attendants became gravely concerned. The doctors reported that a cardio-pulmonary collapse was setting in. They did all that their medical skill would allow, but it was evident to them that death was near. The Church officials prepared for the worst. Into the room, with loving solicitude came the Pope's three nephews, the Princes Carlo, Marcantonio, and Giulio Pacelli; Count Enrico Galeazzi, special delegate of the Pontifical Commission for the State of Vatican City; Father Virginio Rotondi, S.J., from the nearby headquarters of the Better World Movement; Father Francesco Pellegrino, S.J., Vatican radio reporter, who kept the world informed hour by hour from the papal residence on the condition of the Holy Father; Sister Pasqualina, the Bavarian nun who had been in charge of the Pope's personal household; Giovanni Stefanori, personal valet of the Pope, and also his chauffeur, Mario Stoppa. The dignitaries in attendance were: Monsignor Tardini, Pro-Secretary of State for Extraordinary Ecclesiastical Affairs; Monsignor Angelo dell'Acqua, Vatican Substitute Secretary of State; Monsignor Federico Callori di Vignale, papal Master of Chambers; and Monsignor Mario Nasalli Rocca di Corneliano, papal privy chamberlain.

The moving, poignant prayers for the dying as found in the Roman ritual were recited. Fervently the apostrophes of the Litany and the impressive words of the oration poured out of the lips of all in attendance in supplication to God that he would yet spare his servant or grant him a peaceful death. In this atmosphere of prayer and reverence, the atmosphere in which Eugene Pacelli had found himself all his life, the great man breathed his last and his soul left the frail, emaciated body. It was 3:52 A.M. of Thursday, October 9, in Italy; Wednesday, October 8, 10:52 P.M. in America. It was in the second floor bedroom of his apartment in the papal summer residence at Castel Gandolfo. He was the first Pope in history to die at Castel Gandolfo. The summer residence had been intended for the health and relaxation of the Pope. It gave to Pius his death and his stiffening in *rigor mortis*.

As soon as he had breathed his last, the sorrowing prelates quietly knelt before the corpse, kissed a hand, and retired. The nephews and the nun wept. Wept as well the crowd that had gathered outside the Castel, and those that had assembled in St. Peter's plaza, and those in so many other parts of Italy together with the rest of Europe. There was weeping too in America, Asia, Africa, and Australia when the news reached these lands. The world wept in sincere grief at the passing of this great man. The mournful dirge tolled out by the bells of the Castel church and caught up by the carillons of St. Peter's, St. John's, St. Mary Major's, and St. Paul's in Rome with all the rest of the Eternal City, found a reechoing response of sadness in the hearts of millions of the faithful and even of millions of non-Catholics.

An iron rule of tradition governs almost every action performed by the Church officials when a Pope dies. All power of government reposes in the College of Cardinals collectively, but it makes no policy nor disposes of any case or problem unless it is of the most imperative nature. It simply administers the routine matters in the interregnum and in particular it is charged with the duty of arranging for the election of a new Pope in accordance with the legal procedures outlined in Canon Law or as decreed by constitutions promulgated by previous Popes.

The first duty of those in charge was to take care of the corpse. After the morticians had done their lugubrious work of embalming the body, the Franciscan Conventuals attached to the Basilica of St. Peter, as by long custom, took up their vigil in the death room. Among them was their American rector, Father Marcello Miller. These friars washed, then vested the corpse with the white cassock of a Pope. Over this they placed a red-velvet cape trimmed with ermine to cover the shoulders, red shoes on the feet, and the camauro, a red velvet cap, trimmed with ermine, on the head. They put a red, silk coverlet over the lower half of the body, folded the hands above this, and placed a rosary in the fingers. The corpses of all Catholics, low and high, hold rosaries in their hands; thus it becomes a fine symbol of the common brotherhood that is theirs, with Christ, as children of the Virgin Mother, the Queen of the Holy Rosary and of Heaven. Finally, they covered the face with a white linen cloth, and began their vigil of reverence in the death-room.

Officers of the Noble Guard in full dress flanked the bedstead standing at attention with unsheathed swords. Four large candle-holders with candles burning surrounded the bed. A kneeling bench, a prie-dieu, was placed beside the bed, and on a table at the head of the bed was placed a large crucifix and a silver holy water font with sprinklers.

Cardinal Tisserant, dean of the Sacred College, in lieu of the vacant post of camerlengo to which the ritual belonged, now performed the ceremony of officially verifying the Pope's death. Flanked by Swiss Guards and accompanied by the cardinals living in Rome with other officials of the Apostolic Chamber, and preceded by the mace bearers, carrying their maces turned to the floor in symbol of the vacant papal throne, he entered the death chamber and knelt at the prie-dieu beside the bed. He then recited the *De Profundis* and sprinkled the body with holy water. Rising, he removed the white linen cloth that covered the face of the dead Pope. With solemn dignity he addressed the body before him, as if presuming it to be alive and able to reply, using the baptismal name. Three times he called out: "Eugenio," and three times he received no response; and so Cardinal Tisserant officially declared the Pope to be dead. Formerly, it was the custom to strike the forehead with a silver hammer. Pope Pius XII himself had discontinued the custom when he acted as camerlengo verifying the death of Pope Pius XI. Instead, Cardinal Tisserant had simply sprinkled the body with holy water. This impressive picture was carried in most newspapers of the world.

The lay notary of the Apostolic Chamber, Guglielmo Felici, then read aloud the *rogito,* a formal document, composed in Latin, recounting the highlights of the life of Pope Pius XII ending with his death now formally verified. Cardinal Tisserant then ordered the Fisherman's ring of the Pope, along with other personal seals with which the Pope had authenticated important documents, to be brought to an assembly of cardinals and broken. This done, he signed the death certificate along with the attending physicians, the notary, the prefect of papal ceremonies, Monsignor Enrico Dante, and other prelates of the Apostolic Chamber.

A most regrettable action was committed by one of these attending physicians, Dr. Galeazzo Lisi. He sold to newspapers information on bedside incidents and words uttered in delirium. For this unethical conduct he was promptly dismissed from the staff of Vatican physicians. A few newspapers used his account but most refused to print it. In December, the Roman Medical Board removed his name from the list of licensed doctors.

After the official pronouncement of death, Monsignors Tardini and Dell'Acqua sent out official notifications of it to the Sacred College of Cardinals and to the diplomatic corps accredited to the Holy See and to the See's diplomats abroad.

Throughout the rest of that fateful morning there streamed into the death-room for a visit of respect a steady procession of cardinals, patriarchs, archbishops, bishops, abbots, generals of religious orders, and other high churchmen, together with officials of the Italian government and diplomats from many countries. Mass was offered in an adjoining room. The majesty of death has seldom been paid as fine an obeisance of a hushed room and a depth of genuine sorrow as attended the sleeping sovereign of the Vatican realm.

Later in the day the body was transferred to the Hall of the Swiss Guards in the Castel to accommodate the increasing flow of visitors. There it remained until the afternoon of Friday, October 10, when it was taken, accompanied by a small cortege, along historic Via Appia to the Pope's Cathedral, St. John Lateran. There, officials of the Italian government, led by Premier Amintore Fanfani, paid formal homage to the memory of the Pope, while the archpriest of the Basilica, Archbishop Luigi Traglia, gave absolution.

Then followed a memorable procession to St. Peter's. Along that four-mile route, its streets crammed with people, all paying their tribute of reverent silence, broken only by sobs that could not be repressed, a two-mile column of religious and clergy, high and low, marched in sad and measured stride to the great Basilica of the First Vicar of Christ.

The body was placed in front of the Altar of the Confession beneath the majestic dome of Michelangelo on a high bier, slanting downward from the altar. The Pope's body faced the people. Even in death the priest stood at the altar facing his flock.

The imposing Noble Guards took up their posts as guards of honor around the remains while twenty-four huge candles shed their eerie light. Countless thousands filed by the bier for one last look at the face they had loved so well. Pius XII had had many gay public audiences in St. Peter's. This one he gave in death was the most numerously attended and made the deepest impression.

On October 13, following the Requiem Mass attended by thousands, among whom were our President's official representatives, the Secretary of State, John Foster Dulles; Mrs.

Clare Booth Luce, former ambassador to Italy; and Mr. John A. McCone, head of the Atomic Energy Commission, he was laid to rest in a vault near the tomb of St. Pius X, a predecessor canonized by Pius XII. Before the actual entombment another embalming was done in line with a new process which is calculated to preserve the body for a hundred years. This may or may not be realized, but it is quite evident that his name will be preserved and lovingly venerated for the centuries to come.

Pius XII left a rich legacy of achievement. His actual last will impressed the world with its simplicity and directiveness. He bequeathed all he possessed to the Holy Roman See. His larger, unwritten bequest was to the flock in general and to the world.

He bequeathed first of all the spirit of peace. He breathed peace in every talk and action. His main diplomatic striving with the nations was to avert the impending war in 1939, the first year of his reign; to restore it to the world during the years of conflict following September 1, 1939; and to ensure its retention when the wars terminated in 1945. In the many tributes that poured into Rome from heads of governments after his death, all mentioned his persistent, valiant work for peace.

He left a legacy of alertness in, and sympathy for, modern needs of people. He was the provident pastor, quickly responsive to the cries of the persecuted, to the misery of the impoverished, the displaced, and the refugee, to the moanings of the sick and to the anguish of the depressed. His charity was unbounded. He gave freely of the resources of the Roman See, he expended his own personal money, and he encouraged the bishops throughout the world to conduct drives for the collection of money, medicines and clothing for the need of every race and creed. Peter's Pence liberally expended has kept many persons throughout the world alive and healthy.

He bequeathed the spirit of brotherhood and tolerance. He appealed to non-Catholics to join him in the crusade against Communistic Atheism; he received most affably the high and low of other creeds, and he encouraged them in all the good work they were doing for the causes of common decency and virtue.

He bequeathed a liberality of attitude towards modern techniques and ways. He approved of the airplane, the movies, TV, and even atomic energy and space flights. He allowed the physical beauties of Vatican City and its liturgical music and ceremonies to be preserved on film and soundtract of the TV camera for the enjoyment of millions who could not travel to Rome. He admitted freely actors and comedians to private audience, enjoying their quips and sometimes returning them. He was the most photographed personage of his time. He allowed this not for personal vainglory but as an instrument of informing an ignorant world that a pope was a human being without hoofs or horns.

He left us an amazing sense of the practical, a virtue seldom attributed to persons of so high a station. Medicine, education, science, politics, economics, labor were all special practical problems besetting his flock. He tackled these problems squarely, pointing out not only the moral ideals for each but their efficient functioning for the welfare of people.

He left us immortal documents to read and ponder over in his scholarly encyclicals. Therein his fine mind and priestly heart enshrined his best thinking on so many subjects, and with his own personal reputation for sanctity, we have a legacy that is wealth indeed for the Church and the world.

He had come to earth's highest office fairly well equipped for it. He left with a reputation for priestliness, for able administration, for leadership, and for personal piety that is admired by all. The papacy had been more liked and respected in the world by his four immediate predecessors. He brought the papacy to the pinnacle of its present popularity, evidenced by the avid interest with which peoples followed the news of his sickness, death and burial.

This is the richest legacy he has left us—a fulfillment of the prophecy of Malachy concerning him. He has left us the blessed memory of a Pastor Angelicus, an Angelic Shepherd.

Pope John XXIII with his brothers and sister on the day before his coronation on November 4, 1958. L. to R.: Giuseppe Roncalli, 64; Zaverio, 75; Pope John XXIII; Alfredo, 69; sister Assunta, 72. *United Press International Photo*

Wearing the Papal robe, Pope John XXIII is caught in a smiling close-up on October 28, 1958. He gave his first Papal address the next day.
United Press International Photo

❀ 6 ❀

How the Pope Is Elected

OUR LORD selected the first Pope on his own personal authority and in view of the need of a certain man with certain qualifications to accomplish the purposes of Divine Providence. He chose not one who was the wisest, nor the oldest, nor even the one he loved best. He chose Peter the Fisherman for the simple reason that this man with his particular qualities could best fulfill the tasks of the office in the days assigned to him. The Lord's ways are mysterious, and humans will never fully understand what he permits to happen. It will help, however, to remember that he promised to be with his Church all days even to the consummation of the world. This promise includes his solicitude for the Vicar who is to keep representing him on earth. It is he who in every succession to the first Vicar permits a certain one to be chosen. He sends the Holy Spirit upon the body of electors and what results may be pleasing or shocking to the world, but it is, nevertheless, the manifestation of his will for the accomplishment of the divine purposes.

St. Paul in I Corinthians, I, 26-29, tells us of God's way in appointing men: "Consider your own call, brethren; that there were not many wise according to the flesh, not many mighty, not many noble. But the foolish things of the world has God chosen to put to shame the 'wise' and the weak things of the world has God chosen to put to shame the strong, and the base things of the world and the despised has God chosen, and the things that are not, to bring to naught the things that are, lest any flesh should pride itself before him."

When Judas vacated his episcopate by suicide, the remaining apostles proceeded to fill with a worthy man the post so horribly disgraced by the traitor. They cast lots under the presidency of Peter, and the choice fell on Matthias. It was a fair and democratic method that readily suggested itself to men who had been under the influence of incarnate justice and charity.

After Peter died in glorious martyrdom on Vatican Hill, June 29, 67, the bishops, priests, deacons and chief laymen, comprising three orders: the episcopacy, the presbytery, and the laity of the Church of Rome, met to choose the successor. They chose Linus, wherefore Linus represented the choice of the whole Church and the will of God through the human action of the particular group qualified at the time to name the successor of Saint Peter.

And so it went for many centuries. Gradually, however, the layman's participation was decreased. The growth of the Church in Rome made it advisable to restrict the numbers of those participating in choosing a pope. After a time the restriction centered about that special class of churchmen called the cardinals. It was this group that had come to represent the three orders that had taken part in the earliest elections as mentioned above: the high churchmen, the bishops; the ordinary clergy, the priests; and the lay people. A council in 769 decreed that only members of the Sacred College could elect the Bishop of Rome, and the part of the laity was reduced to acclamation. Since a cardinal is pastor of one of Rome's churches, they verify the ancient rule that the clergy of a city elects the bishop.

The cardinals, restricted to the number of seventy, were, and still are, divided into three orders. Six are cardinal bishops, fifty are cardinal priests, and fourteen are cardinal deacons. This latter class formerly admitted laymen in its ranks but at present one must be a priest. (Canon 232) This same Canon prescribes that a cardinal must qualify as a man of outstanding learning, piety, judgment and ability. In their three orders, the cardinals fairly represent the whole Church functioning as the flock of Christ intent upon the virtue of its members and the spread of the faith to other peoples. The six cardinal bishops are in charge of the seven suburbicarian sees immediately adjacent to Rome, namely, Ostia, Palestrina, Porto-Santa Rufina, Albano, Velletri, Frascati and Sabina-Poggio Mirteto. The Dean of the Sacred College always has attached to his own see that of Ostia, so that while there are seven suburbicarian sees, there are only six cardinal bishops. They represent the immediate coadjutors of the pope in the top-level administration of the whole Church. The cardinal priests are usually the archbishops of sees in various parts of the world, as our own Cardinals Spellman in New York, McIntyre in Los Angeles, O'Hara in Philadelphia, and Cushing in Boston. These, obviously, are the actual workers in the vineyard. The cardinal deacons, in the main, perform the vast clerical work entailed in so huge an organization. Thus the three orders embrace and represent the population and functions of the living Church much like the way our congressmen represent us, the people.

The right to elect a pope belongs exclusively to the cardinals. Even an oecumenical council does not enjoy this right. In fact, were a council in session when a pope dies, it is by law suspended. All cardinals, unless they have resigned or have been deposed, are electors, even if they happen to be under censure at the time. All cardinals are duty bound to exercise their franchise unless lawfully excused, and if present in the conclave they must, under pain of excommunication, respond to the summons when called to the balloting. (Canons 32-42 of Constitution of Pius X, December 25, 1904, *Vacante Sede Apostolica*)

This electoral college of cardinals is often compared with our own presidential electors together with the Electors of the Holy Roman Empire. The principle in both is the same, namely, the chief members act for the whole body to elect the head. Should all the cardinals be killed, as is possible now in the face of the atom bomb, the right to elect the Bishop of Rome will revert to the body which originally enjoyed it and of which the cardinals are representatives, namely, the clergy of the Eternal City.

Nine days of official mourning for the dead pontiff are prescribed, after, or during which, the pope is buried. In the case of Pius XII, as we have seen, the death occurred on October 9, his funeral was held on October 16. During the nine days of mourning, the cardinals appeared with uncovered rochets. All cardinals not yet in Rome were journeying to that city to attend the conclave. They had been officially summoned to it by the Substitute Secretary of State, Monsignor Dell'Acqua.

The word, conclave, stemming etymologically from *con*, with, and *clavis*, key, means that which is under key, or locked up, and has an interesting origin which is useful to cite at this point. After the death of Clement IV in 1268, it took the cardinals two and three-quarter years before they elected Gregory X; and that long, scandalous period would have been protracted had not the people of Viterbo, where the election was taking place, taken it upon themselves to tear the roof off the quarters of the cardinals, thus exposing them to the cold. This accelerated the election. The success of locking up the cardinals and making access to food and communication with the outside world difficult prompted the elected Pope to promulgate that a conclave should be the method of future elections. This constitution was announced in the fifth session of the Second Council of Lyons in 1274.

Assisted by the heads of the three orders of the Cardinals, the camerlengo, or one acting as camerlengo—Cardinal Tisserant in our present case—made preparations for the holding of the conclave. The recommendations of these three were then referred to the General Congregation of Cardinals which collectively was administering the Church in the interregnum. The Cardinal Dean (always the Bishop of Ostia), in the present case Cardinal Tisserant, presided at the meetings of the General Congregation which began to meet daily. In the first of these meetings, called "preparatory congregations," the various constitutions which govern the conclave were read and the cardinals took an oath to observe them. Pius XII himself had issued the latest constitutions on what was to be done during an interregnum. They enjoined the two provisions just mentioned, their reading and the oath taking, with these following:

The election of a chamberlain if that post was vacant;

The making of arrangements to begin the conclave fifteen days after the death of the pope, and, if necessary, to have it begin eighteen days after;

The fixing of the day and manner for taking the pope's body to the Basilica of St. Peter's for the paying of respect to the remains by the faithful;

The arrangement for the nine funeral Masses and the determination of the time for the first six meetings of the cardinals;

The designation of who was to give the eulogy for the departed pontiff and of who was to give the exhortation for the choosing of a new pope;

The naming of two or three cardinals who would supervise the examination and selection of the conclavists, the construction of the walls needed for the sealing off of the area of the Vatican Palace to be used for the conclave, and the assignment of cells to conclavists;

The examination and approval of expenses involved in the period of the conclave;

The reading of letters from heads of state, reports from apostolic nuncios and of any other document that might be of interest or usefulness to the College of Cardinals;

The reading of any documents left by the dead pope for the cardinals;

The breaking of the fisherman's ring and the other official seals used in authenticating the documents of the Holy See;

The drawing of lots for apartments to be used by the cardinals in conclave, except for those whose infirmity or advanced age made it advisable to grant them the better ones before all others;

The fixing of the date for the beginning of the conclave.

Also at this first "preparatory congregation," the Cardinals elected Cardinal Aloisi Masella, the Prefect of the Sacred Congregation of Sacramental Discipline, to the office of Chamberlain of the Catholic Church. They decided that the nine-day period of mourning for the late pontiff should begin on October 10. Monsignor Alberto di Jorio, regent of the Secretariat of the College of Cardinals, was named Secretary of that body, and thus Secretary to the conclave which was to elect the Pope. Since it was traditional for the new Pope to create the Secretary of the conclave a cardinal, the selection was carefully made.

The new Chamberlain, Cardinal Masella, was now in charge of the regular administration of the Church during the interregnum. He acted with the advice and consent of a committee of the heads of each of the three cardinalitial orders in routine matters, while for extraordinary problems he had to consult with the entire College of Cardinals.

Further, according to the 1945 Constitution of Pius XII, the Chamberlain had the right and duty of examining all writings going into and out of the conclave. In this he took precedence over the secretary of the conclave within, and the marshal without.

During the days that followed the first meeting, the various officers and persons required for services in the conclave, called the conclavists, among them the Secretary of the Sacred College, the Sacristan of the Apostolic Palace, the Master of Apostolic Ceremonies, confessors, physicians, guards and servants of various kinds, were examined for discretion by a special commission. Each cardinal had the right to two attendants, lay or clerical, but only one, a layman, could enter the conclave with him. All who were approved to enter the conclave had to take an oath to keep secret anything that happened within the area of the conclave.

While all these legal preparations were going on, a physical one had begun as well. A large part of the Vatican Palace was sealed off from the rest of the edifice by a brick wall especially constructed for the purpose, with, of course, a door that could be shut separately from the outside and inside. The floors walled off had as many living quarters and service rooms as were needed. Each cardinal had the use of an apartment, each apartment having three or four small rooms or cells for himself and attendants. Austerity marked these rooms. There were simply a modest bed, a prie-dieu, a crucifix, a desk with lamp and writing materials, a few chairs, and practically nothing else. Access to the conclave was through one door only, a door locked from without by the Marshal of the Conclave, Prince Sigismondo Chigi Albano, and from within by the Cardinal Camerlengo, the Chamberlain. There were four revolving shelves which permitted the passage of food and other necessities without chance of looking through. These were guarded from within by a prelate assigned to this task by the camerlengo, and from without by the marshal and majordomo. Once the conclave began, this door was not opened again until the election was announced nor was anyone permitted to leave the area of the conclave until the conclave was officially declared ended. All communication with the outside world was strictly forbidden under pain of loss of office and excommunication.

Very faithfully the officers in charge of the various details, high and low, performed their duties of preparing for the conclave. It can readily be appreciated what work was entailed to house, feed and serve the cardinals; to provide rooms and other necessities for the officers and servants of the conclave; and to ensure the smooth functioning of the important business at hand. It is to the credit both of the dead pontiff and to the skill of the camerlengo that all preparations were well handled. The former had chosen able, dedicated men for offices which, in time, had to function in the handling of a conclave; while the latter showed a grasp of detail that was amazing. Most foreign observers, particularly the newsmen, marvelled at the ease and dexterity with which orders were given and carried out by the Vatican officials.

The General Congregation had fixed Saturday, October 25, for the beginning of the momentous conclave.

On the morning of that day, fifty-two cardinals, the whole complement except for two, Mindszenty and Stepinac, detained behind the iron curtain by the enmity of the Communists, gathered in St. Peter's majestic basilica for the first ceremony, a spiritual one. They attended the Mass of the Holy Spirit. It is the faith of Catholics that the Holy Spirit inspires every good work and in elections, particularly, directs the will of men, while keeping it free, to make the choice in line with God's decree as it emanates from his absolute will in some cases or his permissive will in others. By his foreknowledge, based on that decree, he knew who the successor of Pius XII would be. The cardinals prayed that their judgment would coincide with their God's. It did. It always does. Can God's will ever be thwarted? Only sin never enters into the province of his decrees. Everything else happens just as he decrees it to happen or permits it to happen.

Cardinal Canali, Dean of the cardinal deacons, celebrated the Mass. An allocation in beautiful Latin was delivered by Monsignor Antonio Bacci, the Secretary of Briefs to Princes. Its substance was to warn the electors of their solemn obligation to give the Church a good shepherd.

The fifty-two cardinals in attendance were:

Cardinal Bishops

1. Eugene Tisserant, Dean of the College, Bishop of Ostia and Porto-Santa Rufina
2. Clemente Micara, Vicar General of Rome, Bishop of Velletri
3. Giuseppe Pizzardo, Bishop of Albano
4. Benedetto Aloisi Masella, Prefect of the Congregation of the Sacraments
5. Federico Tedeschini, Bishop of Frascati

Cardinal Priests

6. Joseph Ernest Van Roey, Archbishop of Malines
7. Emmanuel Goncalves Cerejeira, Patriarch of Lisbon
8. Achille Lienart, Bishop of Lille
9. Pietro Fumasoni-Biondi, Prefect of the Propaganda
10. Maurillo Fossati, Archbishop of Turin
11. Elia Della Costa, Archbishop of Florence
12. Ignatius Gabriel Tappouni, Patriarch of Antioch, Syria
13. James Louis Copello, Archbishop of Buenos Aires
14. Peter Gerlier, Archbishop of Lyons
15. Gregory Peter XV Agagianian, Patriarch of Cilicia
16. Edward Mooney, Archbishop of Detroit
17. James Charles McGuigan, Archbishop of Toronto
18. Emile Roques, Archbishop of Rennes
19. Carlo Carmelo de Vasconcelos Motta, Archbishop of Sao Paolo
20. Norman Gilroy, Archbishop of Sydney
21. Francis Spellman, Archbishop of New York
22. Jose Marie Caro Rodriguez, Archbishop of Santiago, Chile

23. Teodosio Clemente De Gouveia, Archbishop of Lourence, Marques
24. Camara de Barros, Archbishop of Rio de Janeiro
25. Enrique Pia y Deniel, Archbishop of Toledo
26. Manuel Arteaga y Betancourt, Archbishop of Havana
27. Joseph Frings, Archbishop of Cologne
28. Ernesto Ruffini, Archbishop of Palermo
29. Antonio Caggiano, Bishop of Rosario, Argentina
30. Thomas Tien, Archbishop of Peking
31. Augusto Alvaro de Silva, Archbishop of San Salvador, in Bahia, Brazil
32. Gaetano Cicognani, Prefect of the Congregation of Rites
33. Angelo Giuseppe Roncalli, Patriarch of Venice
34. Valerio Valeri, Prefect of the Congregation of Religious
35. Pietro Ciriaci, Prefect of the Congregation of the Council
36. Maurice Feltin, Archbishop of Paris
37. Marcello Mimmi, Archbishop of Naples
38. Carlos Maria de la Torre, Archbishop of Quito
39. Georges Grente, Archbishop-Bishop of Le Mans
40. Giuseppe Siri, Archbishop of Genoa
41. John D'Alton, Archbishop of Armagh
42. James Francis McIntyre, Archbishop of Los Angeles
43. Giacomo Lercaro, Archbishop of Bologna
44. Stefan Wyszynski, Archbishop of Gniezno and Warsaw
45. Benjamin de Arriba y Castro, Archbishop of Tarragona
46. Fernando Quiroga y Palacios, Archbishop of Santiago, Spain
47. Paul-Emile Leger, Archbishop of Montreal
48. Cristanto Luque, Archbishop of Bogota
49. Valerian Gracias, Archbishop of Bombay
50. Joseph Wendel, Archbishop of Munich and Freising

Cardinal Deacons

51. Nicola Canali, Grand Penitentiary
52. Alfredo Ottaviani, Pro-Secretary of the Holy Office

Seventeen were Italian, six French, three Spaniards, three Brazilians, three Americans, two Argentinians, two Canadians, two Portuguese, two Germans, and one each from Cuba,

Columbia, Ecuador, Chile, Ireland, Belgium, Poland, Armenia, China, Syria, India and Australia—a fair cross-section of the world.

After the Mass, the cardinals were free to make their last preparations before being enclosed. Seventy minutes before the cardinals were to enter solemnly into conclave, Cardinal Mooney of Detroit suddenly died. His death reduced the number of electors to fifty-one and the number of American cardinals to two. The unexpected death of that kindly prelate in that dramatic moment stunned the world and a pall of gloom settled over the conclave which, though serious in nature, nevertheless has its joyous aspects.

At mid-afternoon the twenty assistants of the marshal of the conclave were clearing the conclave area of all persons who did not belong there. "Extra Omnes," they called out, (Out All). When the area was cleared, about 5 P.M., the cardinals entered the conclave in solemn procession and by 5:20 the doors were locked. Only death could release them until a pope was elected. The marshal of the Vatican shouted his order to the Vatican guard, "Hoist my flag!" It was done and the marshal was now in complete charge of the Vatican outside the conclave.

Inside, Monsignor di Jorio was in charge. With the fifty-one cardinals, some two hundred conclavists were enclosed. At one time, each cardinal had to provide his own food, but since 1878 the kitchen has been a part of the conclave. All meals are taken in private but are served from a common kitchen.

Great care was taken to prevent written communication from the outside world through food served to a cardinal, as had sometimes been done in past conclaves. In fact, all instruments of communication—the telegraph, the telephone, the microphone, the radio, the camera, even the mirror—are strictly forbidden. (Canons 47-52 of the Constitution of Pope Pius X, Dec. 25, 1904.)

At this time, when all were enclosed, the Constitution regulating the election of a new pontiff was again read to the cardinals and they again took an oath to observe it. Each conclavist was carefully identified and oaths were administered to the chief officials of the conclave. The following is the oath taken by the cardinals:

> I, standing in the presence of this man of God (the Monsignor who administered the oath), touching with my hand the Holy Gospels, promise that I will observe a rigorous and inviolable secrecy on each and all of those things which in any way come to my knowledge concerning the election of a new pontiff.
>
> I will keep secret all matters dealt with and defined in the Congregation of Cardinals, in the conclave, or in the place of the election, all matters which concern the voting, nor will I in any way whatsoever directly or indirectly by words, writing or signs or in any other manner communicate to anyone what I have learned during the conclave.
>
> I promise that I will bear no radio, telegraph, microphone or any other instrument for the transmission or reception of messages, and no photographic or cinematic equipment.
>
> I will observe this pledge under penalty of excommunication which can find absolution only by special ruling of the future Pontiff.

It was Saturday night, October 25. On the morrow, the feast of Christ the King, the cardinals would proceed to vote. Well known is the story of that little stove in the voting chapel, whose chimney protrudes to the heavens in order to make the smoke of the burned ballots indicate to an anxious world outside if the balloting has resulted in an election or not.

That little chimney became the world's center of attraction for the next two days.

7

The Election of John XXIII

ON SUNDAY, October 26, the cardinals assembled in the Pauline Chapel to attend the Mass of the Cardinal Deacon. It is prescribed by law that all vocals receive the Sacrament. After the Mass, the cardinals retired for a spell. Meanwhile the Sistine Chapel, where the voting was to take place, was made completely ready for the occasion. Six candles were lighted on the altar. On the altar they placed a large chalice covered with a paten. The papal throne had been removed; in its place, the canopies over the throne of each cardinal had been spread to signify that he shares sovereignty with the others until the pope is elected.

The Constitution of Pope Pius XII, "Vacante Apostolica Sede," issued December 8, 1945, was to govern the election, since it was the last legislation to be enacted on the subject of the election of a new pope. It first nullified all previous laws on the subject, for the sake of avoiding any encumbrance from some unremembered law that could be resurrected, and then confirmed and established most of the norms in extant canon law with the exception of this: The votes necessary to elect were to be two-thirds of the vocals present, *plus one*. It had always been abhorrent that a cardinal should vote for himself. To prevent its occurrence, the elect, in previous conclaves, was pointedly asked if he had voted for himself. This procedure was embarrassing and far from satisfactory. The election was null and void if the man admitted he had voted for himself, his vote having constituted the required two-thirds. Under the circumstances, could it be expected that a man incriminate himself? The expedient of Pius XII solved the perplexity. He required a two-thirds vote plus one, so that if a man had fallen so low as to vote for himself, the two-thirds majority was still present and legally entitled him to the office.

When layfolk heard through newsmen who delved into all phases of papal elections and reported their findings to the public that there were no qualifications in law other than that one must be a male and enjoy the use of reason, they were simply amazed. For this highest office on earth the least qualifications? But so it is. Prudence had dictated not to restrict the electors beyond the barest essentials. Their own prudence could be relied upon to select one who possessed all the expected, though unwritten, qualifications for this high office.

Into the famed Sistine Chapel, on the altar wall of which shines forth the tremendous painting of Michelangelo, "The Last Judgment," sufficient in itself to instill awe and a sense of solemnity into anyone, the cardinals filed shortly after the Mass to begin the process of electing a new pope. It was about ten o'clock.

Three forms of election were possible. The first is called *per inspirationem,* by inspiration, which results when there is a unanimous *viva voce* selection, the name of a man being called out aloud by one cardinal and repeated by the rest of the college. The second is *per compromissum,* that is, by pre-arrangement or compromise delegation. In this case, by unanimous consent of the cardinals beforehand, three or five or seven are delegated to do the actual choosing with the understanding that the cardinals will abide by the choice of these delegates of theirs. It is similar to what prevails in an organization's nominating committee. The third is *per scrutinium,* by secret ballot. This is the usual procedure, and it prevailed in the election of John XXIII.

Pope Pius XII had left no private instructions nor had he expressed any preference as to who should succeed him. The post, then, was freely open to all cardinals and there was talk of the college selecting a non-cardinal, Milan's Archbishop Montini's name being prominently mentioned in this connection. As usual, all newsmen had begun guessing beforehand. Several had been proposed as "the most likely to succeed," among them prominently Cardinal Agagianian, the Armenian, on the theory that his selection would entice the Greek Orthodox Church back into the fold of Rome. Cardinal Roncalli's name, too, was whispered about as a possibility, although more prominent were the names of Cardinals Masella, Costa, Siri, Ruffini, and Ottaviani of Italy, with that of Tisserant of France. Even Cardinal Spellman was mentioned here and there. The thought of an American Pope was very sweet in the minds of many in the States.

All candidates for the office are forbidden to make or accept any pre-election pledges. Simony in the election is severely punishable by excommunication, although it would not invalidate the election. If pre-election pledges have been made by the unsuccessful candidate, they are rendered null and void. Promises to vote for or against any particular candidate are nullified and subject the one who made them to excommunication. Furthermore, to correct an old abuse, no cardinal is to accept for transmission to the Sacred College or to any member of it a veto of any civil government. Better than any campaigning by an individual is the injunction to the whole Church to pray earnestly for the speedy, peaceful, and worthy election of a new pontiff. (Canons 79-85 of Constitution of Pius X.) The Holy Spirit, invoked by clergy and laity alike for this purpose following the death of a pope, is the best means of insuring what is best for the Church.

A new stove had been placed in the Sistine Chapel for the burning of the ballots. The old stove had disappeared since it was last used in 1939. The ballots were on hand, secretaries at their desks, the cardinals on their thrones. All was in readiness for the momentous action.

Three cardinals were chosen by lot to act as tellers or scrutators, that is, to verify the validity of a ballot, three others were chosen to be revisors, that is, to verify the number of votes cast, while three others were named as infirmarians, whose duty it was to go to the cell of a cardinal too sick to come to the Sistine Chapel, accept his vote and bring it back to the scrutators.

The ballot is a simple one. It is a piece of paper, oblong in shape, on which is printed:

> Eligo in Summum Pontificem R. (for Reverendissimum) Meum D. (for Dominum) Card. (for Cardinalem), ______________________.
>
> I elect as Supreme Pontiff the Most Reverend, My Lord Cardinal ______________________.

This piece of paper is then folded over, thus showing the top on which is embossed either the seal or the motto of the cardinal who is voting.

The cardinal on his throne simply writes on the ballot the name of the one he wants to have as pope. He folds the ballot without signing or sealing it. Then, in order of precedence, each cardinal files up to the altar holding the folded ballot between the first two fingers of his right hand. When he reaches the altar, he kneels for a moment in prayer, then he rises, and in a loud voice pronounces the following solemn oath:

> "I call to witness Jesus Christ, who will judge me, that I am electing him who before God I judge should be elected."

He then places the ballot on the paten which he tilts to allow the ballot to slide into the bowl of the chalice.

When all the cardinals have finished this procedure, the ballots are emptied out of the chalice by the tellers and are simply counted. If the number of ballots taken out of the chalice does not exactly correspond with the number of the cardinals in the chapel with those who might have voted from their sick cell, the ballots are immediately burned. If there is agreement of number and persons, then the tellers record and announce the vote as they find it written on the ballot. After this the ballots are strung together with a thread, the needle of which passes through the word, "Eligo." This secured bundle of ballots is then put aside for a moment, after which the tellers again go through the names on the ballots to verify their first tally. If they find agreement, they pass the string of ballots to the reviewers.

If a two-thirds majority plus one has been achieved, the ballots are immediately burned, but if it has not been achieved, the ballots are put aside to be burned with those of the succeeding ballot, which is immediately taken. This is what happened in the first ballot taken on October 26, and it was the same with the second ballot. Whereupon, the morning session ended and the two sets of ballots were burned together. It is recalled that there was much confusion outside when the smoke of that burning began to rise from the chimney outside the window of the Sistine Chapel. The smoke looked white as it first arose, and great excitement prevailed. But the smoke soon turned black and it was evident that no pope had been elected.

Two other sessions, each taking two ballots, were held that day. All day long the world awaited for the fateful wisp of white smoke. At one point it seemed to come, and even the Vatican radio announced that an election had taken place, but it proved to be an error. Thus Sunday passed, and Monday passed, with no results.

On Tuesday, October 28, the cardinals met for a ninth ballot. This and two more proved unsuccessful. Rumors were flying thick and fast throughout the world: "there is a pope"; "no, there isn't." "It is Cardinal so and so"; "no, it is this other Cardinal."

All throughout—but then who knows the story of what went on in the Sistine Chapel that day?—the cardinals kept diligently at their task trying to select a worthy successor to the revered Pope Pius XII. This we can presume to state. The proceedings were and remain a strict secret. As we write this a few weeks after the election, there is an item in the papers to the effect that the pope who was elected has rebuked newsmen for trying to pierce the secrets of the conclave. The Church has cast too well a cloak over the proceedings for even the gimlet eye of a star reporter to penetrate.

All we know is the main result as has been told to the world.

On the twelfth ballot, taken towards the evening of Tuesday, October 28, the feast of Saints Simon and Jude, Apostles, white smoke definitely was seen to pour out of that little chimney, the focus of the world's attention for days. The crowd in the piazza stirred. "We have a Pope, we have a Pope," became the joyous chant of the horde, and its ranks were very quickly swelled to enormous proportion as the news spread throughout the city with lightning speed.

What had happened in the Sistine Chapel? When the tellers counted the votes of the twelfth ballot, they discovered a two-thirds majority plus one. The fact was duly announced to the assembled cardinals. The man who had attained the required majority was the Patriarch of Venice, Angelo Giuseppe Cardinal Roncalli.

At this point the Secretary of the conclave, Monsignor di Jorio, ordered the doors to be opened, so that the Masters of Ceremonies could witness the act that was to follow and perform some necessary services.

Cardinal Tisserant then went to the throne of Cardinal Roncalli and put to him the important question: "Do you accept the election?" The pope-elect answered "yes" promptly and firmly, following the usual protestation of unworthiness. From that moment when he said "Yes," he immediately acquired by divine law the full and supreme power of jurisdiction over the whole flock of Christ. (Canon 219) Thereafter, all his acts became valid, even before he was to be crowned in formal ceremony.

Upon the acquiescence of the elect to assume the post of the Vicar of Christ over the flock, the second question was put: "By what name do you wish to be known?" The new Pope answered as promptly: "By the name of John XXIII."

Once this was accomplished, the Master of Ceremonies saw to it that all the canopies except that of the new Pope should be lowered. The new Pope was then escorted to an adjoining room where there were a number of white papal soutanes of varying sizes. He put on the size best fitted to his figure, a ceremony called the *immantatio*, the vesting, and returned to the Chapel, where now he sat on the portable papal throne set in front of the altar.

The touching ritual of the *adoratio*, the paying of homage, or obedience, followed. Each cardinal approaches him and professes his loyalty quite markedly by kissing first the toe, then the hand, and finally receiving and giving the double embrace. It was reported that the new Pope went at this a little awkwardly and apologized for it, saying: "You see, I am not used to this sort of thing; forgive me."

After that, the Pope appointed the camerlengo, who put on his finger the Fisherman's Ring. The Sistine Chapel ritual was over. All had been done decorously, canonically and expeditiously.

What followed was perhaps something that cannot be fully described as decorous, but it is typical of the spirit which is in the people of Rome. The crowds in the piazza, with the Vatican Palace and the Sistine Chapel in view, had grown to immense size and impatiently waited the public announcement of the name of the new Pope. Speculation ran rife. All sorts of guesses were made, all of them more or less according to preconceived notion or desire.

At last—it was dark outside now—a light played on the central balcony of St. Peter's. Into the light stepped Cardinal Canali, the Dean of the Cardinal Deacons. The eyes of two hundred thousand human beings were focused on him, and the ears of uncounted millions glued to radios all over the world were intent on hearing him. He cleared his voice and recited the ancient formula:

"Gaudium magnum annuntio vobis. Habemus Papam, Eminentissimum et Reverendissimum Sanctae Romanae Ecclesiae Cardinalem, Angelum Josephum Roncalli!"

"I announce to you a great joy. We have a Pope, the Most Eminent, the Most Reverend Angelo Joseph Cardinal Roncalli!"

The response of the people to the announcement was thunderous. No one who has not been in St. Peter's piazza can appreciate the exuberance of a Roman crowd. Salvo upon salvo of *vivas* followed. The people waved their handkerchiefs, they embraced each other, they shouted their unrestrained joy. It would have mattered not who had been elected Pope. The essential point was that the Church had again a chief shepherd. This was the primary joy. On top of this was the relief of the Roman crowd that it was again an Italian. Since the year 1522 the peninsula has had a son on the throne of Peter. In the back of its mind is the realization that someday it will have to yield that privilege to other nations again, but it has national pride enough to feel that the Church is safer in the hands of one whose blood is the same as the inhabitants of the peninsula. On top of this secondary joy was the third one: the respect they had had for the Patriarch of Venice. Many in the crowd might have expected another, but they did take joyously the news that it was this kindly and able Metropolitan of Venice.

Long and loudly lasted the *vivas*. It was Italy's reaction to the election, and it was largely repeated throughout every Catholic center in the world. The conclave seemed to be ended but the crowd did not stir. It kept shouting its *Viva il Papa,* with one imperious aim: it demanded an immediate sight of the new Vicar of Christ, and his first blessing.

John XXIII appeared on the balcony that is the heart of the beautiful façade of St. Peter's. As soon as the people saw him a new and more enthusiastic roar of delight rose from the throats of the quarter-million people. He smiled on them warmly and affectionately, so typical of the Italian temperament. They were his people, and he their father, not only canonically but by ties of common national blood. "Bless us, Bless us," they shouted in unison, and so the new Holy Father, the Father of all Christendom, on that notable night of October 28, 1958, raised his consecrated hands to bless for the first time, *Urbi et Orbi,* the beloved City of Rome and the world.

Sit nomen Domini Benedictum!	Blessed be the name of the Lord!
Ex hoc nunc et usque in saeculum!	Now and forever!
Adjutorium nostrum in nomine Domini!	Our help is in the Name of the Lord!
Qui fecit coelum et terram!	Who made heaven and earth!
Benedicat vos Omnipotens Deus Pater, et Filius, et Spiritus Sanctus!	May Almighty God bless you; the Father, the Son, and the Holy Spirit.

And as he mentioned the Names of each adorable Person of the Blessed Trinity, he made the sign of the cross over the host of humans before him. Each one blessed himself in turn, and each sensed a divine somethingness in the blessing of this great priest whom it had pleased the Lord to place over his people.

8

His Antecedents and Background

WHEN a girl brings a young man to her home with the intent of interesting her people in accepting him, the question invariably comes (in private) to her later, "What's his background?"

We may at this point ask the same question, and attempt to answer it for the benefit of the world. The world is interested in knowing the background of this man whom Providence has unexpectedly propelled into the foreground of the great personages on earth.

As soon as his election was announced, many headlines such as these were spread on the front pages of newspapers: SON OF THE SOIL BECOMES POPE SHARECROPPER'S SON RISES TO PAPACY PEASANT TO PRIEST TO POPE FARMER ELECTED POPE HUMBLE CONTADINO NAMED BY CARDINALS

His background, then, is very evident. He is a man of the soil, the descendant of a long line of farmers ekeing out their living by the work of their hands.

This is the general background. Let us expand it before we go into the particulars of such a background.

Lombardy is Italy's fertile plain nestling at the foot of the towering Alps. It produces a great variety of crops and lends itself well to the raising of important live-stock.

Fertile as it is, with rich soil and an abundance of water, Lombardese farmers have to work as hard as any farmer in any other region. The glebe is somehow always stubborn and a man has to bend his back opening up the reluctant crust of earth for the implanting of seed which theoretically is to yield a hundred-fold, but which yields only that portion of the hundred-fold commensurate with the vagaries of the weather and the human sweat expended in the period between harrowing and harvest. The Lord had decreed: "In the sweat of thy brow shalt thou eat bread," and no one realizes more the truth of that punishment than does a farmer. He realizes too well that there are many thorns and thistles to contend with before he can bring to market his wheat, rice, potatoes, beans, broccoli, barley, cabbage, corn and the like.

He becomes much more impressed than others with what Christ tried to convey through his parable of the cockle. Weeds are cancers that eat away the substance of the good crops and hard work in uprooting them is the farmer's lot if he wants a fair yield. Animal husbandry is very rewarding, but it requires a seven-day week of vigilant toil. The cows must be milked, the horses must be stabled, all living things have to be fed and watered, and yard and barn area must be kept clean.

Farming is as old as man and it remains his hardest chore. The other great basic callings, building, carpentering, fishing and hunting, hard as they are, allow for periods of rest. Not so farming.

We cite this to bring to our readers' attention the fact that the background of John XXIII is one calculated to have trained him to persistent vigilance, on top of the virtue of laboriousness. He had to keep his eye on the weather, he had to watch for the mating of the stock, the laying of the hens, and the nesting of the birds. One of the finest descriptions of the nature of God is given in the verse: "Are not two sparrows sold for a farthing? And yet not one of them will fall to the ground without your Father's leave." (Matthew X, 29). The farmer learns to imitate this divine solicitude for the least of creatures. He worries about the colts, the kids, the lambs, the chicks. Did we say lambs? This particular farmer's boy has now the divine commission to "Feed my lambs," and what background could be better calculated to ensure that they will be cared for solicitously and fed properly?

Still in general background, he is of Italian blood. Many had hoped that the five hundred and thirty-five year period of occupancy of the papal throne by an Italian would be ended. Many have felt that such an Italian possessiveness is monopolistic and unfair, and that while it had its need and merit for a period to obviate another recurrence of a Babylonian Captivity, that danger is now long past. We shall not enter into the substance of these arguments. We simply wish to point out that his possession of Italian blood is of great advantage. History sustains the contention that Italians have a fair record in ruling as Popes. They are diplomatic, paternal, affable, and flexible, to mention a few characteristics. They are not inclined to harshness or to despotism. They are generally willing to listen and grant what favors they can. These are qualities that are admirable in high places. It does not mean that all Italian popes have had these qualities, but in the main it has characterized them. They bring quite a bit of heart into an office that must have heart as well as brains. Furthermore, it retains the genial relationship that must exist among neighbors. The seat of the Church is in Italy, and Italians live in Italy. When Europe was very Catholic and catholic, when nationalism was not a prepossessing prejudice, the papacy suffered nothing if its occupant was a Spaniard, a Frenchman, a German, a Hollander, or a Greek, but nationalism is rampant now in Europe and even a novice in international relations sees the awkwardness during a war should the occupant of Peter's throne be anything but an

Italian. The Communists would have quite a propaganda gem to exploit.

In future years it may be proper to change. It might have been very smart to have done it now. But it is certainly safer not to have done so and it can be presumed that the cardinals preferred to be on the safe side rather than smart.

For the details of background, we should consider the economic, social, moral, cultural and spiritual elements in his family's history.

Some farmers are rich, others are poor. A rich farmer owns his land, which is of considerable size, and enjoys good labor and an eager market. The Roncallis were not in this class. For several generations they tilled the soil that belonged to Count Ottavio Mogliani. Sharecroppers they were, as so many Italians are, getting a bare portion for their living out of the crops they coax from the soil.

The house where they lived was in a beautiful vale between the Adda and the Brembo Rivers in the village called Sotto il Monte (Under the Mountain), a short distance from the provincial seat, the City of Bergamo. The house was very plain, built, as most Italian farmhouses are, of rough stone with little ornamentation. Animals are quartered quite near the house, and sometimes in the very precincts of it.

Their fare has been described in the journals and it should make anyone marvel that in a civilized country such frugality has to be borne, not by the most desperate of the population, but by hard workers of the soil that produce food in prodigal abundance. When they arose, for breakfast they had a bowl of cereal or a slice of the regional dish, polenta, a sort of corn mush made into a cake. For dinner, a mixed vegetable soup followed by a bit of cheese or salami. At night, more of the polenta, with orders to leave a bit of it for the morning. They rarely could indulge in meat or wine.

So they were poor, quite poor, a fact that was freely admitted in conversations when as bishop and cardinal he spoke of his childhood to friends. It is hard for us Americans to accept that farmers in Italy use very little milk and eggs on their table. Milk is converted into cheese because there is no refrigeration and eggs are jealously kept for the sick or for traditional cakes. They produce few eggs at best, because hens in Italy are not the spoiled darlings of farmers, bulging as they do here with purina chow, but have actually to scratch for a living 'mid the refuse of the barnyard. It is a sort of vicious circle of scratching. The human has to scratch for his living and because thereby he cannot give to the animals too generous a supply of fodder, the animals have to do their own scratching or foraging, and they do not produce enough for the farmer to be relieved of the need of scratching.

Economically, then, it was a dismal situation. It was a sort of continuation of the feudal system which kept a select class very rich and the majority very poor.

Socially, the position was a little better. The Roncallis are first mentioned in 1429 as likely to be belonging to the lower nobility. There is a family crest which dates back several centuries, a stone tower in a field of three horizontal bars rouge and blanche, in the upper bar a fleur-de-lis on either side of the tower which juts into the top bar. The legend or motto of the family is *Obedientia et Pax,* Obedience and Peace.

The Roncallis have many branches of the family in other parts of Italy and in France. The Roncallis of Sotto il Monte stem from an ancestor, Martin, for which reason they are called "The Martini." It seems that the ancestral seat of the family was Valle Imagna near Bergamo. There and elsewhere for some centuries they enjoyed the title of Count. The family name was held by Counts in Montorio, nicknamed the Bragini, who achieved some fame, and by Counts in Foligno and Rovigo, while without the title they are found in Peretti, Frosio and Parolini.

The family produced in its various branches religious, priests, painters, doctors, and other professional men. One of them, Stephen, nicknamed Pamarancio, achieved a great fame around 1600 in France as a painter, while another, Cristoforo, did some painting in St. Peter's in Rome.

Hence, while the economic situation of the future Pope's family was miserable during his childhood, socially they were far from the lowest rung. Italy has a long memory for those who carry an honorable name. The Roncallis were respected in their little village despite their poverty.

This respect was grounded on their moral character even more than on their social status of gentry. They had maintained a good reputation as law-abiding citizens. They lived a sober, moral life, free from anything that might be alluded to as a scandal. They were peaceful, friendly neighbors setting the good example of Christian living. When we remember the feuds, turmoils and wars through which Lombardy emerged after the Napoleonic campaigns in the region and the long years of revolutions that kept the land in ferment until unification of the peninsula was achieved in 1870, the fidelity of the Roncallis to the moral standards of Christianity is a remarkable achievement. While other families became delinquent, indifferent religiously, and even anti-clerical, the Roncallis kept on being highly moral, decent and pious folk.

The ordinary Italian, no matter how low his economic condition may be, has a love in his soul for the fine, lofty and beautiful things of life. He appreciates art, he is moved by good literature, and he becomes rapturous listening to sweet music. The Roncallis were not rude men. Poor, but like so many others, aspiring to bring the nobility of culture into their lives. They read the classics of their land whenever time permitted them, they visited art galleries and museums, and they loved to hear the concerts played in Bergamo on occasions of a feast or holiday. The opera music enthralled them while the gay folk songs of Italy would lift their souls to heights of enjoyment seldom reached by those who follow concerts for the sake of impressing people as devotees of music.

Like most Italians, they had a keen appreciation of the architecture and art it was their opportunity to enjoy as they made the rounds of the churches and public buildings in the environs of Bergamo. They may not have taken professional courses in art appreciation, but they could discourse warmly and intelligently on the gems of art that they saw in the cathedrals, churches, palaces and municipal edifices of the region. We have mentioned that several of them achieved some fame in painting. This love of beautiful things is a fair indication of the beauty of one's soul within, which in the main is the essence of true culture.

The speech of the Roncallis might not have had the elegance of the salon, but they had a gentleness and an old-world courtesy that harken back to the courtliness and refinement of the better families.

The true strength of the Roncallis lay in their deep spirituality. For them, the Catholic faith was not just a social habit or a badge of conformity and respectability in a community predominantly Catholic. It was an unshakable conviction and a gladly accepted way of life which bore its natural fruits in persistent acts of piety and service. They had a deep reverence for priests; they saw in the Mass the supreme act of worship to God Almighty in which they were privileged to participate and draw from its table the nourishment they needed to keep their souls aglow with health.

That Italian womenfolk are normally devout is accepted as commonplace, but this is not true of the menfolk. The Italian male has grown largely lax in religious observance. He has developed the notion that going to Mass regularly and attending devotions should be the concern of the women only. He usually retains a deep attachment to the Church, but scandalizes his co-religionists of other lands, particularly of

America, by being so indifferent in the matter of Sunday Mass and frequent reception of the Sacraments.

Not so the Roncallis. The women were always intensely pious and devout, while the menfolk were not too far behind in giving evidence of a lively, practical faith. They attended Mass regularly, they approached the Holy Table, they lived the life of a dedicated, fervent Catholic. With unerring insight, they knew that the strength they needed to confront successfully the various problems of life could come only from the Bread of Angels. They were not ashamed to be seen going to the altar rail. Rather, they were proud to stand up and be counted as sentinels of the Sacrament and their satisfaction was immense whenever they were chosen to carry the baldachino for the Corpus Christi or the Forty-Hours Devotion processions.

They always showed a warm, sincere loyalty to the papacy, particularly at a time when in the revolutionary turmoil of the nineteenth century, the papacy was unpopular in northern Italy. It took courage to speak up for the rights of the Church at a time when the trend was to despoil her. It but revealed the true sense of the supernatural and the relish of spiritual things that this breed of the Roncallis possessed. They were fine, simple, God-fearing people, not only basically sound and beyond reproach as must characterize "a Caesar's wife," but definitely dedicated to the living exemplification of Catholic action.

Background is important. This background of John XXIII is as good as one can find to assure the world that he possesses as a heritage from his ancestry all the qualities needed for his arduous office.

❁ 9 ❁

His Pre-priestly Life

GIOVANNI BATTISTA RONCALLI courted and won for his bride the modest and attractive Marianna Mazzola, and proudly he brought her to the house in Sotto il Monte started originally by the known ancestral head of his family, the Martin, mentioned in the previous chapter. The house is known as the Ca' Martino, or Camaitino, and was a simple but adequate structure for the newly-weds. Some others have called it Cascina Colombera. It is of stone covered with mud-brown stucco, and is of three floors. A patio has been built at one side, looking out on a courtyard.

The house is located on what is now the Via Brusico, and if one proceeds a scarce fifty yards from the house he will arrive at the town square of a half dozen small shops. From this square radiate several dirt roads which wind to other clusters of farm houses to constitute the commune known as Sotto il Monte, a town boasting of the enormous population of 1,773 souls.

The young husband worked hard on the terrain allotted to him to cultivate so that he could maintain his bride in reasonable comfort and be prepared for the expenses (not enormous) involved in the hoped-for birth of the first baby. The first baby came in due time, a girl. Then another girl.

There is always a great deal of friendly ribbing by relations and neighbors when the first child is not a male. It increases when the second is distaff as well. Whatever embarrassment Giovanni Battista might have felt at the teasing he received was finally dispelled when on November 25, 1881, he was presented with his first-born son.

He was a robust, healthy infant, and it was providential that he was strong at birth. The piety of the Roncalli family and, in particular, the spiritual anxiety of the devout mother impelled the counsel to have the child baptized immediately. This may seem astonishing to our American women: the mother rose from her bed a few hours after delivering the child and insisted on carrying it to the parish church. It was a bitterly cold day. Aided by her husband and a woman neighbor, she dressed, covered herself with a woolen shawl, and off she trudged to church. No appointment of course. A telephone? Who had even heard of one in that region? She expected to find the parish priest in the church and he would baptize it promptly and she would bring it back to its warm crib, a Christian in God's grace. Her anxiety was a real one because the infant mortality in the region was high. No Roncalli would ever die unbaptized.

When she arrived at the parish church, to her dismay she learned that the pastor had had to go on a sick call with Viaticum. So she had to wait. She had to wait in a sacristy that would have competed favorably with a meat-packer's cold room. The chilling wind raced through the creaks in the stones and the chinks of the woodwork. Four hours they waited there, chilled to the bone. Papa Battista kept the child as warm as he could under his jacket, his own teeth chattering in unison with that of his wife and neighbor who was to be the sponsor. Snow had started to fall around noon. They were all very cold and hungry and it took stamina for them to remain there. The stamina was physical, but also drawn from the spiritual conviction of the necessity of having the child baptized. How that child survived that ordeal on the very day of his birth will remain a marvel to recount.

Finally, the parish priest returned, and started to baptize the child. "What name is it to have?" he inquired. "Angelo Giuseppe," replied the father. "Angele Josephe, quid petis ab ecclesia Dei?" (Angelo Giuseppe, what do you seek of the Church of God?) ritualistically asked the priest. And the response came sincerely from the infant through the mouth of the sponsor: "Fidem" (Faith).

Angelo did receive the Faith, a faith that never left him, a faith that never lessened but increased as the years sped on.

The baptismal font has been shown in the newspapers. It is one of the simplest imaginable. But what are fancy accoutrements worth in contrast to the imperishable wealth of the spirit accrued through baptism—the removal of original sin, the infusion of sanctifying grace, the incorporation into the Mystical Body of Christ and its indelible mark to witness for all eternity, a heavenly heritage.

The child grew and waxed strong. No expensive formulae or pablum, no Gerber's baby food—only his mother's breasts and the softer foods of the family table. He had no pretty little clothes, no blue for boy—only the white of peasant swaddling, no silk coverlets, no fancy crib, no baby carriage. His cot was an iron one in a corner of the parents' room, with no fairy-tale characters prettily painted on the walls, with no rattle and no teddy bear. A teething ring instead of paregoric and for medicines no gentle castoria or children's aspirin, but a tummy rub and a mother's crooning. That he had. There are old familiar lullabies that an Italian child hears and never forgets. In this he shares a wondrous fraternity with the Irish infant who is charmed with the Tura-lura, the American infant with "Rock-a-bye," and every other infant in the world who is fortunate to have a devoted mother hovering over his crib.

We cannot refrain from the reflection at this point that humble as was the crib of the future Pope, it was richer by far to the manger of the Child of whom he has become the Vicar. And devout as Angelo's mother, Marianna, was, sweet as was her song to her sleepy child, she must yield to the Mary, daughter of Anne, who hovered over the crib of the Babe born in Bethlehem.

A child in Italy gets much love, but as a rule is not fussed over as much as is an American child. On a farm, particularly, with the parents occupied in many chores, the child is left often to his own devices. This does not usually make for delinquency, however, as is too often the case here, because while the attentiveness is not minute, it is regular and constant. The child plays in the vicinity of the house with other companions. When the weather is pleasant, unabashedly they shed much of their clothing. Barefootedness is common. The games they play are of a gentle sort: kicking a ball, hide-and-seek, berry hunting, school, and the like. A farmer's boy would have a dog and there is much fun in goading a goat, pulling a sheep's tail, trying to milk a cow, and riding a colt.

Little Angelo enjoyed the sunlight and green of his pleasant valley over which towered the foothills of the Alps. He had much to make him happy: kind parents; the company of many brothers and sisters, for the Roncallis in time had thirteen children; the open country; pleasant neighbors; and work. Work was his lot from earliest years commensurate with his growth and strength. This is usual on all farms of the world. The young boy can be put to clean a part of the stable, feed the chickens, lead the horses, bring the swill to the pigs, and carry the milk into the house. Later on, he would ride with his father on the farm wagon, bringing things in from the fields and delivering other things to neighbors. He would be put to weeding; then to a bit of plowing and harrowing, the mending of fences, the pruning of trees and bushes, and to the eternal problem of supplying water for the tubs and wood for the fireplace, the only source of heat for cooking the food and warming the house.

Angelo, the boy, enjoyed all this round of work and play on his paternal farm. He had grown into a sturdy lad, well capable of sustaining a day's labor. As the oldest boy, he took command of the children and acted as a sort of foreman over them, conveying to them the father's orders of the day. The father eyed him with much pleasure, for he was growing in the best tradition of the Roncallis, strong, dependable, industrious, and quite bright.

He grew very pious and religious. He loved to say his prayers, loved to steal into church for a visit. His attachment to a church was, first, because of its spiritual inspiration and, second, because he was stimulated by its art and beauty. He thus began to receive a liberal education in the arts from earliest years as he plied his father and the priest with questions on painters and architects.

He began to visit sanctuaries farther than those of his village. He has the most delightful memories of the Abbey of Pontida, of the Marian sanctuaries in the Province of Bergamo —the Madonna of the Fields, the Madonna of the Cornabusa, the Madonna of the Rose. He visited often the conventual chapel of the Franciscans in Baccanello, a short distance from his home. When the angelus rang in the friary tower, it would signal the time to his mother, who would invariably then put on the hearth the pot for the evening polenta.

At the banks of the Somasca river, to which his father's cart sometimes carried him, he heard of the saintliness of Girolamo Miani, and he conceived for that saint a great personal devotion. His most tender memory is that of the shrine of the Madonna of the Woods, which, later as Patriarch of Venice, he had the joy to crown on September 30, 1954, since Cardinal Shuster of Milan in whose territory it was, was unable to perform the ceremony due to illness.

The father had seen to it that the boy obtained his reading, writing and arithmetic in the only school available to his children, the little private school run by the parish priest. After doing the morning chores on the farm, which required early rising, the boy would trudge to the village church for several hours' session with the pastor. The pastor was a patient man with children and, as must be evident from the good foundation of education possessed by the lad, he was quite a competent pedagogue.

When the boy was nine years of age, after finishing all that the little parish school could afford to give him, his father registered him for the sixth grade in the superior school of Celano, a village fairly near Sotto il Monte. The father was determined that his first-born son should not remain a farmer. He saw talents in him that would easily fit him for the medical or legal profession. He appreciated the physical strength and farming sense of his son, invaluable aids to him in running the farm, but he was willing to sacrifice that aid to himself for the benefit of the boy. He envisioned him a professional man who would restore the tarnished prestige of the Roncalli name. (What a modest vision in contrast to the reality that was to be.) His brothers laughed at this idea of Giovanni Battista, claiming that the boy's bull strength fitted him for farm work, a bird-in-the-hand advantage, and that the bird-in-the-bush dream of artist or professional should be discarded. But the father was a resolute man and despite criticism determined to have the boy attend the school in Celano.

So, to Celano, Angelo went and there he achieved an enviable record as a student. He loved the books given to him to read and absorb; he was keen on history and mathematics, he proved proficient in letters, and he showed a marked aptitude for languages. He was rather exceptional for a farmer's boy and his teachers quickly painted to him the advantages of pusuing higher studies rather than returning to the farm.

What higher studies? His father had spoken of the usual professions, doctor, lawyer, engineer, notary; or the arts—painter, musician, sculptor. The farm boy had an inspiration. We will call it this in lieu of the word "vocation" which is more proper, but about which we will speak more formally later. On the farm the boy had often to keep a watch on sheep. Well, then, let him keep watching sheep, only another kind of sheep—the sheep about which the Master had so often mentioned as belonging to him.

He was now eleven years of age. For a farm boy, he had matured far beyond the mentality of the ordinary American school boy of eleven whose horizon is limited by bicycle, hockey and baseball. He had the mind of a grown man. The physical work on the farm had toughened him physically, while the studies at Celano had progressed him mentally.

There came into his heart the determination to follow the Master in the shepherding of souls. He would be a priest. This, he felt would satisfy his father. His father had wanted a son of his to be something better than a farmer. A priest is better than a farmer. But even more than this wish to satisfy his father, whom he loved very much, was his own need to satisfy the imperious urge in him to dedicate his life to the priesthood. He had read: "The fields are white for the harvest." That was language he could understand.

Far more important for the world than a harvest of grapes or corn was a harvest of souls. He had seen many a harvest blighted by a storm's sudden fury or by a long-drawn-out drought. He had heard of many peoples and nations that had been spiritually blighted through one sudden storm of revolt or by long spiritual dryness. He would try to restore these harvests. He had been particularly distressed by the fact that many of his fellow Italians had fallen from the faith. No Italian had any business outside the fold shepherded by Christ's Vicar. It was a stout and holy resolve in the lad's mind, a true vocation granted by God and fostered by personal prayer and the counsel of good friends. The apostles had physically heard the call: "Come, follow me." Angelo heard it just as truly in his soul, and with as great a determination as affected any of the original twelve, he resolved to follow it.

When he spoke to his father about it, the man was surprised, had a spasm of disappointment, but thereupon readily consented. His mother—well, like any Italian mother—was overjoyed. All devout Catholic mothers have a secret longing to see their boy at the altar. So it was agreed. The boy was to go to the seminary in Bergamo.

To Bergamo he went, spending there eight years of his life, 1892-1900. It must have thrilled him to put on the clerical garb for the first time. It thrilled him more as he plunged into the classical studies required of him. On the throne of Peter at the time was the bright luminary, Leo XIII. He had issued that immortal encyclical, "Rerum Novarum," the charter of liberty for the workers of the world. Already Angelo, the seminarian, learned of the conflict of the colossi—the materialism of Marx versus the spirituality of the gospel message, or Communism versus Christianity. He entered enthusiastically into the conflict. He was still only a boy, but a boy who had a man's brain and heart: a brain to see clearly the eternal principles at stake in the conflict, and a heart courageous enough to want to enter into the lists on the side of the Preacher of the Sermon on the Mount.

He successfully finished the courses prescribed in the seminary at Bergamo, which introduced him to the delights of Philosophy, Church History, Liturgy, Canon Law, and others.

He was not too quick in mastering his subjects. The professors early spotted that he lacked certain fundamentals, but because he was so spiritual and likable a fellow, they conspired to help him, and so he got through.

They sent him, in 1900, to the Lateran Athenaeum in Rome,

for his theological studies, and for special courses in the Apollinaris. This school is noted for its theology, and we can well appreciate that Angelo, now a young man, found in theology the most satisfying of all his studies. It is the science of God, and is the most sublime of the sciences by reason of its "subject," the Supreme Being, directly studied and because of the rewards to the soul that accrue from the study of Supreme Truth and Goodness. It can be said that the formation of a priestly heart is in ratio to its appreciation of the beauties of theology. Angelo had loved God from infancy. He had often meditated on the infinite majesty of the Eternal Spirit; he had formed a personal, intense attachment to the Christ, the Savior of the World, in whose priesthood he wanted to participate, and he had constantly increased his love and devotion to the Mother through whose most pure and virginal body the Savior had come from heaven to dwell amongst us.

Theology had enriched his knowledge of God, of Christ, and of Mary, and with this enriched knowledge there had come a deeper love. The young man had learned the Theology of the Mass—how it is the continuing, though bloodless, perfect sacrifice of Christ "unto the remission of sins," and of the Theology of the Sacraments which apply to man the infinite merits of that perfect sacrifice.

Into his soul had come the firmer resolve: since Sacraments are for men, let them be administered to men. From his heart came the fervent prayer: Lord, accept me as thy priest, so that I, in thy name, can administer to them the Sacraments thou hast established for their salvation.

Angelo had developed the heart of a true priest. He had his degree in theology, so his mind was ready; he had taken the discipline of the seminary, so his will was ready. "My heart is ready, O Lord, my heart is ready." (Psalm 107, 2)

All that was heeded now was the call by a bishop. This call came on August 10, 1904. The deacon Angelo knelt in the sanctuary of the Church of Santa Marie in Monte Santo, Rome, and heard the call of the ordaining prelate, Bishop Ceppetelli. He stepped forward. Hands were imposed on him. His own hands were pressed on chalice and paten and he heard the unforgettable words: "Receive the power to celebrate Mass for the living and for the dead, in the Name of the Father, and of the Son and of the Holy Spirit."

The farmer boy had become a priest; the shepherd of a few farm sheep was now the shepherd of countless souls.

10

His Priestly Life

AS AN *alter Christus* he ascended the altar in St. Peter's in Rome, on the day following his ordination, to celebrate his first Mass. It was the altar over the confession of the first Pope. Can anyone describe the sublimity of the first Mass of a priest? Years of yearning and striving, years of studying and praying, years of anxiety with alternate moods of wonderment and doubt, a sustained sense of unworthiness, an ever resurgent confidence that it is God's mercy to impart the eternal dignity. The palms are still redolent of the consecrating oil and the words of the consecrator keep ringing in his ears: "Whatever you shall bless shall be blessed, whatever you shall consecrate shall be consecrated." Then, resolving any doubt, he remembers the words of the Eternal Priest himself: "You have not chosen me, but I have chosen you and have appointed you that you should go and bear fruit, and that your fruit should remain." (John XV, 16). So he ascends the altar of his God, to the God who gives joy to youth. Father Angelo has offered his first Mass, and as in the case of all priests in the world, it is the unforgettable day of his life.

Sotto il Monte duly celebrated on the day of their pride's ordination. A good dinner was had, music was played, and fires were lit that burned for the night. It was open house at the Roncallis—which pleasant social event was repeated the day the young priest arrived home to say his first Mass in his native village. Unfortunately, at that particular time the village church, the parish of St. John the Baptist, was being repaired and redecorated. So he had to be content to say Mass elsewhere for a while.

What would happen to him now? A newly ordained priest always wonders as to the assignment he will get after his brief vacation is over. Will he be sent to a big parish or a small one; a city one or a rural one; will he have a friendly pastor or a tyrant? Providence had prepared a surprise.

The bishop of the diocese of Bergamo, Giacomo Count Radini-Tedeschi, had followed the studies of his young subject with great interest. The reports from the professors in his own seminary and of the faculty of the Apollinaris convinced him that he had in Don Angelo a discreet, able, and industrious cleric, whereupon he determined to appoint him as his secretary.

This post of secretary to a bishop has its advantages and disadvantages, with the disadvantages usually getting the edge. The advantage is that you immediately come under the notice of the superior and learn the inside working of a diocese, an invaluable source of information that synthesizes in one month what it takes years of classes of Canon Law to impart. The disadvantage is that you lead a life of dull routine, always under the eye of the superior, and woe to you if you forget what the bishop wants you to remember, or remember what he wants you to forget. To those whose temperament is for pastoral ministry the business of working in an office day in, day out, with a bit of traveling now and then, wherein one acts as a sort of sublimated altar boy or valet for bishop, is most unpalatable. But it is a post badly needed in any diocese. For some it means recognition and promotion after a period of drudgery while in the case of others it proves too hard for their temperament.

Don Angelo proved to be a good secretary, and while faithfully attending to his clerical chores, he zealously saw to it that he would perform some priestly function. He found time to teach Church history, Apologetics, and Patristic Philosophy in the seminary, and he helped out in parish services. In this connection he thought it would be helpful for the parish to have a news bulletin. Such a publication, he asserted, would serve admirably in acquainting the parishioners with the activities planned by the pastor, and avoid tedious announcements during Mass which consume much of the time that should be devoted to preaching. His clear, practical mind saw so many advantages in this idea, novel in his day, and it did prove successful. Today, as most readers know, it is almost usual procedure in parishes.

His relations with his bishop were cordial. He must have learned much from his superior, not only in ecclesiastical procedure, but in classical learning and social graces. Whatever might have been lacking to him from his simple living in Sotto il Monte was now being steadily supplied as he performed his duties as secretary. There were people to meet, places to visit, situations to smooth over, dinners to attend, and so many other opportunities for the shy country boy to acquire the poise and the facility of social acts, that is, treating people politely and confronting difficult situations with equanimity. He had been teased in the seminary about being a country bumpkin. He was fast losing bucolic awkwardness while he kept retaining a farmer's simplicity and warmth. He was growing to a good stature of the man in public life. His secretary's desk was proving to be a splendid seminary for the acquisition of the many items of knowledge and of the smooth diplomatic ways one needs for his own personal maturity and for successful relations with the public.

He came in contact with many people of low and high

degree. It all helped him to appreciate the problems which bothered each class. He had to treat with the Cardinal of Milan and with the peasants of the commune; he had to meet the officials of the government and the humblest subjects of the crown; he had to interview the monsignori and pastors of the diocese and the tradespeople. All classes passed in review before him and from each he learned something of ruling men and of their behavior under rule.

He was impressed very much, and fortunately it turned out to be reciprocal with the studious librarian at the Ambrosian Library in Milan, a certain Don Achille Ratti. Brief chats now and then with this man kept our young priest ardent in reading. The librarian of the Ambrosian, as everyone knows, became Pope Pius XI in 1922, and, as we shall see, had confidence enough in him to promote him to a high post.

The association with all sorts of persons was a liberal course in psychology. His contact with his own bishop, particularly, was a joyous flight into the sublime reaches of theology. He often has described his relationship with his ecclesiastical superior in these memorable words: "He was the polar star of my priesthood." Don Angelo meant this in its best spiritual sense. Bishop Radini-Tedeschi was a very saintly man, as well as being an able administrator of the diocese. The "polar star" allusion was the secretary's way of saying that the bishop had constantly edified him, and that such episcopal piety had constituted a challenge to the secretary to emulate it.

This is an ideal relationship between bishop and priest, and it recalls the many fine incidents in early Church history when a saintly bishop would be the model on which a priest or deacon would pattern his own way of living.

This happy schooling in both spirituality and sociality lasted ten years. Ten years are a good part of one's life. These ten years for Don Angelo were to prove the last decade of what we may term his private, peaceful life of preparation. Henceforth, it was to be no longer private, quiet, or peaceful. He was through with preparation as such. He was now to get into action on his own.

Among his many side activities in this period of his life was the one of arranging and conducting pilgrimages of the people of Bergamo to various shrines in Italy. This, too, broadened him both culturally and socially. At the same time it brought to his attention many practical problems that were confronting the people.

In this period, too, he produced his first book, an analysis of the life of Cardinal Baronius, the great Church historian. He was reading voraciously, and no one who does that can for long resist the urging of his writing fingers.

In 1914, as most of our readers will recall, Europe engulfed herself in the horror of World War I. Italy, striving at first to stay out of it, was inevitably drawn into the conflict. Her diplomacy had put her into a most unenviable position. She had been a member of the Grand Alliance with Germany and Austria. These two countries were immediately in the war through the refusal of Serbia to come to terms, and expected Italy to join them. Italy determined not to, claiming that her alliance was for defense only, not for offense. Her joining the war later, on the side of the Allies, earned her the bitter enmity of Germany and hardly anything less than suspicion and contempt from the Allies. Her position, therefore, was not the most pleasant, and it demanded more sacrifices in men and material than would normally be the case.

The necessary and complete mobilization of the Italian kingdom gathered into the maw of its insatiable military machine many elements which, in our nation, would not be touched. It may come as a surprise, and even a shock, that a supposedly Catholic nation such as Italy would actually go to the expedient of drafting priests to serve as soldiers in war.

But so it was. France did the same thing. The drafting of soldiers, started in France in the throes of the revolution's counter-attack against royal armies assembled to crush liberty, had changed the pattern of wars. Heretofore they had been affairs conducted by mercenary soldiers hired wherever obtainable, leaving the citizens of a country free to go about their business. Now war involved all citizens and it increased enormously the burdens on a country and its casualties.

From his peaceful life as secretary to his bishop, Don Angelo was rudely snatched. He was drafted into the Italian army and ordered to serve as a sergeant in the medical corps. He had studied a good bit of medical lore and practice and it now began to prove very useful to him.

The campaigns were bloody and arduous. We can imagine the anguish that was his as he saw the wounded, the crippled and the mutilated brought to the center for treatment. On the farm, he had felt for a lame horse and a bruised sparrow. He felt keenly now the misery of men whose bodies were racked by disease or torn asunder by bullet or shrapnel. He did what he could to alleviate their physical pain. What he did was notable because he had become an expert in pathology and as a dispensary technician. He was allowed to work side by side with the doctors. As priest, he was able to help even more in their mental and spiritual anguish. God's providence had placed him in a spot where he could do a great deal of good to the rank and file.

In time, he was promoted from sergeant in the medical corps to the post of chaplain with a lieutenant's commission. In this new capacity he was able to function more openly as a priest, and his ministry, both spirtually and physically, was fruitful of many satisfying results. The experience of the war put that necessary bit of iron into him which he needed to give him the final strength of character to deal with difficult people.

The war ended with Italy impoverished and inglorious. Wearily, the soldiers made their way home to try to resume their civilian occupations. This "farewell to arms" period has been the theme of many a poet and novelist and is an epic in itself.

Upon his quitting the army, Don Angelo returned to his diocese. The bishop in 1919 appointed him spiritual director of the seminary. In this place of learning, where twenty years back he had been teased as a backward country cousin, he was now in high honor. And he did credit to his post, which was one of great importance in the training of priests. The seminarians found in him a practical counselor, a man whose own spiritual solidity made it easy to pass on to others that spark of inspiration which no amount of mere book learning could ever do.

Next to becoming a priest, the noblest calling is to help a boy advance to the priesthood. Most Catholics do this by their prayers and contributions. This, teachers and administrators can do by imparting knowledge and enforcing discipline. But, particularly, the spiritual advisers do it by keeping the noble aims and objectives of the priesthood of Christ constantly vivid in the young aspirant's mind, by guiding him over the rough recurring periods of spiritual sterility, depression, and rebellion, and by being the living model of the actual holy priest right before his eyes.

While at the seminary, performing his spiritual services for the future spiritual leaders of the diocese, Don Angelo's fertile mind saw the practicality of starting or providing student homes for the middle-class students who were attending the state schools. Rich students could provide for themselves without difficulty in homes or pensions of their choosing, but the middle-class student had to seek lodgings which often represented either a corporal hazard or a moral one. A student home, either one actually built for the purpose, or at least rented and supervised, was the answer of practical-minded Catholicism to an old problem of keeping the adult student in the fold.

He also played an active role in the Catholic Action movement which was then in its infancy and which he was destined to spark into vigorous growth. Catholic Action appealed to his sense of apostolicity which, as a mark of the Church, has to be found in heads and members. It is not enough to believe. True belief must manifest itself by action—an action which would tend to spread the faith or defend it.

So notable was his work in this field that it came to the attention of Pope Benedict XV, who was trying to bring both economic and social order out of the shambles that was postwar Italy. In 1921, he invited Don Angelo to come to Rome to work with the Congregation of the Propagation of the Faith.

Thus, back to Rome he went—the beloved Rome of the scene of his final priestly studies and of his ordination, the beloved Rome, the prime see of the world, whose bishop was shepherd not just of that great city, but of the whole earth.

He was made a monsignor and put in charge of the project of reorganizing the whole Congregation. New fields were opening following the World War. God always compensates for losses in Europe by opening up promising fields of conversion elsewhere, and the Propaganda was to rise to the occasion. The robust priest from Bergamo diocese had a fine flair for organizing various services. The Propaganda had labored too long with antiquated methods of procedure. This slow technique, bogged down with musty tradition and red-tape, reduced the efficiency of this great arm of the Militant Church. Monsignor Angelo's task was to expedite means and missioners to the fields ripe for the harvest.

This was a job he liked and he tackled it with his accustomed enthusiasm. He worked hard at it for four years. He pointed out easier ways of accomplishing the purposes of the Propaganda, and he was doing a very creditable piece of work when, in 1925, by the grace of God and by favor of the Holy See, he was raised from the status of a priest to become truly a successor of the apostles by being selected as a bishop.

❀ 11 ❀

His Episcopal Life

THE episcopacy is the fullness of the priesthood. He who receives this order becomes formally a successor of the apostles and enjoys great spiritual powers and honors.

The words, *epi scopus,* from which episcopacy or bishopric is derived, are Greek and together mean one who looks over, or oversees. Thus, in the very wording we see indicated a power to rule. The Scriptures pointedly state that bishops are "to rule the Church of God." (Acts XX, 28) The bishop is the ruler of that portion of the Church to which he has been appointed or elected. On this point there arises one of the fundamental differences between the Catholic concept of the episcopacy and that of those Protestants who acknowledge an episcopacy. The Catholic concept is to the effect that each bishop, having a diocese to rule, rules it by divine right but not purely independently since his diocese is a portion of the whole; for the sake of order and unity he must abide by those decisions which affect the whole, the whole being under the jurisdiction of the Bishop of Rome. (Canon 329) In a sense each bishop is pope in his own diocese, but since confusion and contradictions would result if each were fully independent, both the divine will and common sense dictate the reposing of the unifying power in the hands of one chief bishop.

Among the main duties of a bishop in his diocese are:

1. To safeguard the purity of the faith;
2. To maintain the faith and spread it;
3. To uphold Christian morality;
4. To punish infractions of Church laws;
5. To promote works of piety, charity, and benevolence;
6. To advance learning;
7. To supervise all religious activities in his area. (Canon 343)

To show these powers, the bishop wears a mitre, the old Mosaic symbol of leadership, and he carries a crosier, whose crook is curved at the end in sign of a bishop's limited pastorate. (The Pope does not carry a crosier for this reason, but in sign of his unlimited shepherding a straight three-barred cross is carried before him.) The bishop wears a ring to signify his marriage to his flock, and a pectoral cross to show both his faith in the Crucified and his willingness to die for the faith.

If a bishop is not to rule a diocese, he is either an assistant to a bishop who does have a diocese or he is selected for some special work. In either case, he is given what is called a titular diocese, that is, he is named as bishop of a diocese which once flourished as such but no longer does since it is in an area where the Catholic faith has been uprooted or abandoned.

Normally one advances from priest to bishop, and later on to archbishop, whose position as a prelate is of higher rank than bishop. An archbishop like a bishop can be named either for an actual archdiocese or for some special work, in which case he is named titular archbishop of a defunct archdiocese.

This is what happened to our Monsignor Roncalli in the Holy year of 1925. Pope Pius XI commanded that he be advanced to the episcopal dignity with the title of archbishop, and since he was not to rule an actual archdiocese but perform some special work the Pope had in mind, he was consecrated as titular Archbishop of Areopolis, a town in Palestine long under Mohammedan rule.

On the feast of St. Joseph, March 19, Monsignor Roncalli was consecrated archbishop and immediately started the work which the Pope had in mind for him, a touchy bit of diplomacy. It was to be the start of a twenty-seven year period of a diplomat on the march, or, as he himself expressed it, a time when he was "a traveler of God."

His first assignment was to be visitator apostolic in Bulgaria. A visitator apostolic is somewhat like an apostolic delegate, who is the representative of the Pope in a country which has no official diplomatic relations with the Holy See, as is the case with our country. An apostolic delegate is a permanent assignment. Witness the span of Archbishop Cigognani who has been apostolic delegate to the United States since 1933, and who has now, November 1958, been named a cardinal. The visitator's assignment on the other hand is for a temporary period, sufficient to take care of an emergency. Usually his duties are simply to inspect the state of the Church in the country confided to him, draw up a report and submit it to the Holy See. His office terminates when this report is filed.

But this did not happen with visitator apostolic Roncalli in Bulgaria. He spent five years in that hostile country as visitator, giving encouragement to the few Roman Catholics in that country, dominated largely by Mohammedan and Greek Orthodox elements, coordinating their activities and protecting their rights before the crown. So important was his work that the Pope changed his status from that of visitator to that of apostolic delegate in 1939.

In this post he became one of the central figures in a bizarre diplomatic mixup. In 1930, a royal match between

King Boris of Bulgaria, a Greek Orthodox, and Princess Giovanna of Italy, a Roman Catholic, was proposed. As is usual in such cases, the Church through her delegate demanded of Boris that he promise in writing to have all children, without exception, born of the union, baptized and raised as Roman Catholics. The "without exception" was included particularly in this case because it was rumored that Boris would insist on having a male heir raised as a Greek Orthodox. The promises were signed and the marriage took place in Italy. The delegate was charged by the Pope to see to it that no ceremony later held in Bulgaria contradicted the Roman Catholic nuptial agreement. Archbishop Roncalli faithfully saw to it that there was none.

Three years later Queen Giovanna gave birth to a baby girl, named Marie Louise. While the royalty of Italy, particularly Queen Elena, the mother of Giovanna, were rejoicing over the birth and en route to Bulgaria for the baptism, King Boris had the child baptized in the Orthodox church. The Apostolic Delegate immediately lodged a vigorous protest, reminding Boris that he had promised in writing not to do that very thing. All Italy was furious at this double-dealing, and sought through the diplomatic channels of both the crown and papacy to have the situation corrected, but very little satisfaction was obtained.

Throughout it all, even though no success in this matter was achieved, Archbishop Roncalli displayed very admirable qualities as a diplomat, quieted down the increasing rancor of both sides, and prevented greater damage to the position of the Church in that hostile land. The experience gave him a better insight into the Greek and Oriental minds. He began making a definite study of the complicated political, canonical and ethnological problems that beset the relations of the Eastern Church with the Western.

On November 30, 1934, Archbishop Roncalli was transferred to the Titular Archbishopric of Mesembris, the ancient name of a seaport on a peninsula in the Black Sea, now called Missivri. It is a town in the province of Roumelia, European Turkey, which province formerly comprised the whole country south of the Balkans and east of Macedonia. Here, he came to know the Mohammedan mind better than before. Turkey had undergone a great change since World War I. It was adopting European ways, and, in a sense, Christian ways. At least it had lost its old ferocious enmity to Christianity and was in friendly relations with Christian nations. The Archbishop's task was to foster more of this new friendliness.

In 1935, the Archbishop's duties were expanded to include that of Apostolic Delegate in both Greece and Turkey. In Turkey, he was also the Apostolic Administrator of the Latin Vicariate Apostolic in Constantinople. He made his headquarters in Istanbul and for nine years, a period which extended to the middle of World War II, he remained at that most sensitive post of the diplomatic world.

He was alert and learned much of that which passes as mystery in the Near East. This farm boy who had never gone to diplomatic school, who never dreamed of making diplomacy his career, by applying to the task the simple triple combination of honest loyalty to one's chief, indefatigable industry, and plain common sense, was able to serve the cause of the Church and of Christian culture very advantageously.

During his period of service in Bulgaria he had gone to the bother of learning that country's difficult language, and while in Istanbul, he had begun to tackle Russian.

When in the Balkans, he noticed at first hand the inroads which Communism was making in that portion of Europe. He saw vast regions come under the influence of the Hammer and Sickle—Roumania, Bulgaria, Yugoslavia, and Albania. Greece and Turkey were on the Red timetable, and they would have succumbed had not the Truman Doctrine been proclaimed.

He made a good impression on the Turkish government by his genial disposition and his willingness to cooperate in anything he could. He pleased the government particularly by his insistence that uniate priests in Turkey celebrate Mass and conduct other services in the language of the country.

So definite was his success as a diplomat in that difficult region of earth in that most trying period of World War II, that in December of 1944, when a diplomatic crisis was boiling in France, Pope Pius XII determined to send this "traveler of God," or diplomat "trouble shooter" to that country. Since France is a Catholic country, Archbishop Roncalli's new title was that of Apostolic Nuncio, that is, ambassador.

They tell the story that one day during a pre-Christmas lull, a coded message came to his delegation headquarters in Istanbul. His code-secretary being away, the Archbishop began to decode the message himself. As he deciphered the code, he learned that he was destined to be sent to Paris as Nuncio. He first thought this was a mistake, and he went back to the task of decoding—but the first version stood up. Whereupon, thinking that the papal secretaries in Rome had made either an error in advancing his name instead of another's or a gross miscalculation concerning his diplomatic ability, he determined to hurry to Rome to clear up the matter. He was astonished to learn when he reported to the Holy See that he had been selected not by any group of high-level secretaries for perfunctory confirmation by the Holy Father, but that Pius XII had himself personally named him to the post.

That post, France, required the best diplomat the Church had. A curious situation had developed which, unless handled expertly, could prove disastrous to the Church. In 1940 France had been conquered by Germany. Northern France, including Paris, was occupied and governed by the German military, while southern France was allowed its own rule, with center at Vichy, provided it would "collaborate" with the German government. This arrangement divided French thinking. One group, headed mainly by General De Gaulle, wanted no arrangement with Germany and preferred to try to fight on until all France was free. Another group, headed mainly by General Petain, thought that a half loaf was better than none; that humiliating as it was, Vichy still allowed some semblance of honor and provided an opportunity for France to keep herself alive politically and to safeguard her culture. The Apostolic Nuncio to France, Archbishop Valeri (now Cardinal Valeri), had gone along with Petain and in doing this kept alive what few rights there were left to the Church in France.

By December of 1944, the "Crusade in Europe" led by General Eisenhower had succeeded in ousting the Germans from France and the liberated French had now turned their full spleen on the collaborators. This spleen included the Church. The French who would never "do business" with Germany, even when Germany had them by the throat, were now in power in France, and began to treat brutally all those individuals and institutions who had gone along with the Vichy philosophy. Despite the great repute of Marshal Petain which he had earned so valiantly in World War I in that memorable defense of Verdun, he was treated ignominiously and imprisoned. The Church was bitterly attacked by patriot and partisan. There was need of a strong, astute diplomat who would be able to blunt the savagery of the attack. Hence, the secret cable to Archbishop Roncalli to hasten to Paris.

To Paris hurried the farmer boy, arriving there January 1, 1945, and without delay presented his credentials to Premier DeGaulle. He was received politely but far from warmly. The farmer boy bided his time—that is, a few hours. The Vatican Nuncio is by ancient privilege the dean of the diplomatic corps in any Catholic country. In this capacity, he was to give the New Year's toast. He gave it—and likely no pleasant cocktail hour arranged for the relaxation of hard-working diplomats or for mutual greetings on the occasion of a holiday, such as this was, was ever more electrified than by the toast the farmer's boy gave to those seasoned diplomats that day. It has gone down as a gem of diplomacy and it immediately won for the churchman a great deal of personal admiration which helped smooth over the crisis that had developed between the Holy See and France.

Patient, plodding work, interspersed with sparkling humor and a genial humaneness made him popular in France and permitted him to gain far more privileges for the Church than through any strict drawing-room technique.

People began to buzz delightfully about him, saying: "He has wit . . . he is humorous—he is most entertaining . . . and oh so clever—nothing escapes his clear, fast eye . . . he is a gem to have for company." This sort of thing helped his personality rating, but its chief result was the important one of establishing cordial relations between the Church and government of France which for decades had been very anticlerical. So charming was the personality of the little man from Lombardy, that he was accepted as the friend and confidant of most of the French politicians. All the while he was a good counselor to the perplexed French bishops. The President of France at the time, Vincent Auriol, became particularly fond of the Nuncio, and this afforded the churchman a fine opportunity of securing more privileges from a country that had learned to be severe and even aloof from her spiritual mother.

While in Paris, the Archbishop served for about seven months as the Holy See's permanent observer in UNESCO. He freely confessed that Catholics could draw inspiration from the announced aims of the international organization. This in itself was a diplomatic act intended to remove the suspicions that had been entertained by some Catholics concerning the real aims of UNESCO. The suspicions became more grounded as UNESCO developed. It did begin to give evidence of being in reality, a "superministry of education," largely in the hands of free-thinkers, who were cleverly steering it to adopt their godless views in education. In an address in 1951, the Nuncio gave a blunt warning that UNESCO should keep to its noble, general aims without attempting to change or suppress the racial, literary or religious values of any people. It should work hand in hand with a Church's missionary activities in a country and not substitute for her. He ended by saying: "On the contrary, it is in order to ensure these values for each country that UNESCO was founded."

Stung by this courageous exposé of the undercover workings of the so-called liberals, the Communist bloc in the National Assembly moved to rebuke the Nuncio, charging that he had unduly interfered as a churchman in a purely lay matter. The French Minister of National Education, André Marie, defended the Archbishop, observing that his remarks had been proper since he was an accredited delegate-observer in UNESCO.

The Nuncio felt they were not only proper, but necessary. He saw in UNESCO a definite international power for great good or great evil. He was becoming more and more conscious of the need of the international approach to the moot problems of these modern times. The little boy born in a very small hamlet of less than two thousand souls had now grown conscious of the two billion human beings on earth.

There had been a story spread that a great deal of the Nuncio's charm in Paris lay in his culinary ability. After all, the way to a man's heart is still through his stomach. Anyone who could interest a Frenchman in a cuisine other than Parisian must have something very savory. A North Italian table will favorably compare with the best dishes on earth, and he must have intrigued the French with the mystery of the Alt'Italia risottos, fungis, ragouts, brodi, pasta and verdura, but it can be equally asserted that the success of any eating party of his, depended more on his own infectious smile and salt in his observations than on any amount of salt in his dishes.

This brilliant diplomatic career of the poor boy of Sotto il Monte, came to an end, when, late in 1952, the announcement flashed over the news wires of the world that the Pope in a coming consistory would give the red hat to his Nuncio in Paris.

The farmer boy of a share-cropping family had achieved a lasting eminence.

12

His Life As Cardinal Patriarch

IT HAS been the usage in Catholic countries that when one living in that country was named a cardinal, he would receive from the head of state of that country the red biretta in anticipation of the formal red hat which the Pope would convey to him in open consistory.

For many years now France had been anti-clerical, and her head of state had very often not been a Catholic, or if he was, not a practising one.

Would Cardinal-elect Roncalli follow the old custom? Everyone wondered what he would do. He very soon resolved their wonder. His sole consideration in the decision was the good of the church. He knew that by accepting the biretta from the head of a state anticlerical in tone, he might be affording an indication or a sign of subservience to a philosophy inimical to the Church, but in his logic he also knew that such an action might be the solvent needed to soften the bitterness that had developed in the officialdom of France toward the Church over the past fifty years.

On January 15, 1953, consequently, he, an archbishop of the Roman Catholic Church, a cardinal-elect and therefore a prince-designate of the Church, knelt before an unbeliever, Vincent Auriol, President of the Fourth French Republic, and received from him the red biretta as a sign of the French people's complacency with the action of the Father of Christendom in making this man a prince of the Church, harking back to those historic days when France was intimate in the councils of the Church.

In the fact that the picture of the cardinal-elect receiving the red biretta from President Auriol has been greatly featured in the plethora of pictures and news items that have appeared since the announcement of the election of Cardinal Roncalli to the papacy is proven the soundness of the reasoning that made the scene possible. Seeing that picture, the most violent enemies of the Church must indeed pull in their fangs. The Church has often been accused of arrogance. But here is a churchman kneeling before a layman. The Church has been charged with arrogating to herself all power on the plea of the superiority of the spiritual realm. But here is a man of God rendering to Caesar the things that are Caesar's. The man's reasoning was indeed sound, and it is this type of reasoning—fresh and clear—that is calculated to bring about happier relations between the Church and all nations.

President Auriol himself indicated this in his brief discourse on the occasion:

> The French Government has been deeply aware of your persevering friendliness, of the solicitude you have shown for the welfare of the French people in line with the noble teaching of the Supreme Head of the Church, and of the generous actions undertaken by you in the cause of peace. I personally recall with a great deal of emotion, Sir Cardinal, our private conversation of January 1. Your words will remain as fine examples of wisdom, of skill and of friendliness.

Further to confirm the good relations which had been cemented, the President presented the Cardinal with the Grand Cross of the Legion of Honor. Conferring this decoration on a cardinal had been a matter of routine in happy days gone by, but since the time when the series of anti-religious laws were promulgated and harshly enforced in the first decade of the century, it had been discontinued. After this honor, although the good-will ambassador was sad to leave France, he departed with the assurance that he had done more to bring France back to the Church than had anyone since the death of the Little Flower, St. Therese of Liseieux, in 1897.

Shortly after his formal reception of the red hat from the hands of Pope Pius XII, Cardinal Roncalli was named Patriarch of Venice. When he heard of this appointment, the new Cardinal was filled with joy. He had loved Pius X, at the start of whose reign he had been ordained and had rejoiced that he had been canonized. Now he was to follow him as bishop of Italy's most attractive city.

The import of the fact that Pius X had been called from Venice to the head see in Rome in 1903 never entered his head. He remembered only that Pius X had been a magnificent priest and set himself out to emulate his excellent virtue. "Here I have a chance to be entirely a pastor," he is quoted as saying. "Everyone says I am a diplomat. The Church's only diplomacy is that of the priesthood."

So this man, burning with zeal both for the inward sanctity of priesthood which he had honored since his ordination and for the active fatherly ministry which in the main had been subordinated to the clerical, pedagogical or diplomatic work of the past fifty years, came to the fantastic watery city of Venice.

The Queen City of the Adriatic welcomed its Patriarch warmly. It went all-out to give its forty-fourth Patriarch and one hundredth and thirty-ninth bishop a princely reception. A gala flotilla of gondolas majestically moved up the Grand Canal 'mid banks of flowers and bunting to the Piazza San Marco, the Cathedral area. In his first sermon from the pulpit of St. Mark's on the occasion of his installation, he assured his people: "Do not look upon your patriarch as a politician or as a diplomat. You will find him only a priest."

This he meant sincerely as revealing his own personal program; but it was accepted better than he realized, for the simple reason that his predecessor, the Patriarch Agostini, had been rough with clergy and people, handling them in a despotic manner. All Venice felt that they would have a calm after the storm, and indeed it proved to be a joyous calm. Venice soon became accustomed to seeing the sturdy little figure of the Patriarch, dressed in modest black outer coat, ambling everywhere, stopping for a chat in the cafés, riding in a motor launch or gondola, pausing before a group of gondoliers and exchanging genial banter with them. Venice was not used to this sort of democracy but she liked it. She liked the man because he was not pretending love of people; she knew he truly loved people.

The Patriarch's secretaries simply could not keep up with him. Neatly arranged horaria or half- or quarter-hour packages meant nothing to him when it was a question of hearing an afflicted tale. He stayed far beyond his allotted time, interviewing all sorts of people, including many disapproved of by his secretaries. Upon their frequent remonstrances that he was allowing himself to waste too much time with anyone who wanted to interview him, he blandly rejoined: "Suppose they want to confess their sins—should I refuse them?"

So he became the People's Patriarch. The desire of many years to be with people he knew—people who were his kind of people; people who needed his ministration of Sacraments; people with whom he could talk freely, familiarly and even jocularly—was at last fulfilled and he was enjoying the goodness of his native element. He had done extremely well as a diplomat and had stood up with the cleverest striped-pants in the profession; but this mingling with working people, the middle class, the backbone of any society, was more in tune with his spirit.

He brought back to the people much that had belonged to them. For instance, in the annual music festival of that year, he filled St. Mark's with music such as had not been heard for centuries—music elevated and classical, yet not stuffy or exclusively provincial. He had a progressive look. Respecting as he did the honor of an ancient regime he still did not stultify himself by closing his eyes to modern needs and ways. Catholic to the core as he was, and supporting naturally the Christian Democrats, nevertheless he was free in advocating what good features there might be in a leftist program.

The problem of Communism is very real in Italy and particularly so in the North. The Cardinal had seen it in operation in many lands, especially in France, so he had learned many of its ways. He was neither fanatically bitter about the situation nor timid. He spoke out forthrightly for the rights of the Church. On one occasion he chided the press very effectively:

> I condemn the bad habits displayed by a certain class of the press which dreams up, confuses or distorts a bishop's intentions, attitudes and words, and which gives a political significance to the mere fact that a bishop has asked his faithful to pray and show feelings of charity and courtesy.

He was forever shocking and bewildering people. They had never heard of a cardinal-patriarch who busied himself with the small problems of people or who gave them anything more than a polite encouragement to be docile citizens. (Fifty years is a long time in the memory of people: they had forgotten Pius X.) He insisted that some marble panels (sacrosanct to the devotee of art) should be removed from St. Mark's in order to afford worshippers a better view of the altar. He naively felt that devotion was far more important than the presence of another gem of decorative art.

His proletarian tendency led some to believe that he would

go to any length to assure people that he was amenable to their wishes. But in truth he knew where to draw the line. Some citizens broached the topic of setting up gambling booths in St. Mark's Square. He opposed it. Some thought him liberal enough not to bother with the scanty attire of tourists who loved to parade around the Square and dart in and out of St. Mark's. He remonstrated; but instead of a bombast, he chose a shaft of wit to preserve the discipline of decor: "People need not come to Italy in furs and woolens. They can come dressed in that modern American silk, fresh and soft, which is a veritable refrigerator at low cost. Italy, on the other hand, is not on the equator, and even there, by the way, lions wear their coats, and crocodiles are lined with their most precious leather." The practical effect of his words was exemplified when the writer's niece visited St. Mark's this summer. Wearing a sleeveless gown, she was politely forbidden to enter. The man of the people first and foremost burns with zeal for the decor of God's house.

Venetians came to love that rotund little fireball who darted all about the city on so many diversified errands, all with one objective: the welfare of souls. He was the shepherd seeking the lost sheep, correcting the wrong opinions of some, fortifying the weakness of others, and keeping all safe from the beasts that would destroy them. The scriptures call these beasts by the generic name of wolf. The specific wolf of our times is the bear that walks like a man and wields a hammer and sickle.

His routine day as Patriarch of Venice, as published in many papers, was terrifying. When we remember that he was in his seventies when he became patriarch, we must remain amazed at the stamina required in following the regimen. Even greater amazement is caused by his persistence in keeping at it so faithfully, although not with the rigidity of a fanatic. He rose at four, whereupon he took care of his devotions, breviary, spiritual reading, meditation. He celebrated Mass at seven. At eight a little breakfast consisting of a glass of milk and some fruit. He then attended to his correspondence, to office routine, and read the papers. This was done in a hurry but little of note escaped his glance. From ten to one he granted interviews. He then had lunch, made a visit to the Blessed Sacrament and took a half-hour's nap. After that it was work again. He attended to diocesan affairs, held his conferences, and made decisions. At seven forty-five with his official family, he recited the glorious mysteries of the Rosary in chapel, the other two parts having been said privately. At eight, supper, after which a stroll through the courtyard or corridors of his residence, a last look at his desk, and bed at ten.

On certain occasions he would vary this routine by staying up till quite late working on an important pastoral or report to the Holy See.

He was faithful in attending the annual retreat of all the bishops of the Veneto region of Italy, a custom started by Cardinal La Fontaine. He never failed to participate in the monthly day of recollection and conference of the clergy. He was edifying not only by his presence but even by his punctuality.

He had an extraordinary love of the liturgy and delighted to arrange for solemn pontificals throughout his patriarchate to which he invited his fellow cardinals and other bishops. The annual panegyric in honor of St. Mark, the Patron of Venice, was always delivered by a bishop. In this fashion, we find that Cardinals Siri, Lercaro, Agagianian, Feltin, Gilroy, Costantini, Ottaviani and others were his guest celebrants or speakers on the occasions of these solemn ceremonies.

He brought a better spirit of harmony and efficiency in his diocese. He saw to it that Masses started on the time scheduled for them (a point very often taken lightly in Italy). He made a visitation of each parish in the five years of his rule, and he often preached at all the Masses on Sunday in a parish. In the big Church of St. Lawrence in Mestre, he did this ten times one Sunday. He was strict about his priests taking proper care of parish records, while, when examining the children on Christian doctrine, he never assumed the air of an interrogator but rather that of a conversationalist. He wanted the children never to fear to approach him or talk to him.

A bishop's difficult task is to handle his own priests, particularly when there is need of rebuke or punishment. The cardinal did this in a most fatherly way. He was firm in denouncing any wrong, but he was kindly with the wrongdoer, feeling thereby that he would the better bring about a correction. He made his observations with tact and was most scrupulous in avoiding the belittling of any clergyman in front of lay people.

The pure simplicity of the man showed itself in his frequent trips to the kitchen to thank warmly the cook who had provided something specially good or novel that day. At table, he was never stiff or formal; he conversed freely with his guests, but did not monopolize the conversation. He would not allow the conversation to get personal.

He liked the hour of Vespers particularly, because he could persuade the organist to strike a key fit for public participation in the psalm singing.

He kept his contacts with the French and it was not infrequent to find the politicians of that land, though differing sharply among themselves and with the Church in particular, harmoniously gathered at table with him. He even joked about it saying that his rotundity was the only point of union that they had.

He kept also his friendships and concern for many peoples and lands. His appointment list looked like a liberal Cook's tour of Europe. He visited the hospitals, schools, orphanages and great shrines of his own dioceses, and branched out into any other that either might have invited him or in which he had some interest. Thus, in a short period, we find him holding a Synod, solemnly inaugurating the Marian Year in his region, conducting a pilgrimage to Lourdes, visiting Beyrut, as Legate of His Holiness to the Marian Congress there and for the crowning of Our Lady of Lebanon, and the consecration of the lower basilica at Lourdes in honor of St. Pius X.

He accomplished a good bit of material expansion in his diocese in the short five years of his patriarchate. He built a minor seminary, he opened thirty parishes, he brought the members of the St. Jerome of Miani Institute to Mestre and put them in charge of the Sanctuary of the Immaculate Heart of Mary; he repaired the quarters of his canons, redecorated his cathedral, and rearranged the vaults containing the remains of his predecessors.

Particularly in the open field of Catholic Action was he the brilliant, energetic leader. He inspired apostolic zeal on the part of his subjects, clerical and lay, in social, cultural, educational, athletic and recreational activities. His fertile brain kept at a good pitch of action the various organizations of his diocese, which actions included everything from a parade in an obscure village for a little-known saint to a Eucharistic Congress across the seas.

He was arranging for the hundredth anniversary celebration of his saintly predecessor, St. Pius X, when the news of his election to the papacy broke. The plans are temporarily suspended, but anyone who had caught a scintilla of the spirit that animates the new Pope will know that so fine an idea will not be long kept suspended.

He has much to do, and he will do what he has to do, the big and the small, because it will all conspire to further the kingdom of the spirit.

Let us explore just why this man of the soil was elected to the papacy.

❁ 13 ❁

Why They Elected Him

WHY did they elect Cardinal Roncalli? Why was he chosen from all the other fifty cardinals—from hundreds of archbishops and from thousands of prominent bishops and priests throughout the world?

The world has pondered this question and would be interested in a definite answer to it. In some cases, the reason behind the election of a pope is patent. At the opening of a conclave a cardinal may possess either an enormous popularity or some great talent that is needed at the time in the papacy, either of which reasons makes his election a foregone conclusion. This, however, is of rare occurrence. Most selections are not of expected men, but are surprises. Even when the man elected was among the "possibilities" advanced by newspapers and commentators, the reason why he was preferred among the other possibilities cries for an explanation.

We do not pretend to know the explanation. We simply are stabbing in the dark with only the light of plausibility to guide us.

In the first place, as we noted in a previous chapter, a pall of secrecy hides the happenings in a conclave. Both cardinals and conclavists take an oath not to reveal to anyone the proceedings, and this oath is religiously observed. Hence we can offer no positive knowledge on why Cardinal Roncalli, mentioned, indeed, as a possibility by several newspapers before the conclave, was elected. His election came as a definite surprise. It is not wrong to try to pierce the maneuvering that preceded the surprise announcement to the world. Our conjecturing will try to be as logical as possible, but we offer it with no certainty that it is what actually occurred in the minds of the electors.

All during the reign of Pius XII, it had been rumored that the time was ripe for a non-Italian pope. The action of the Pope in reducing the number of Italian cardinals seemed to confirm the impression that the Church was ready to change. It would not have been too surprising if a non-Italian had been elected.

During his reign, the great Peace Pope gave no indication of any preference for a successor. Some were close to him, some reflected quite sharply his ways and personality, yet no one could be pointed out as definite heir of the mantle.

Hence, upon the death of Pius, no cardinal emerged as "the sure man" to succeed. There were enough of the "possibles," with most newspapers agreeing on about six, while the various others mentioned, for reasons of local pride possibly, amounted to twenty.

The sensible way of looking at the problem is to study the composition and mood of the College of Cardinals as the conclave opened, to remember certain statements made before the conclave started, especially by those close to the throne, and to try to interpret logically the why and wherefore of twelve ballots in three days of deliberation.

There was a suspicion that the College was divided into two camps, the one, Pacellian and conservative, the other progressive and reformist. The division was not a sharp one, nor could it be characterized as definitely political. It simply represented truthfully the age-old disagreement between those who want to hold on to the ways of the past and those who want to try new methods, such as have divided Whig from Tory, Liberal from Conservative, and, for that matter, the progressive elements in both our Republican and Democratic Parties as opposed to the traditional stalwarts of each.

It is surmised that there were twenty-five Pacellians, seventeen innovators, and nine neutrals as the conclave opened. Thirty-five votes were needed for election. From that set-up, even if all the nine neutrals joined the larger group of Pacellians, it would not be enough. This fairly explains why there was no election on the first ballot. Each side was feeling out the strength of the other side, and for that matter each side might have had to take some time to decide which one of its group should be the sole standard bearer and around whom the group could rally.

There was no electioneering in the conclave, no campaign speeches in support of any candidate, no soliciting, no open discussions. Each cardinal had to weigh the problem by himself, and while there could be some private seeking of information on points either of law or of a person's qualifications, the decision had to be made in line with one's personal conscience.

The result of each ballot as announced set off a swarm of reconsiderations in the mind of each cardinal whose vote had been for anyone else than the one who showed a plurality. Should he switch to the leader, or should he adhere to his first choice writing in his ballot the formula, *accedo nemini,* I agree to no one else (than the one for whom I first voted). Naturally, switches of votes were made. What motivated the switching which finally grew to the size sufficient to garner the required two-thirds plus one?

In the beautiful discourse delivered by Monsignor Antonio Bacci, Secretary of Briefs to Princes, during the Solemn Mass of the Holy Spirit on the morning of the opening of the conclave, which we can compare to a keynote speech, it was pointed out to the cardinals that they had the solemn duty of electing "not only a teacher and pastor, but a father as well."

In effect, it was a pointed recommendation. It was a counsel to give to the Church a priestly pope rather than a political one. "One," the Monsignor had continued to say, "who will take to his heart, as Christ Jesus had done, the cause of the poor, and of the distressed of earth." He ended by calling for the election of a "holy pontiff," thus stressing the primary qualification that a candidate must possess, since his piety was a need greater than any political sagacity, administrative genius, or diplomatic skill.

It is quite certain that the cardinals remembered the words of Monsignor Bacci after their first vote, which likely, in many cases, went for a sort of "favorite son." Their duty was to remember the needs of the Church and thus give her that type of pontiff best calculated to meet the problems of the times. Different ages require different types of leaders. While all cardinals are *papabile,* that is, qualified to be popes—for surely they are chosen deliberately because they possess the necessary abilities—not all might be suitable in a given period.

Many factors had to be studied and appraised. What is the political condition of the world? What is the religious mood of man? What power has arisen that has to be dealt with, either by show of power or by diplomacy? What moral dangers are present? What are the missionary needs? What persecutions confront the Church? Would this particular cardinal be acceptable to that sizable and influential bloc of nations? Is he presentable for audiences? Does he speak a variety of languages? Is he old enough or young enough?

The grapevine has intimated that fulfilling all the essential conditions was Cardinal Siri, Archbishop of Genoa, and that the Pacellians were solidly behind him. It even named the Pacellians: the Italian Cardinals Ruffini, Tedeschini, Fumasoni-Biondi, Pizzardo, Siri, Mimmi, Micara, Canali, Ottaviani, Cigognani; the American Cardinals, Spellman and McIntyre; the two German ones, Frings and Wendel; the two Portuguese, De Gouveia and Cerejeira; the two Brazilians, De Barros Camara and Da Silva; the two Argentinians, Caggiano and Copello; the two Canadians, McGuigan and Leger; the Cuban, Betancourt, the Ecuadorian, Torre and the Irish, D'Alton. It has not been asserted that all these so-called Pacellians voted solidly and persistently for Cardinal Siri from the beginning. The strategy was to entice the neutrals to their camp, so it is likely many of their votes went to Cardinal Masella, the most prominent of the neutrals, and at times even to Cardinals Ottaviani and Ruffini so as to entice those neutrals favorable to these cardinals to the Pacellian side and to avoid the impression that it was too rigid for one candidate. If you will, it is politics at its best or worst. This human element, this earthly mode of doing things, is inseparable from human affairs whether it be the question of electing an asemblyman, passing a money bill, or electing a pope. Each side wants to draw the "free votes" to itself and uses a variety of techniques, called adroit or slick, depending on one's partisanship.

The other camp, the so-called *riformisti*, reformers, included, it is presumed, Cardinals Lercaro, Ciriaci, Dalla Costa, and Valeri among the Italians; all the six French Cardinals, also the Belgian, the Syrian, the Chinaman, the Indian, the Pole, the Chilean, and the Armenian. The Polish Cardinal Wyszynski drew much sympathy by reason of the persecution his country was suffering which put him in command of some votes, while Cardinal Agagianian with his strong personality was in a position to swing a few votes to any favorite of his. It is likely that this group at first concentrated their votes in favor of Cardinal Valeri after giving a token vote for the Syrian. Cardinal Valeri possessed eminent qualities of leadership, was greatly admired by the neutrals as well as by his own group, and seemed a fair contender for the crown against the more powerful Pacellians.

It is not known for certain if, in the deadlock of the early ballots, there was an attempt to break it by inserting the name of a non-Cardinal, Archbishop Montini of Milan. He was regarded as a *riformisto,* was highly esteemed, and, to all intents and purposes, accepted as a cardinal because he had been offered the red hat but had declined it. It is likely that his candidacy was advanced with frankness, and succeeded in attracting some of the votes of the Pacellian bloc. Once a dent was made in this bloc, it was easy to guide the voting to a more acceptable neutral. The leading candidate of the Pacellians, Cardinal Siri, for all his qualifications, including his age, 52, discovered that this very virtue of youth was militating against him with the arch conservatives. They felt that it just would not do to have so young a pope. Furthermore, he had the reputation of being too austere. This encouraged a further break in the big bloc. By the third day, it became apparent that if a worthy compromise candidate could be offered, he would stand a good chance of success in short order.

It has been suggested that the compromise would be in electing an elderly pope among the neutral group. An elderly pope, not calculated to live too long, would be acceptable to the two groups, who then would hope to consolidate their respective positions before the day of another conclave. The human element again, of course, and this technique inevitably brings to mind the election of the elderly Pope Leo XIII in 1878 for the same reason. The plan in that case did not work, for Leo lived to celebrate his silver jubilee as Pope, and he survived most of the cardinals who had hoped to have an easier time in electing the person they had in mind.

The compromise candidate was now put forward. He was the Patriarch of Venice, Cardinal Roncalli, classed as a neutral. With him as neutrals were the Italians, Cardinals Masella and Fossati; the three Spaniards; the Australian, Gilroy; the Brazilian, De Vasconcellos; and the Colombian, Luque. Cardinal Masella, able as he was, had failed to attract enough votes from the Pacellians and the Riformisti.

Cardinal Roncalli succeeded in this. He had a fine reputation as a man of good common sense, an indefatigable worker, a charming personality perfectly at home with brilliant diplomats and with peasants and factory workers. His captivation of the French nation and his administrative record in Venice pulled great weight. The Church had enjoyed the fine services of an aristocratic pope. The times counselled a change. The proletarian world had to be assured that the Church is not an exclusive champion of the rich and lordly. Abraham Lincoln had wisely said that God must love the poor since he makes so many of them. The Church had been given the charge to preach the Gospel to the poor. Roncalli was a poor man's priest. In this age when Communism is attracting the lowly and laboring class, the Church has to give assurance that she is the Church of the poor man. The background of the Patriarch of Venice was admirably suited to the need, and the more the cardinals reflected on it, the more it became apparent to them that they had in this sharecropper's son the man to win the masses.

How soon after his name was seriously presented did the trend to accept him show itself? We do not know. All we know is that when the twelfth ballot was taken Cardinal Roncalli had won the necessary two-thirds majority plus one, and the white rings of smoke that poured out of the chimney told the world that the cardinals had agreed on a successor to Pope Pius XII.

It has since been rumored by the *voci*, the voices, a name employed to designate the Roman indoor sport of piecing together certain bits of information quietly whispered, that Cardinal Roncalli had secured forty of the fifty-one votes on the twelfth ballot, five more than necessary to be elected.

All the above reasons are human ones, and a mixture of surmise and fact. Other considerations were his likable qualities, his approachability, his fairness, and his evident sense of priestliness. He would be a priestly pope. Further, the cardinals were aware that he would be far more accessible to the hierarchy of the Church than had been the case with Pius XII. It was also believed that he would be more liberal in satisfying the legitimate ambitions of the curia prelates for advancement. Pius XII had frequently by-passed these faithful servants and had given the red hat to outsiders for the purpose of emphasizing the international character of the Church. This was laudable, but it could do damage to the spirit of the official family that has to do the plodding work of the Holy See. The business of having it run by under-secretaries is not wise if continued too long.

Cardinal Agagianian had been mentioned as a possibility because, as we said, he might make a reality of the dream of the desired union of the Eastern and Western Churches. But the prelate who had gone to Bulgaria, Turkey, Greece and Syria as a diplomat had worked hard towards that end and was as keenly desirous of achieving the dream, with even more promise through superior charm and ability, than any other, including Cardinal Agagianian.

They knew he had ability to simplify the workings of the Holy See; they knew he could handle the Communist menace; they knew he understood the disciplinary problems in the dioceses of the world; and they knew that he could attract the friendly cooperation of governments to further the activities of the Church.

They had confidence that this man of the people would

win the hearts of the people of the world. After all, the Church had been established for the spiritual welfare of people.

All these are the human reasons based on a mixture of fact and surmise to explain plausibly why the Conclave of 1958 gave us as Pope that particular priest, Cardinal Roncalli.

But the truer reason is the divine one. It was God's will. God disposes all things sweetly—in the way he wants and in his own good time. His Providence had decreed that in 1958 there should succeed to the post of Vicar of Christ on earth this humble man of the soil. Cardinals at the start might have had their own ideas. God brings about circumstances to have them freely change these preconceived ideas to fit his own plans. We pray, without too much attention to the depth of it: "Thy will be done on earth as it is in heaven." It is done, indeed, and because it has been manifestly God's will that John XXIII should sit on Peter's throne, we accept it gladly.

❁ 14 ❁

The Ceremony of His Coronation

THE Nazarene, of whom the Pope is acknowledged by Catholics to be the Vicar, wore a crown of thorns placed rudely and painfully on his brow in a gesture of contempt by the sneering soldiers of Caesar. When the first Crusade succeeded in liberating Palestine, Geoffrey of Bouillon, who was named to be Christian King of Palestine, refused to wear the traditional gold crown of kings in the region where his Lord had worn the circlet of sharp thorns.

Why then should one who claims to be Vicar of the Crucified be willing to wear any crown at all, let alone the triple one which is the regal adornment of the Pope?

The simple answer is that while the Church was in hiding, her chief bishop indeed had nothing hanging over his head except the sentence of death. Later when the papacy was acknowledged by the Caesars and accorded the title of spiritual sovereign, it was proper that the Pope should wear a symbol of this sovereignty. His Lord indeed had worn a crown of thorns in his passion, and that crown will gloriously and forever symbolize the depth of his love for man, but the fact is he is now in glory at the right hand of his Father Almighty, crowned King of Kings and Lord of Lords, of whose kingdom there will be no end.

The Pope is his Vicar, the Vicar of Christ who is in glory. It is for the purpose of reflecting the grandeur that is due to Christ, the triumphant Savior, that his Vicar allows himself to be dressed in majestic robes and appear among men in the habiliments of royalty. Judas once hypocritically complained: "That ointment could have been sold for much and given to the poor." The Master had replied: "The poor you have always with you, but me you have not always." (Matthew XXVI, 9-11) Christians have interpreted these words to mean that while it is noble to give to the poor, it is equally noble, and even more so, to provide for the glory of God's house. This explains the instinct to build lordly cathedrals and to lavish on the altar the costliest materials available. It is all intended to glorify Christ the King.

The objection that it offends Christian simplicity and tends to make the priest vain and pompous is not valid. Our Lord did rebuke Judas and praised the action of Mary Magdalene who poured on him the costly ointment. Simplicity must always prevail in the heart of a person, but exteriorly he must respond to the dignity of his office, remembering that the honor is not due to him personally but to the Lord he represents. God's majesty is better brought out by building him a magnificent temple than by worshipping always in a stable or plain meeting hall. Similarly Christ's priestliness and kingship are better brought out by his priest being robed in garments befitting his office and dignity. The danger that the priest might arrogate to himself the honor and grow vain is present, and some indeed may have succumbed to the spirit of vanity, but, for all that, the decor of God's house and altar permits the risk. The primary intent is to give glory to God by the use, in the worship of him, of the best materials we have. If man's weakness or wickedness twists the pattern by making him personally enjoy the magnificence of the materials, it is peradventure, and does not affect the goodness of the primary aim. In the building of a cathedral there is always danger that some of the money be misappropriated. This is never a warrant to forbid the construction of the cathedral.

A definite warrant, by clear analogy, for the magnificence of the ceremony of the coronation is found in the Scriptures themselves. The priests of Israel were divinely ordered to wear rich gowns in their ceremonies, and the high priest was especially enjoined to present himself in adornments of vestments which fitted his unique rank. Should the shadow which was Israel be grander than the substance which is Christianity? The Levitical priesthood is no more. It served in its day to prepare the world for the reality to come, the everlasting priesthood of Christ in the Order of Melchisedec. It is proper to show its interior superiority over all ancient priesthoods by external manifestations. Exteriors should always conform as far as possible to the interior dignity.

This is why, then, the Catholic church proceeded to conduct a magnificent pageantry of coronation once she had selected her new high priest. She would show to the world by exterior display the grandeur of the office that she had bestowed on Angelo Roncalli.

Contrary to expectation, John XXIII appointed Tuesday, November 4, to be the day of his crowning instead of Sunday, November 9, as had been predicted. By coincidence, it happened to be the day of elections in the United States.

By eight in the morning the Basilica of St. Peter's was filled with fifty thousand people, high and low, while more than two hundred thousand jammed the plaza outside. There were representatives of all governments friendly to the Holy See, of all royalty, and of great houses. Our country was represented by our Under-Secretary of State, Robert Murphy, by our Secretary of Labor, James P. Mitchell, and by Claire Booth Luce. Tribunes had been erected near the main altar for the Pope's relatives, for the various representatives of government, for royalty, for distinguished persons, and for prominent religious superiors.

At eight-thirty the ceremonies started. The Pope, in white cope with jeweled clasp, and wearing a precious mitre, flanked by the members of the noble guard, was met by the cardinals in the vestry. A procession of some 400 persons was formed, consisting of the noble guards, knights, religious, clergy, mitred bishops, cardinals and attendants. Heading the procession was Monsignor Ovidio Bejan, carrying the papal cross. Monsignor Bernardino Bocchini carried the papal tiara on a cushion of white silk. Prince Giuseppe Aspreno Colonna, as chief lay assistant at the throne, followed the cardinals, as did other noblemen of the papal court.

When Monsignor Enrico Dante, Prefect of Apostolic Ceremonies, gave the sign that all was ready, the Pope mounted his *sedes gestatoria*, a mobile throne, and the procession filed to the atrium of the basilica, the great lobby of St. Peter's. Here a gilded throne had been erected which the Pope ascended, and thereupon received the formal homage of the basilica staff, the Canons of St. Peter's. The combined Sistine and Julian choirs sang the stirring greeting: "Tu es Petrus" (Thou art Peter).

After the obedience of the basilica staff, the Pope remounted the portable throne and was borne into the basilica proper. The peal of silver trumpets warned the congregation of his coming, and at the first sight of him on the portable throne the whole mass of humanity in St. Peter's kept shouting in a frenzy of enthusiasm, *"Viva il Papa,"* "Long Live the Pope." This kept up till the Pope reached the Chapel of the Blessed Sacrament, where he dismounted and knelt in reverence before the Sacramental Presence of His Lord. His mitre was removed, so was his zucchetto: he was now but a humble man kneeling in prayer. This reverence of his to God would remind him of his true status of *servus servorum Dei,* servant of the servants of God, and dispel any tendency to personal vainglory, far more than the precautionary ritual which was being carried out by attendants who in the procession were carrying in front of him plates on which was burned flax, and as the smoke of the flax arose, he was reminded: "Holy Father, thus passes the glory of the world."

After his homage to the Eucharist, the procession moved to the Chapel of St. Gregory, where another throne had been set. Here he formally received the obeisance of the cardinals, archbishops, bishops, and abbots. It was a touching scene of filial respect and of paternal affection publicly displayed. They kissed his foot and his ring, whereupon he imparted to all his apostolic blessing. After this act of homage, the cardinals proceeded to their choir stalls behind the main altar, removed their cappa magna of ermine and appeared in their liturgical rank, the cardinal bishops with cope, the cardinal priests in chasubles and the cardinal deacons with dalmatics. Each wore his precious mitre, while archbishops and bishops wore precious copes but a white mitre. When all of them were thus vested and ready, the Pope rose from his throne and intoned the start of the canonical hour of Tierce, nine o'clock, corresponding to the hour of the ceremonies. The prelates, assisted by expert religious choristers, chanted Tierce while the Pope, who had repaired to his throne beside the altar, began to vest for Mass. He put on buskins, amice, alb, cincture, stole, tunic, dalmatic, and chasuble, on which was folded the *fanone*, a white, silken cloth in whose center was embroidered a gold cross, an apparel exclusively papal. Crowned with the precious mitre, he washed and dried his hands, Prince Colonna offering him the water and towel. He then put on gloves over which on the proper finger was inserted his episcopal ring. By arrangement both actions ended simultaneously, so that now all was ready for the actual liturgical ceremony of the coronation Mass, which was to be celebrated on the high altar above the confessional of St. Peter. Attending him were Cardinal

Tisserant as assistant bishop, Cardinal Wendel as deacon, the two Cardinal Deacons, Canali and Ottaviani, as assistants at the throne, and Monsignor Staffa as subdeacon.

The first action in the celebration of Mass is the humble confession of the priest that he is a sinner with his plea to be forgiven, so that "we may be worthy to enter with pure minds into the Holy of Holies." Thus the Pope, as celebrant of his coronation Mass, acclaimed as he was by the world as "His Holiness," now acknowledged himself before the whole Church as a sinner with these words:

> I confess to Almighty God, to the blessed Mary, ever Virgin, to blessed Michael the Archangel, to blessed John the Baptist, the holy Apostles, Peter and Paul, to all the Saints, and to you, brethren, that I have sinned exceedingly in thought, word and deed, through my fault, through my fault, through my most grievous fault. Therefore, I beseech the blessed Mary, ever Virgin, blessed Michael the Archangel, blessed John the Baptist, the holy Apostles, Peter and Paul, and all the Saints, and you, brethren, to pray to our Lord God for me.

It has been charged by some non-Catholics that the Church claims that the Pope is impeccable in her assertion that he is infallible. The above clearly shows how she distinguishes between the private man and the official teacher.

After the recitation of the "Confiteor" (I confess) at the foot of the majestic altar of St. Peter's and the placing of the maniple on his left arm by the subdeacon, an unusual feature occurred: each of the first three Cardinal Bishops sang a special oration proper for the coronation Mass. The Cardinal Deacons then removed the mitre from the pope and imposed on him the pallium, the special white stole of an archbishop, cut circularly to fit over the shoulders with two pendants dropping symmetrically from it on front and back and interspersed in loop and ends with six black crosses, one each over breast and back, one on each shoulder and on each pendant. To keep the pallium from sliding off the chasuble, three gold pins, one topped with a ruby, the others with emeralds, were used to affix it to the vestments. The three pins symbolize the three nails of the crucifixion. Vested thus, the Pope mounted the altar, incensed it, and was incensed in turn by Cardinal Tisserant. He then recited the Introit and the Kyrie, which were sung in unison by the choir, and at the end he intoned, in a voice surprisingly vigorous for his age, the *Gloria in Excelsis Deo.* After the choir had finished it, Cardinal Canali led in the singing of the Litany of the Saints.

The oration of the Mass followed, after which, while the Pope read the Epistle at his throne, the subdeacon, Monsignor Staffa sang it in Latin, while Don Pietro Tamburi, of the Greek Pontifical College, sang it in Greek. After the Pope had read the Gospel, Cardinal Wendel sang it in Latin, while Don Nicola Psaltis, also of the Greek Pontifical College, sang it in Greek. This is done out of respect for the Eastern Church and to show universality. The Gospel, as was natural for the occasion, was taken from Matthew XVI, 13-19, containing the promise of Our Lord: "Thou art Peter, and upon this rock I will build my Church."

After the singing of the Gospels, the Pope greeted all in Greek: *Eirene pasi,* Peace be to all of you, after which he sat down and read a beautiful homily in Latin. He showed great emotion doing it, but his voice was clear and resounding. In substance it reminded his hearers that before all things the Bishop of Rome was a pastor, the shepherd of the flock of Christ; that no one could properly advance to Christ except through this established door of the fold, the primacy of Peter; that for all exclusive honors which might surround him, and for all estrangement that human vicissitudes might have affected the relation with those sheep who have left the fold, the words of Joseph to his brethren hold true—"It is I, Joseph, your brother, fear not"; that he had chosen November 4 for his day of coronation because it was the feast of St. Charles Borromeo, the great Shepherd of Milan, his priestly model, at whose altar in Rome where the saint's heart is preserved he had received his episcopal consecration thirty-four years ago. He ended by urging all to keep praying for him lest his faith fail not.

After the homily he intoned the Credo. The choir took it up with the beautiful notes of Palestrina's music. At the offertory which followed, three hosts were submitted, one accepted by the deacon for the Mass, the other two consumed by the sacristan in the Pope's presence. Similarly, the wine was tasted beforehand by the sacristan. This ritual was a lugubrious reminder of some of the wild periods in papal history when there was a danger of some partisan poisoning the Pope. Far from suppressing this sad page in her history, the Church has retained it in her coronation liturgy. When the bread and the wine had been accepted the Pope made the offertory, and thus continued the Mass normally through incensation, secrets, preface and sanctus. All the guards and noble knights now stood at rigid attention, the silver trumpets blared forth to warn of the impending consecration, and all others knelt with heads bared. The Pope took the wafer of bread, bent over it, and whispered, following the sequence of the words of the Canon in which he placed himself as a priest in the role of Christ, the High Priest: "This is my body." It is Catholic Doctrine that transubstantiation immediately takes place, the substance of the bread, while its accidents or visible qualities remain, being replaced by the substance of the Body of Christ. He then knelt in reverence, lifted it up for all to see, and knelt again. Similarly, he bent over the chalice containing wine, and whispered: "This is the chalice of my blood, of the New and Eternal Testament, the Mystery of Faith, which is shed for you and for many unto the remission of sins." The wine thus became the Precious Blood. The separate consecration mystically makes the Lord die again, for as his physical death occurred by the blood becoming separated from his body, so the separate consecration disunites his blood from his body. Again he knelt, lifted the chalice, and knelt anew.

There followed the rest of the Canon, terminating with the Our Father, and so to the Communion. Ordinarily the celebrant of a Mass gives Communion to himself. In the coronation Mass there is a change. The Pope went to his throne after kissing the chalice and giving the kiss of peace to his attendants, who in turn conveyed it to all the attending prelates. At his throne, in the sight of the whole church, on his knees, bareheaded, he received the Host from the hands of Monsignor Staffa, who carried it on a gold paten covered with a pall in the form of a twelve-pointed star. Then Cardinal Wendel brought to him the chalice from which the Pope drank the Precious Blood. All the while, the choir sang the strains of the *Adoro Te*, the beautiful Eucharistic hymn composed by St. Thomas Aquinas in 1264.

The rest of the Mass followed: communion prayer, post-communion prayer, the blessing, and the last Gospel. It was now past noon and the four-hour ceremony had been taxing. But other rituals remained. First, the archpriest of St. Peter's advanced and offered to the Pope a stipend for the Mass he had celebrated, a purse of white, embroidered in silk and containing twenty-five silver Julians, a coinage dating to the time of Julius II. Then, processionally, all left the Basilica. All except the cardinals and the Pope left by way of Scala Regia, some to find places in the balconies, others to issue outside. The cardinals and the Pope went to the Hall of Benediction where they rested while final preparations were made on the central balcony of the facade of St. Peter's. Here the blue-white drape had been let down bearing the Pope's coat-of-arms. A crimson-decked throne had been placed in the center, and the flags of the Papacy, the sign of the Church's joy, were fluttering in the breeze. In front, a vast horde of humanity, estimated to be 300,000, crammed every inch of the huge plaza of St. Peter's and the Via della Conciliazione up to Hadrian's tomb. The steps of the basilica, kept clear by the Roman police and the pontifical guards, were now taken by the mitred bishops and other high church dignitaries. The air was tense with expectancy. Everyone's gaze was centered on that empty central balcony. The cardinals stepped out on the loge off the Hall of Benediction. The drama of the coronation was about to unfold.

At last the three-barred papal cross appeared, followed by the selected participants of the coronation ceremony, and finally the Pope himself. He seated himself on the throne while a tremendous roar of welcome rose from the throng in the streets below. The roar subsided as six golden voices sang the famous composition of Dominic Bartolucci, *Corona Aurea super Caput eius,* "A crown of Gold upon his Head." After it, Cardinal Tisserant chanted the Pater Noster, the Our Father, with the following oration prescribed:

> Almighty and Everlasting God, who art the dignity of the Priesthood and the Author of Government, grant thy grace to thy servant, John, our Bishop, so that he may fruitfully rule thy Church, and since by thy clemency he is constituted and crowned as the Father of Kings and Rector of the Faithful, may all things be successfully governed by him under thy direction.

Cardinal Ottaviani then removed the mitre from the Pope's head. Cardinal Canali advanced with the tiara, the triple crown of the papacy. The Pope bent his head slightly. A great hush came over the crowd. In the solemn silence, Cardinal Canali expertly placed the tiara on the Pope's head, and said aloud and ringingly these words of the ritual:

> "Accept this ornate tiara of three crowns, and
> remember that you are Father of the Princes

> and Kings, Rector of the world, and Vicar on earth of Jesus Christ, Our Savior, to whom is the honor and the glory forever."

The whole action was but four minutes in duration, but its effects will be felt for many generations. After his coronation the Pope blessed lovingly *urbi et orbi* the Eternal City and the World, and from the throats of thousands swelled *vivas* and good wishes. The Church had a crowned head, the world a spiritual leader.

The tiara, materially, is not very costly; historically, it stands for little except that it is a sort of adaptation of the headgear of the Mosaic High Priest, or a transformation of the Phrygian cap which had been given to Pope Saint Sylvester by Constantine as symbol of the liberty of the Church; artistically, it is disputed as an imposing adornment; and it can be easily conceded that it is far from convenient as an ordinary item of wear. But symbolically it stands for much. It is the sign of the awe and majesty which surrounds the man, the external indication of a triple kingship he enjoys. He is king of an earthly realm, Vatican City; he is king over all earthly kings because of the superiority of his jurisdiction in spiritual matters; and he is the visible king of that spiritual visible kingdom, the Church, established on earth by the Master, now in heaven invisible to us. The eternal head of the Church, Christ, chooses a man to be his vicar, a visible head, and this vicar, as any viceroy of an earthly king, properly assumes the dignity and power of his principal. The vicar, or viceroy, or prime minister, as you will, has the task of ruling in the name of the king and properly puts on the external habiliments of his office. The Vicar of Christ has the task of preserving the truth of the words of the Master, "Go teach all nations," and dispensing the wealth of the merits of his passion, "Feed my lambs, feed my sheep." He is entitled to the externals of such a high office, and thus an earthly crown becomes him.

In joy, the Church has placed a crown on the head of the man who is the Vicar, and in love and loyalty hails him her divinely-appointed leader.

15

His Titles and Honors

OVER the cross of Christ, a title was written in three languages, Hebrew, Greek and Latin. It was a title given partly for historical record and partly for derision. As everyone knows, it read: Jesus of Nazareth, King of the Jews.

"What I have written, I have written," haughtily replied Pilate to the protesting Jews. They wanted the title changed to: "He said that he was the King of the Jews." They did not recognize him as their king; they wanted nothing of him. In fact, they had brought about his crucifixion on the charge that he had elected himself to be their king. They had no king but Caesar, they said with tongue in cheek.

But the title, given in derision, fitted admirably. They had so often wanted to make him king, but he had refused to be an earthly king, wanting only to be their spiritual emperor in a kingdom that would include all the nations and races of earth.

He laid the foundations of this spiritual kingdom while he was on earth. After he ascended into heaven, he began bringing about the spread of this kingdom from a mere handful of some one hundred and twenty followers huddled in fear in the cenacle to greater numbers in Palestine first, and then to even greater numbers in other regions of earth.

He had charged his followers, "Go ye into the whole world and preach the Gospel to every creature." (Mark XVI, 15) They obeyed, their sound going forth through the world, and in time the spiritual kingdom became a good-sized visible congregation of believers in every country. It was his Church made real and living.

As the Church grew, and as she pondered over the majesty of her Founder, she discovered many titles to add to his name. She found some in the sacred pages, she arrived at others by deep meditation, and from all this study she has composed that beautiful Litany of the Sacred Heart which is a grand description of the character and mission of the God-Man. He had been called by his enemies during his earthly life: the Nazarene, the carpenter, the Galilean, and, alas, the pretender. John the Baptist had called him the Lamb of God; the disciples had lovingly called him Master. He had described himself as the Way, the Truth, the Life, the Door, the Light, the Vine, the Resurrection, the Good Shepherd. All these titles fitted him, and every title that will ever be coined denoting his power, his goodness and love, will always fit him.

Likewise, as the Church grew, as she pondered over the extraordinary prestige and power granted to her chief priest and over the events that began to surround his person, she began to realize that he had a right to many significant titles and honors. These were either in direct relation to his office as Vicar of Christ or side accumulations indirectly flowing from some of his historic activities or acquisitions in the course of time.

In the ceremony of coronation which we have just reviewed, when the tiara was placed on his head, he was entitled:

Father of Princes and of Kings
Rector of the world on earth
Vicar of our Savior, Jesus Christ

These are the stately, kingly titles accorded to him in line with the triple crown placed on his head.

Let us explain their meanings.

He is called Father of Princes and of Kings because he is the vicegerent of the King of Kings, Jesus Christ. To the Christian, Our Lord is the King of men and of angels. From him all kings take their government and dominion. This includes all who in one way or another possess the power or prerogatives of kings, such as parliaments, oligarchies, presidents, dictators, and the like. In the Middle Ages and up to rather recent times, the kings were acknowledged to rule by divine right. In abusing this prerogative, their power was curtailed by people so that today what kings remain rule by what is called the mandate of the people, and they must conform to constitutional limitations. But the fact remains, as St. Paul has pointed out, that all power is from God. (Romans XIII, 1-2) Christ had clearly indicated this truth when in answering Pilate's boast that he had power to crucify or release him, he said: "Thou shouldst not have any power against me, unless it were given thee from above." (John XX, 11)

The power and dignity, then, of earthly rulers primarily comes from God who allows to people, to custom or circumstances, the actual selection of the person to rule. At times he directly makes the selection as in the case of David.

The Son of God, in becoming man for our salvation, is king of all men, and king of all kings. This is indisputable Christian doctrine.

When, then, he appoints a vicegerent to act in his name in his earthly absence, that vicegerent assumes the title and prerogative of his principal just as any viceroy does. It is Catholic doctrine that Christ appointed Peter to be his vicegerent, and this office of Peter has continued in his successors. Wherefore, properly, the Pope is Father of the Princes and Kings. Christ's kingdom was a spiritual one.

Peter's power then is spiritual. He cannot assume a political supremacy over the princes and kings of earth—what is of Caesar shall belong to Caesar—but he does possess the pre-eminence of honor over them since the spiritual realm is superior to the material one, and in any conflict between spiritual matters and political ones, the superior needs of the spirit should prevail.

This truth was gladly recognized, though not always obeyed, in the Catholic Middle Ages. The kings of Europe regarded the Pope as overlord and they paid him due deference. The position of the Pope has not changed, although the mentality of Europe's rulers has. The Kings of England continued to entitle themselves "Kings of France," even when it became apparent that France did not belong to them. The Pope is entitled to be Father of the Princes and Kings of earth, not because they may or may not accept him as such, but because he has a divine right to the title as the alter ego or viceroy of him who is constituted the King of Kings and the eternal King of the World.

It may be pointed out, as well, that the truth and retention of this title has been, and will continue to be the rallying point of all men of good will for the formation of a true Christian brotherhood. The bond that ties a United Nations is a human one. The bond that could tie a United Christianity is a spiritual one.

For the same reasons, the second title, Rector of the world on earth, is a proper one. It does not mean that the Pope assumes all political and physical mastery over nations, but it does mean that he is constituted the teacher and moral guide of all men. Christ died for all men, and he left a Gospel that spells the salvation of all men. The preaching of this Gospel and the application of its spiritual power was reposed in his apostles, and their successors, with Peter and his successors as chief. He had said it clearly: "on this rock I will build my Church." (Matthew XVI, 18) He is the invisible ruler or rector of the world; his visible representative is therefore the visible rector ruling in his name.

A Christian should feel more confident than otherwise in this wise disposition of the Savior. The world needs and looks for a leader, a leader in the higher levels of human living—in virtue, truth, morality, and in the spiritual and supernatural. It has this divinely appointed leader.

The third title of the tiara is that of Vicar of Christ. This is the whole essence of the papal position. All the dignity and power of the Pope stem from this cardinal fact. In the Chapter on the Origination of the Papacy, we have shown that the Catholic contention is that Christ actually appointed St. Peter his Vicar and that this office was not to perish with Peter but was to continue with the existence of the Church, since her mission requires the visible unity that stems from Peter, to the end of time.

In a formal listing by the Church of the Pope's titles and honors, as can be found in her official books and in such a ready one as the Catholic Directory, we find the following:

Bishop of Rome
Vicar of Jesus Christ
Successor of St. Peter, Prince of the Apostles
Supreme Pontiff of the Universal Church
Patriarch of the West
Primate of Italy
Archbishop and Metropolitan of the Roman Province
Sovereign of Vatican City

The second of these we have already discussed. The first is most important because it gives rise to the second, which is the paramount title.

A man becomes the Vicar of Christ because he succeeds St. Peter in that office. He succeeds St. Peter because he becomes, as St. Peter chose to be and so continued to his death, the Bishop of Rome. When Peter died, as we saw, the clergy of the City of Rome, his See, met to elect his successor. This was Linus. After his death, again the clergy of Rome met to elect their bishop. And so it has continued to this day, since the cardinals, as we have noted, are the chief clergymen of the City of Rome, each a legal pastor of a church in Rome. The man they elect becomes bishop of that particular city, and that particular city happens to be the See founded by St. Peter, so that the elected Bishop of Rome becomes automatically the successor of St. Peter, and consequentially the Vicar of Christ.

The Cardinals met in conclave October 25-28 of 1958, and on October 28 elected Angelo Roncalli as Bishop of Rome. Hence the title fits him, and the consequential one of Vicar of Jesus Christ as well.

The third title, Successor of St. Peter, Prince of the Apostles, is, for the same reason, properly his. The whole theory of the authority vested in the Pope rests on this Catholic position that he is the *Petrus redivivus,* the Peter living anew in him. The legend inscribed on the inner rim of the cupola of St. Peter's, the constant references to him in the liturgy, and in the official chant of the Church, *Tu Es Petrus,* Thou art Peter, all clearly indicate the firm faith of Catholics that John XXIII is Peter, as all his two hundred and sixty predecessors have been. This is why the papacy is a dynasty. It goes on, not by blood, nor by will of the flesh, nor by will of man, but by the power of God. It is a spiritual bond among them all, a pure continuity resting on one sublime, unifying reality, the will of Christ, to ensure for his Church her visible unity, her sure fountain of holiness, her clear apostolicity and her definite universality.

Once these three titles are acknowledged, the three being intimately connected, the others easily become apparent. The Pope is not only a pontiff, a bishop, of his own proper see, but the supreme pontiff of the universal Church, because he is vested with the power of Peter who had jurisdiction over the other apostles. While all bishops rule by divine right, their right, by divine dispensation, is subordinated to the authority of the chief bishop, a dispensation humanly necessary to safeguard the unity and holiness of the Church.

The title, Patriarch of the West, is a subordinate one to the others. A patriarch is chief bishop of a large area of earth. The Church started in the East. St. Peter himself had been Bishop of Jerusalem and later Bishop of Antioch. When he translated his See to Rome, his successor at Antioch was considered to be the chief bishop in the East, and the title of Patriarch was given to him. Later, this diocese was engulfed by the Saracen invasion and did not function too well, but the city of Constantinople rose to great eminence and its bishop assumed the title of Patriarch of the East. The Western Roman Empire still centered at Rome became subordinate to the Eastern Roman Empire centered at Constantinople. The title, Patriarch of the West, refers chiefly to this division of the Roman Empire, but does embrace the spiritual authority which the Western Patriarch had over all other Patriarchs, including the Patriarch of the East. We saw in the brief history of the Papacy that an Eastern Patriarch dared to call himself Universal Patriarch, for which he was rebuked. The only Universal Patriarch is the Bishop of Rome for he alone, as successor of St. Peter, holds the plenary power over all bishops.

The title, Primate of Italy, is a natural one, since a primatial see is the one first established in a country, such as Canterbury in England, Armagh in Ireland.

The next title, Archbishop and Metropolitan of the Roman Province, also follows properly. Dioceses are grouped into provinces which take their name from the archdiocese of which the dioceses are suffragans. Rome is an archdiocese around which are grouped the sees, suburbicarian so called, and others. Hence, the Bishop of Rome, the head diocese of the province, is an archbishop. The term metropolitan is indicative of the fact that he is bishop of a large, metropolitan city, the principal see of the area known as a province.

The last title in the official list, Sovereign of Vatican City, is a newly-acquired one, following the Lateran Treaty of 1929. Before that, the Pope was King of the Papal Territory or States, a political area civilly governed by the Pope. The Treaty surrendered to Italy all the territory except that little area of Vatican City, in which area the Pope continued to be the civil ruler, or king.

In the course of history, there have accrued to him several other titles distinct in terminology but correlative with the main ones above. The first we may mention is that of *Papa,* from which the word Pope is derived. *Papa* is father in Italian and in several other languages. In the Eastern churches, the term was given to all priests, even as we give the term Father to our priests, but in the course of years, while the Eastern Church retains it for all priests, in the Latin Church the term *papa* became proper only for the Pope. It is, obviously, a term of familiarity, bespeaking family affection, as we would call our own physical father, papa. For Catholics, he is *the* Father of the Faithful, the papa of Christ's visible kingdom.

He is called the *Summus Pontifex,* the Supreme Pontiff, as well. It is commonly known that the office of Pontiff stems from the days of the Roman Republic. He was the civil engineer who built bridges. The word *pons* in Latin means a bridge, and with *facere,* to make, the etymology is clear.

Julius Caesar in his day assumed the office of Pontifex Maximus, a variety of Summus Pontifex, meaning similarly the Supreme Pontiff, or chief bridge-builder. The word pontiff thus derived from a purely civil origin has, in the course of history, been associated exclusively with a spiritual bridge-builder, that is, a bishop. Pontiff in ordinary Christian parlance now means a bishop. The translation from the purely civil to the spiritual is very appropriate, for the word pontiff indicates rather well the function of a spiritual leader who stands midway between God and man, and, as it were, bridges the distance between them.

In most documents that emanate from Rome, and, indeed, on most buildings in Rome, the abbreviations Pont. Max., standing for Pontifex Maximus, are frequent. The Popes have adopted the phrase in their *stylus curiae,* their style of chancery writing. It is an apt title for it succinctly conveys the Catholic doctrine concerning his person. He is the chief bishop of Christendom.

The Jews had a high priest, the chief of all the Levitical priests of the Mosaic dispensation. This high priest had great honor and power. Now that the Mosaic dispensation has been replaced by the Christian, the term high priest is properly appropriated by the Pope. All bishops are high priests, and it is always rather thrilling to hear the strains of the "Ecce Sacerdos Magnus," "Behold the High Priest," played at the entrance of a bishop into his church or into any hall where he is to preside at a function. However, the term is, without being exclusive, more properly applied to the Pope, the head of all the high priests. They are high indeed, but he is the supreme one among them, the Summus Pontifex.

A title most exclusive is that of *Servus Servorum Dei,* the Servant of the Servants of God. As we saw in the brief history of the Papacy, St. Gregory I originated this title as a rebuke to the Archbishop of Constantinople who had illegally and pompously entitled himself, Patriarch of the Universal Church. It is with this title that the Pope addresses himself to all his fellow bishops and to the faithful in important documents.

It fits him well, because it is so redolent of him who had said to the apostles at the last supper: "He that is the greater among us, let him become as the younger; and he that is the leader, as he that serveth." (Luke XXII, 26)

Finally, his official title of address is, Your Holiness. This sums up the exalted character of his office. He is the Holy

Father, the Good Shepherd pointing the way to holiness of doctrine and to holiness of living. Christ came into the world to make men holy, and he left his own power to make men holy in the hands of certain men, his priests, and pre-eminently in the hands of the visible priest of priests, the Pope, the Holy Father of Christendom. Possibly, he may not be personally holy. History tells us that some were not holy men, but the point is, the office is holy. Peter was not always holy, but he and all his successors have taught men to be holy, wherefore each is properly called Your Holiness.

❁ 16 ❁

His Prerogatives and Powers

OUR Founding Fathers wisely separated the possession of authority in the three branches of government, the legislative, executive, and judicial. They felt that to repose the full power of government in one man was dangerous to the nation's liberties. Their bitter experience with the English king, and their knowledge of Europe's history, prompted them to divide the powers. A congress of appointed (later elected) senators, and of popularly elected representatives, should be the law-making body; a president should be the executive of these laws; a supreme tribunal should be the interpreter of these laws. It was a system of checks and balances.

The system has worked well. Our country is fairly a model in government. So true is this that many nations have adopted our form of government.

The papacy is a government. It governs the spiritual life of millions of human beings scattered all over the world. In this spiritual government there is often inextricably connected the authority over some temporal matters.

Is there in the papacy a division of powers such as in the Government of the United States? The answer is, no.

In the hands of the Pope are reposed all legislative, executive and judicial powers. He is, in this sense, an autocrat.

Why?

Simply because it was the divine will for him to have these powers. The proof? The words of the Master addressed to Peter: "I will give to thee the keys of the kingdom of heaven. And whatever thou shalt bind upon earth, shall be bound also in heaven: and whatever thou shalt loose on earth, it shall be loosed also in heaven." (Matthew XVI, 19) Again, "Simon, Simon, behold Satan hath desired to have you that he may sift you as wheat. But I have prayed for thee that thy faith may not fail; and do thou, when once thou hast turned again, strengthen thy brethren." (Luke XXII, 31-32) Further, in John XXI, 17: "Feed my sheep."

It is of Catholic faith, from these texts and others, and fortified by the common understanding of the other apostles and disciples of Our Lord, and from the acceptance of the first Christians, that all power, legislative, executive and judicial, is reposed in Christ's Vicar.

We have said it was humanly wise for our Founding Fathers to separate the powers. Why was it not wise for Christ to do so? Simply because it is of itself wiser to repose all authority in one man. It is only through the historic abuse of the power by the autocrat that it became necessary for people to separate the powers. Peter's powers are primarily spiritual, and hence do not involve themselves in all the complexities of human lust or avarice, the cause of the autocrat's despotism. Some Popes, indeed, may have yielded to the urges of avarice and partisanship, but that was exceptional. Philosophers have generally conceded that the best form of government is that of a monarch with supreme authority. When we remember that Christ promised to be with his Church all days even to the consummation of the world, the danger latent in authority being reposed in one man is inapplicable in the case.

The authority stems from God and is not the grant of any civil power. The Church is a perfect society, sovereign and independent in her own realm. She is not obliged to any state for her existence. She has a divine commission which transcends in importance the aims of the temporal power. She has been instructed by her Founder to give unto Caesar the things that are his, but she must preserve and uphold the things that are God's. To do this effectively, she must be free in her own field. The story of the Papacy has been one of continual struggle against the encroachments of the civil power which would reduce her to a mere arm of the State if not to complete oblivion.

It is wise, then, both for the mission and for the attacks against the mission, for the leader of the Church to possess all power so that he can move swiftly and effectively against the enemies of the spirit.

Let us review these powers in some detail.

In the field of legislation, the Pope is the sole lawmaker. As a sensible man, he naturally consults experts in various fields; he may even establish bodies which can legislate in minor or routine matters, but in all cases the final decision is his to promulgate a law or a decree, to recall previous laws or to amend them. In this particular field of law, we may state the following prerogatives:

1. He legislates for the whole Church, with or without the aid of a general council.
2. It is his right alone to convoke a council. If by chance it has been convoked without his consent, its acts are invalid unless he approves and legalizes the meeting.
3. He presides at the council personally or by his chosen delegate; he directs its deliberations and either confirms or vetoes its acts.
4. He can make new laws that are not in contravention with divine or natural laws, and he can revoke any law of his predecessors.

5. He can dispense individuals from the obligations of purely ecclesiastical laws.

6. He can release one from all vows, both public and private, solemn and simple, when he deems it expedient. He delegates to bishops authority to dispense in simple vows.

7. He can reserve to himself whatever powers might ordinarily be left in the hands of the bishops.

Still in line with his legislative power, he holds the supreme magisterium or teaching office in the Church. Wherefore,

1. He alone proclaims a dogma that is to be accepted and believed in under pain of heresy by the universal Church.

2. He alone issues the official text of the Creeds of the Church, such as the Apostles' Creed, the Nicene, the Athanasian.

3. He determines when and by whom and under what circumstances an expression of faith shall be made.

4. The Church is infallible in her teaching of the Gospel of Christ, and so is he personally infallible when he proposes *ex cathedra,* that is, officially as teacher, a point of faith or morals to be the doctrine of the universal Church. (This prerogative is quite misunderstood by non-Catholics and generally shocks them to the point of violent opposition. We shall explain it in detail later.)

5. He recommends and approves text-books for catechetical teaching and for study in theology.

6. He condemns the publishing, reading, and keeping of books detrimental to faith and morals.

7. He condemns certain propositions as heretical or deserving of censure, or warns when they are offensive to piety.

8. He safeguards the Sacred Scriptures in the integrity of its books and in the purity of its text.

Still in the field of legislation, but in the department of direction of proper worship to God, he has the following powers:

1. He alone prescribes the liturgical services in the Church in worship of God. He issues the pontifical, the book of rules for episcopal functions, and he approves the missal which contains the norms for the celebration of Mass, the supreme act of worship.

2. He institutes the universal feasts of the Church and suppresses those which he deems expedient to do so; he fixes the degree of their solemnity, raising it or lowering it as the devotion of the age may warrant it.

3. He alone canonizes saints, placing on this action the seal of his infallibility, and he alone raises a departed servant of God to the title of Blessed.

4. He alone can give the privilege of a private chapel wherein Mass may be celebrated.

5. It is his prerogative to dispense the spiritual, limitless treasury of the Church, accrued from the infinite merits of Christ's passion, by the grant of indulgences, plenary or partial.

6. It is his right to give to simple priests the power to administer the sacrament of confirmation and to bless the oil of the sick and that of the catechumens.

7. It is his right to permit abbots and other prelates who are not bishops to administer minor orders.

8. He can establish the diriment and prohibitive impediments to marriage which are not already dictated by natural or divine law.

9. He can prescribe the matter, form, the manner of administering and the minister of a sacrament unless they have already been determined by their Founder, Jesus Christ. What the Lord has explicitly determined in sacraments cannot be touched by the Pope, but in those matters not determined by Christ, such as the matter and form of the minor orders, the matter and form of confirmation, the form of extreme unction, and of marriage, the Pope can determine.

10. He can legislate in *perpetuam rei memoriam,* that is, in perpetuity, or for a stated period, in all fields purely spiritual or definitely involved in the spiritual.

As an executive, his main responsibility is to see that all laws, divine, natural, ecclesiastical, and even good civil laws, are obeyed. He establishes congregations, which correspond to our cabinet posts and other offices or bureaus, to help him in the actual enforcement or running of the papal government. He has a Secretary of State, sends out his ambassadors, called nuncios or legates, and, in most ways usual with civil governments, keeps his eye on world happenings. So wide and accurate is the information that comes to him that our President Roosevelt asked to utilize it for the purposes of the war and sent to the Vatican Myron Taylor as a special envoy. His relations with Pope Pius XII have been one of the prides of American Catholics. Mr. Taylor, an Episcopalian, reported glowingly of the splendid cooperation he received from the Vatican, all of which aided our war effort.

In details of governing, the Pope has the following powers:

1. He can establish universities possessing the status and privileges of a canonically erected Catholic University.

2. He directs Catholic missions throughout the world.

3. He appoints bishops, transfers them, accepts their resignation, elevates or deposes them.

4. He establishes new dioceses, restricts or enlarges them, suppresses them as circumstances warrant.

5. He can approve a new religious order or congregation, and suppress any.

6. He can grant exemptions in obedience normally due to a bishop on the part of an institute or an individual.

7. He has the supreme administration of the goods of the Church whether of lands, buildings, or furnishings, and can dispose of them as he sees fit.

8. He can require a levy on the clergy and the faithful for

ecclesiastical purposes and he has a right to a "Peter's Pence" for his personal expenses or for charitable donations.

9. He creates cardinals.

In the realm of the judiciary, the following are his prerogatives:

1. He has the right to interpret the natural law and to give official interpretations of the divine law.

2. He can set up what tribunals he deems necessary for the adjudication of all cases dealing in matters directly or indirectly connected with the spiritual.

3. He may deal with minor cases in the first instance, and he disposes of all appeals since he is the court of last resort.

4. He may impose censures, that is excommunications, interdicts or suspensions, either by judicial sentence or through general law.

5. He may reserve to himself what cases he deems wise to reserve.

6. He can punish and degrade any cleric for grave infractions of canon law.

7. He may call for answering before his tribunal any nation, prince, or bishop for impairing the good name or welfare of the Church.

All these powers may sound terrifying in their summation, but it must be remembered that they are not as formidable as they seem. The Pope does not act on whimsy. He is, in the first place, hedged in by many restrictions and restraints of the divine law. He cannot make any new doctrine, a new sacrament, a new decalogue. He simply executes the mandate given him by Christ. This office of his must be free from interference both from civil authorities outside, and from internal dissent. He must have free communication with his bishops throughout the world. This is why he must be sovereign. He should not be impeded by any clique that might arise within the Church. This is why he must possess the supreme authority. It is all a very sensible arrangement.

Is it not too big a task for one man? Well, if we were to list all the duties incumbent upon the President of the United States, we would equally tend to feel that they are too much. They are unless they are parcelled out to officers, the cabinet members, the bureau chiefs, and others, who are responsible for certain portions of the work. The President attends to the very big problems, leaving the minor or routine ones to his subordinates. That is what the Pope does. He has his correlative cabinet, the congregations, and his bureaus, the chancery offices, and the tribunals. He has as his senate, or counselors, the cardinals. The work is huge but it can be done and it has been done.

As to the tremendous sweep of his powers, besides the restrictions of the divine law already noted, he is circumscribed by tradition, ancient statutes and customs, the rights of a Council, of bishops, of religious orders, and of others. He is not arbitrary, whimsical, or fickle. Human, yes, and he will make his mistakes in policy and procedure, but he is a priest vowed not to arrogate the power for his own personal advantage, but for the good of the flock. There have been a few exceptions, but in the main the Popes have vindicated the trust reposed in them by God. A devoted monarchy is the best form of government, and the papacy is a dedicated institution.

Are there any checks should a Pope forget his dedication? In strict canonical legality there are none. He is unanswerable before any Council of the Church or human court. However, there are many intangible checks as history has shown: the opposition of saints, the remonstrances of the collective episcopate, the *vox populi,* the voice of the people, which has always been a powerful deterrent to despotism. Above all is the check of the Master Himself, who knows how to correct any bad situation as it may develop. The Pope is responsible to the Master Himself, who knows how to correct. The faithful, and, for that matter, the non-Catholics, need not fear that the vast power resident in the Pope will ever seriously or for long be abused. So many of them have been saints; so many of them have been wise, able administrators. Even those who might not have been too edifying in their personal lives have retained a fine consciousness of their duties to the Church in general and have provided a rule that has been just and progressive.

Finally, a word about his infallibility. This word scares many people. How can a human being be infallible? The point is the Church does not claim that the Pope is infallible in all things. He can be mistaken about many things. Cardinal Gibbons delighted to tell this story of Leo XIII. Whenever he was presented to the Pope, Leo XIII would invariably give his name the ordinary Italian pronounciation, calling him Cardinal Jibbons. No matter how often he was corrected, he kept on with "Jibbons."

The Catholic doctrine is simply this: because it is inconceivable that Christ's Church could fall into error of faith, the chief spokesman of the Church, when, and only when, speaking for the whole church and enunciating a doctrine that is to be held by the whole church, is protected from error by the Holy Spirit. If he, the supreme teacher, could teach error, the Church would then be in error on a matter of faith, and so falsify the words of Christ. On all other occasions, even if he were preaching a sermon in St. Peter's, the Pope could enunciate an error. Only when he is speaking as the official teacher to the whole church is he immune from error, not by personal virtue, but by power of the Holy Spirit, the Guardian of truth.

The Popes have a remarkable record on this point of infallibility. In the almost two thousand years of their rule, with so great a variety among them of saint and sinner, learned and unlearned, headstrong and mild, proud and humble, no Pope has ever contradicted another on a matter of faith or morals. A Pope has contradicted another in discipline, policy and procedure, but never in doctrine. The enemies of the Church have searched hard for one clear case of doctrinal contradiction, but have never succeeded in finding one.

The word infallible should terrify no one. The Catholic Church is not afraid to use the term, but the fact is all churches must assert that their teachings are infallible, otherwise they are admitting that what they teach need not be true. If they do that, can they hope to convince anyone of the merits of their claim to be the true church? The true church, obviously, must claim to be infallible in her teachings, and her chief spokesman when talking officially for his church, must be infallible himself. Remove infallibility from him and you remove the ground of conviction, substituting in its place the liability of error. A church that admits the liability of error in her teaching cannot be Christ's Church.

❁ 17 ❁

His First Acts

IT IS commonly believed that the first happenings of a new regime are presages of its succeeding history. Ancient soothsayers looked for omens at the start of any reign and generally interpreted them favorably or unfavorably in line with their own personal attitude toward the king. We have discarded the old superstitions. Nevertheless, we do pay some attention to the first acts of a new leader because we feel they reveal something of character and purpose.

His very first act was his acceptance of the result of the twelfth ballot. The acceptance itself is not significant, but the words he used are. The acceptance is the one essential act which immediately confers on him the fullness of the papal office. When Cardinal Tisserant approached him and put to him the formal question: "Do you accept your canonically performed election as supreme Pontiff?" Cardinal Roncalli answered: "Listening to your voice, 'I have been made to tremble and am afraid.' " (This quotation is from the ninth response, the *Libera*, in the office of the Dead). "What I know of my poverty and littleness suffices for my confusion. But seeing in the votes of my very eminent brother Cardinals of our Holy Roman Church the sign of the will of God, I accept the election that has been made and I bend my head and back to the chalice of bitterness and to the yoke of the Cross. In the solemnity of Christ the King we all sang, 'The Lord is our Judge; The Lord is our Legislator; The Lord is our King; he will save us!' "

The canopies of all cardinals except his were then lowered. This was his first papal throne, and on it he received the first homage of the cardinals and of the papal court. Cardinal Tisserant then asked him: "By what name do you wish to be known?" The world awaited this answer because it would give the first clue of his purposes. His answer was surprising, solid, and sweet:

> Venerable Brothers, I shall be called John.
>
> This name is sweet to Us because it was Our father's; it is dear because it was the name of the humble parish in which We received baptism.
>
> It is the solemn name of the innumerable cathedrals spread about the world, and, first among them, of the sacrosanct Lateran Basilica, Our cathedral.
>
> It is the name which in the long series of the Roman Pontiffs has been most used.
>
> Indeed, there have been twenty-two unquestionably legitimate supreme Pontiffs named John. Nearly all had a brief pontificate.
>
> We have preferred to shield the smallness of Our own name behind this magnificent succession of Roman Pontiffs.
>
> And was not St. Mark, the Evangelist, the glory and protector of Our most dear Venice, he whom St. Peter, Prince of the Apostles and first Bishop of the Roman Church, loved as his own son, also called John?
>
> But we love the name of John, so dear to Us and to all the Church, particularly because it was borne by two men who were most close to Christ the Lord, the divine redeemer of all the world and founder of the Church.
>
> John the Baptist, the precursor of our Lord, he was not, indeed, the light, but the witness of the light. And he was truly the unconquered witness of truth, justice, liberty, in

his preaching, in the baptism of repentance, in the blood he shed.

And the other John: the disciple and evangelist, preferred by Christ and by his most sweet mother, who, at the last supper, leaned on the breast of our Lord and thereby obtained that charitable love which burned in him with the lively and apostolic flame until great old age.

May God dispose that both these Johns shall plead in all the Church for Our most humble pastoral ministry, which succeeds that so well conducted one to its end by Our lamented predecessor of venerable memory, Pius XII, and those of his predecessors so glorious in the Church.

May they proclaim to the clergy and to all the people Our work by which We desire to "make ready the way of the Lord, make straight his paths. Every valley shall be filled, and every mountain and hill shall be brought low, and the crooked ways shall be made straight, and the rough ways smooth; and all mankind shall see the salvation of God." (Luke III, 4-6)

And may John the Evangelist, who, as he himself attests, took with him Mary the mother of Christ and our mother, sustain together with her this same exhortation, which concerns the life and the joy of the Catholic Church and also the peace and the prosperity of all peoples: "My children, love one another; love one another because this is the great commandment of the Lord."

Venerable Brothers, may God in his mercy grant that bearing the name of the first of this series of supreme Pontiffs, We can, with the help of divine grace, have his sanctity of life and his strength of soul unto the shedding of Our blood, if God so wills.

This reply was written on parchment by the prefect of the Pontifical Ceremonial Congregation, with the two masters of ceremonies acting as witnesses. It should equally be written in the consciousness of all interested in the papacy, because it sets forth clearly the true character of his person and the purposes of his reign.

After he had declared his name, Monsignor di Jorio, Secretary of the Conclave, placed on his head the white zucchetto, or skull cap, of a pope. John took his cardinal red skull cap and placed it on di Jorio's head, thus creating him a cardinal on the spot, as had been the custom. Pius XII had ignored it. He then retired to a sacristy to vest in his white papal robes. In passing to the sacristy, he blessed the assembled cardinals. When vested, he mounted the throne placed in front of the altar of the Sistine Chapel and there accepted the second obedience of the cardinals. There was reported the human story of his embarrassment in receiving the embrace of each after the kissing of his foot, and he apologized very sincerely: "Pardon me if I appear to be embarrassed. I must get used to this new state of things. Yesterday, I was a cardinal. Today I am Pope. Pardon me." After the obedience, he accepted from Cardinal Tisserant the Fisherman's Ring, by which a pope authenticates all his official documents.

Later he appeared on the balcony of St. Peter's after Cardinal Canali had officially announced the election, and imparted to the multitude of people his first public blessing.

Surprisingly, he extended the conclave, requiring all, including the cardinals, to remain in their Vatican quarters over night. Many of the conclavists, assigned to service, presuming that the conclave was broken following the news of the election, had left their quarters to witness the giving of his first public blessing. According to law, they immediately incurred excommunication. When it dawned on them that they had incurred the excommunication because they had left before official leave had been given to them, these conclavists —among them some priests and nuns—realized they were really outlaws. When the new Pope heard about it, he called them together and started sternly with: "You have all incurred excommunication." Then, seeing how penitent and crestfallen they were, he smiled and took the black cloud away with: "I shall use my new authority in your behalf. I free you of the excommunication."

The conclave was declared over at ten o'clock the next morning. It is reported that the Pope spent the night in the apartment of the former Secretary of State.

Weather omens cannot be relied on, but it is usually more comforting if they tend to encourage confidence. On the night of his election, a beautiful moon near its full streamed soft, silvery rays over Rome, lending an enchantment to the majestic group of buildings which is Vatican City. The air was light and semi-cool, good to breathe and feel its softness on the cheek. The next day was one of those incomparably lovely autumn days in Rome with a warming, golden sun beaming down its bright benediction. All sensed in these things a happy augury of success for the new pontificate.

Clerical matters had to be attended to promptly, first of which in importance were the letters to be sent to the sovereigns and heads of state in diplomatic rapport with the Holy See informing them officially of John XXIII's election. He had also to confirm all officers of the papal court and renew the credentials of his envoys. This included the confirming of Cardinal Masella as Camerlengo, since his choice by the College of Cardinals in the interregnum was a temporary one. He appointed Monsignor Tardini Pro-Secretary of State, a post that had been vacant since 1944. He made other appointments, all in line with his declared policy of bringing the Holy See to the peak of its efficiency.

With all the serious matters that claimed his attention the first day in office, he found time to greet warmly the many unauthorized visitors who had succeeded in evading the Swiss Guards in the confusion of the swift events following the election. He kept patient, even warm and paternal amid all the pressure of duties. In passing through the Vatican to take a glance at the papal apartments, he spotted the masons tearing down the wall they had erected for the conclave and he chatted amiably with them. For him it wasn't condescension. It was simply his ordinary way of being pleasant with the humble from whom he had sprung.

He promptly sent messages of thanks to heads of state from whom he had received congratulations on his election. It is natural that his message to the Italian President should contain warmer effusions than usual:

> With vivifying pleasure, We have received the fervent expressions of the congratulations of Your Excellency and of Our beloved Italian people extended to Us in the happy circumstance of Our elevation to the Supreme Pontificate, and We appreciate the noble sentiments that prompted them.
>
> In Our soul, which now must beat with paternal solicitude for all men, there is an ear for the cry which comes to Us of the anxiety and hopes of that particular Nation which is Our own Fatherland.
>
> We desire to reply to your devoted message by expressing Our Profound gratitude and by raising to God Almighty Our ardent prayers for Your Excellency's health and for the spiritual and civil prosperity of the whole Italian nation, in the bright hope of peace, nourished by a sense of Christian justice and Charity. As a pledge of Our benevolence and as a happy augury of abundant favors from heaven, We impart on Our beloved Italy a most special apostolic blessing.

He startled the world by resorting to the radio for a world-wide address twenty hours after his election. The papers gave excellent publicity to this speech which he delivered from his throne in the Sistine Chapel immediately after he had received the third obedience from the cardinals. It was a clear, ringing message to the Church and to the world leaders.

His message to the Church was to the effect that cardinals, bishops and priests everywhere should keep in mind the high vocation that is theirs to spread the Truth of Christ and administer his Sacraments to people needful of them for their eternal salvation. He then paid a tribute to, and implored help for, the many bishops, priests, brothers, nuns, and laymen in persecuted lands, "where there is no liberty, or too little of it," for the exercise of the Catholic faith. "We participate in their sufferings, their sorrows and pains; and We implore God, the giver of all good things, to put an end to this inhuman treatment."

He then pleaded for Christian unity, appealing to the Eastern Church and to Protestants to come back to the harbor of truth and unity of faith, in one fold under one shepherd. He said that he would be all charity, and would welcome them back with open arms if they showed a willingness to return.

> Therefore, let all come, We beseech them, in full and loving will, and let this return be as soon as possible, with the help and inspiration of grace. They will not enter into a foreign house, but into their own, that same house that once was illumined by the doctrinal sign of their ancestors and made precious by their virtues.

Then, turning to the problems in the world, he said:

> Let Us now be permitted to direct Our appeal to the leader of all nations in whose hands are placed the fate, the prosperity, the hopes of the individual peoples.
>
> Why should not discords and disagreements be finally composed equitably? Why should not the resources and the ingenuity of man and the riches of the peoples, used frequently to prepare arms—pernicious instruments of death and destruction—be used to increase the well-being of all classes of citizens, particularly of the needy?
>
> We know that it is true that in bringing about so laudable,

so praiseworthy a proposition and to level the differences, there are grave and intricate difficulties in the way, but they must be victoriously overcome, even if by force.

This is in fact the most important undertaking, mostly connected with the prosperity of all mankind. Put yourselves, therefore, to the task with confident courage, under the reflection of the light which comes from on high, and with divine assistance turn your gaze to the people who are entrusted to you and listen to their voices.

President Eisenhower included his praise for this particular appeal to the heads of government when he sent his congratulatory message. It read:

Upon this auspicious occasion in your life and in the history of the Roman Catholic Church, I send you, through my personal representatives, greetings and best wishes for a successful stewardship as Supreme Pontiff.

The trust and responsibility that have been bestowed on you are great. In these troubled days, the hopes of the world for peace and justice require confidence in its leaders. Your broad experience and wide travel will serve you well in this new and difficult task.

I have read with great interest your appeal to the leaders of all nations for peace. I share with you the fervent desire for a peaceful solution of the momentous problems that beset mankind.

The Pontiff's speed in going before the radio to give his thoughts to the world, and his positive, forthright, dynamic message are clear indications that his reign is going to be a strong one. He knows what he wants and he knows how to go about getting it.

The strength of his coronation homily and clear declaration that he would be a pastoral pope rather than a political one have already been alluded to. Among other acts of his in his first days, we may mention:

1. He ordered the heads of the various congregations and their offices to prepare for regular meetings with him. These would resemble the cabinet meetings of governments, a procedure which had fallen into disuse in the Vatican.

2. He gave indication that he would not simply represent "a continuity" of the papacy, or of the policies of his predecessors, but would initiate a progressive program that would better reflect the supple youthfulness of the Church.

3. When Pope John went out to the balcony of St. Peter's to greet the huge crowd and to bless it and the world, he walked instead of being carried on the portable throne. He went out to the balcony with little or no ceremony. He showed a sincere embarrassment at the overwhelming acclaim given to him. He had been of the people, and applause had been very remote from him. When he began to receive it as legate, nuncio or cardinal, he took it not to himself but to his office. He still gives signs of accepting it—and marvelling at it—not for his own person, but for his position.

4. He surprised everyone in Vatican City by making an inspection tour of the entire 108.7 acres of his realm. This had not been done in forty years.

5. He has astonished everyone in Vatican circles by his free and open manner of treating the people. He is master of protocol and diplomacy but dispenses with it whenever he can. He instructed the editors of *L'Osservatore Romano*, the official Vatican newspaper, to discontinue the use of the traditional polite phrases, "illuminated discourse," "words of wisdom," and to substitute simply: "The Pope said." Papal secretaries who used to kneel to take notes when the Pope spoke were told to sit down at a desk as all good secretaries do.

He showed both independence of tradition and respect for the convenience of many by fixing his coronation day not for Sunday, November 9, as was expected, but for Tuesday, November 4, only a week after his election.

He took formal possession of his Cathedral of St. John Lateran on November 23. Capping a busy week, he also spoke to leaders of the men's section of Italian Catholic Action, visited the papal summer palace at Castel Gandolfo, and sent a special message to the people of Venice. Incidentally, he had promptly appointed a successor to that See left vacant by his own elevation.

Clearly, he took the world by surprise on November 17 when he announced that he would hold a consistory on December 15 for the creation of twenty-three new cardinals, which would increase the number beyond the traditional number of seventy to seventy-four. Some of the new cardinals created were long due for the promotion, such as Montini of Milan and Cicognani, Apostolic Delegate to the United States. Others were surprises. Americans were happy to learn that two of the new cardinals are from the United States, Archbishops Cushing of Boston and O'Hara of Philadelphia. He gave one to Mexico and one to Uruguay, which were surprises. Did he name twenty-three deliberately to coincide with his name?

On December 1, upon hearing of the fire in a Chicago parochial school which took the lives of ninety children and three nuns, he sent a message of condolence to Archbishop Meyer.

On December 15, in secret consistory with twenty-three cardinals who met to approve the twenty-three cardinals-elect, the Pope again vigorously spoke out against the persecutors of the Church. He cited particularly the insidious attempt in China to divide the Church by illicit consecration of bishops, an act coldly calculated to divide, frighten and weaken the faithful.

On December 17, he appointed Archbishop Egidio Vagnozzi as Apostolic Delegate to the United States to succeed Amleto Cardinal Cicognani. He also appointed Bishop John F. Dearden, of Pittsburgh, as Archbishop of Detroit to succeed Cardinal Mooney, and Bishop William E. Cousins of Peoria as Archbishop of Milwaukee to succeed Archbishop Meyer who went to Chicago.

On December 23, he delivered over the radio his first Christmas message to the world which was rebroadcast in thirty languages. It was a beautiful address, from which, as the most salient remarks, we may cite or quote the following:

1. He acknowledged gratefully the enthusiasm with which his election had been received.

2. He paid a glowing tribute to his predecessor, saying that "We already like to regard him as joined in heaven with God's saints, and from there continuing to dispense renewed strength to those Christians who survive him." He confided that much of the acclaim he was receiving was due in reality to the great esteem people had for Pius XII.

3. Pius had wisely inaugurated the Christmas messages, which hitherto had been mere exchanges of greetings with courts of the world. Into the nineteen of them he had poured "a depth and breadth of theological and mystical insight, skillfully directed at practice, and his deepest thoughts regarding the changing circumstances of discipline, and often of the lack of it, in the personal, domestic, civic and social spheres." He said he could do nothing better than to echo those messages of Pius, each of which was a "masterpiece of theological, juridical, ascetical, political and social learning. Each and every discourse was set in the splendor of that doctrine which has for its central theme, Jesus of Bethlehem, and for its chief point of guidance, the mysterious star which proclaims the eternal truth of the spiritual life."

3. He then made a plea for unity, saying: "The birth of the Lord is an announcement of unity and peace in all the world. It is a renewed pledge of good will put to the service of order, of justice, and of fraternity toward all Christian nations, come together in a common desire for understanding, and of great respect for the holy liberty of collective life in the three-fold religious, civil and social order." He went on to say vigorously: "The Tower of Babel was built

in the first centuries of history on the plain of Senaar, and which ended in confusion. Other such towers are being built even now in several regions of the earth, and they will certainly end as the first. But the illusion for many is great and ruin is threatening. Only unity and the strengthening of the apostolate of truth and true human and Christian fraternity will be able to halt the impending new dangers."

4. He ended by saying: "May this be a constructive Christmas. May as many as hear this voice over the airwaves... wish to reinforce their good intentions for the sanctification of the New Year, so that it may become for all the world a year of justice, of blessings, of goodness and of peace."

On Christmas Day, he visited the infants and children in Gesu Bambino Hospital. He was quite at home with these innocents. On the next day, he visited the non-innocents—the criminals in Regina Coeli jail, breaking all precedents. He was not too much at home with them, but he did offer good comfort and inspiration to them, even quipping that since they could not visit him, he had come to visit them. He revealed to them that when he was a boy one of his relatives was "sent up for a month" because he had been hunting without a license and his imprisonment had made a deep impression on him. He spoke to them about the fourteen works of mercy "which help to make life sweet and serene," and about respect for just laws and acceptance of their sanctions. When photographers at the Gesu Bambino Hospital the day before had been distracting him with constant explosions of flashbulbs, he said: "One should probably add a fifteenth work of mercy—that of enduring annoying people. I am very fond of photographers, but by these words I want to explain that I want to enjoy a little peace." Then, in good humor, turning the table on himself, he added: "But now I do not want to be the one forcing you to practice the fifteenth work of mercy by making you listen to a long discourse."

That day, December 26, when he visited the prison, was a Friday. He dispensed from the law of abstinence out of a practical consideration for the much meat left over from all the tables of Christendom. Besides, it was a civil holiday in Italy.

He has approved the filming of a book on the life of Pope Pius XII by Dr. Oscar Halecki, professor of History in Fordham University. He has appointed Monsignors Cesare Zerba as Secretary of the Congregation of the Sacraments, Pietro Palazzini as Secretary of the Congregation of the Council, and Dino Staffa as Secretary of the Congregation of Universities and Seminaries and as legal counsel of the Secretary of State. Importantly, he named as Secretary of State, an office long vacant, a newly-created cardinal, Domenico Tardini. He has consecrated him with three others as archbishops and four others as bishops.

He has delighted Italians by receiving a circus troupe, by leading in the recitation of the Rosary from his apartment window, and by granting to the citizens of Vatican City their very first audience. As the 200 of them crowded into the Clementine Hall, he reminded them that as theirs was a special honor of being quasi-members of his family, so was it their responsibility to be better Christians than the rest. He astonished most by violating an old papal tradition that the Pope eats alone by having some of his relations at dinner shortly after his election and by having Archbishop Angelo Rotta, one of the newly-created cardinals and last Apostolic Nuncio to Hungary, as his Christmas dinner guest. He has particularly delighted Britons and Americans by attempting a few words in English and promising that he will master English. He has appointed Monsignor Thomas Ryan to be his instructor, with lessons beginning on Jan. 6. When he first tried it, he said: "I do not speak it very well, but I will do better in the future. If anyone here is an expert in the language, he should know that I am taking my novitiate." A novice at seventy-eight! But of such is the stuff in John XXIII.

New Year's Eve proved to be a very busy day for the Pontiff. At noon, he appeared at his window, recited the Angelus with the mass of people gathered in the plaza of St. Peter's, gave them his blessing and wished "A Happy New Year to all." The crowd shouted back its own good wishes. Later, during the regular Wednesday audience, which fell on December 31, and was attended by 10,000 of the faithful, he said: "How many are the reasons for gratitude We must have toward the Lord for benefits conferred during 1958. The goodness of the Lord makes Us hope for new graces and assistance during the New Year." He lightened the solemn occasion by teasing the nuns: "Sisters are always so quiet in the convent, but when they go out, they are full of enthusiasm and are always found right up in front." He ended by recommending to all increased devotion to the Blessed Virgin and to the Angels, while revealing that he had only recently added to his chapel a beautiful new painting of the Madonna surrounded by twelve Angels. Later, that day, he again appeared at his window to acknowledge the homage of the street car workers of Rome. "You are all young compared to myself who am so old. Yet my office as Vicar of Christ, which I unworthily hold, allows me to participate a little in the eternal youth of Christ." He then asked the men to recite four Hail Marys with him: "The first for you, the second for your children and the sick, the third for your fellow workers, and another for the Church."

The last hour of 1958 he spent in prayer in the privacy of his personal chapel. It had been an eventful, unforgettable year for him, so he could not forget his Lord who had made it possible.

On New Year's Day he received the good wishes of his staff and of the prelates in Rome. He gave the traditional New Year's Day audience to Rome's Mayor and Municipal Council with other national and local dignitaries.

He has voiced several thoughts of moment in various audiences and interviews since this year of 1959 began. He spoke to members of the International Institute of Liturgical Art and defended modern art in churches. "Art, when inspired by truth and beauty, and when animated by the true spirit of Faith, has a legitimate function . . . it can be as a source of spiritual inspiration, giving a foretaste of what happiness there will be in paradise on seeing God face to face."

In his interview with teachers of Catholic private schools he spoke of the need of preserving effective freedom in the schools. "The mission of teaching is a particular participation in the merits of the Christian apostolate."

On January 5, with the diplomatic corps and his aides he witnessed a private performance of the opera, *Murder in the Cathedral,* which portrayed the martyrdom of St. Thomas á Becket. He is a devotee of the opera and enjoyed the performance immensely.

Rome is still chuckling over a recent pleasantry of his. In meeting with the Italian bishops, as he came to the Chaplain-in-Chief of the Italian armies, he saluted, saying: "Sergeant Roncalli reporting, General!"

On January 25, the feast of the Conversion of St. Paul, and the last day of the Unity Octave, the Pope announced, during a visit to the Basilica of St. Paul, that an Ecumenical Council would be held. This tremendous news immediately attracted the keen interest of the Christian world. The purpose of the Council would be the grand one of trying to unify Christendom. Thus, within three short months of his election, he has put into motion a mighty movement intended to marshall the strength of Christianity against its common foe, Communism.

In all, his first acts have been a mixture of the surprising and the expected, of the bold and of the conventional, of the progressive and of the conservative. What does his rule promise?

Before that can be answered, His burden must be reviewed in more detail.

18

His Burden

WHEN a priest puts on his chasuble in preparing for the celebration of Mass, he recites quietly to himself: "O Lord, who hast said, 'My yoke is sweet and my burden light,' grant that I may so bear it as to gain your grace." The priestly stole is linked with the yoke of old put on the shoulders of beasts or men for the carrying or pulling of a heavy burden. A priest carries a heavy moral burden. The chief priest of Christendom carries the heaviest burden.

In the Chapter on the Pope's powers and prerogatives there were enumerated his rights and dignities. There is no right or dignity which does not carry a corresponding responsibility. If the powers of the Pope are terrifying in their sweep, his burdens are more terrifying in their accumulated weight.

The father of a large family today has the hard task of providing for the temporal needs of his little ones. The President of a large country such as ours has the backbreaking job of keeping order in the land and of providing for its general welfare. The Pope has a large realm in numbers, in territorial extent, and in aims that transcend the material welfare of men. He is directly responsible not to a people who can be assuaged or hoodwinked at times, but to God who knows all the secrets of a man's heart.

A summation of the main burdens that are now Pope John's should be helpful in appreciating the pressure that is on him and it should lead to our affording him at least a charitable understanding of his actions.

He voiced the heaviness of his burden in the first allocution to the Church on October 29, the day after his election:

> This hour of trepidation in which, through the mysterious will of Divine Providence, there has been imposed upon Us the most grave honor of the Supreme Pontificate after the death of our predecessor, Pius XII, of immortal memory, which has such great merits for the Catholic Church, oppresses and weights upon our heart.

His essential burden is the divinely imposed one "to preach the Gospel to every creature, to teach all nations, to feed the lambs and the sheep of Christ's folds."

The gains made in these fields by his predecessors must be retained and even advanced. The Pope must try to see to it that not one soul is lost. His is the same charge Christ acknowledged for himself: "Those whom thou hast given me, I guarded." (John XVII, 12) Primarily, he must be the good shepherd bringing the sheep to good pasture, bringing back the strayed lamb, protecting all from the wolves of the world. It is on his conscience if any human soul is not given the opportunity of knowing about God and being invited into the fold, if anyone, having been in the fold, strays away from it, and if any evil which can be prevented threatens the welfare of the flock. This is his gravest of burdens and the one he himself acknowledged when he declared at his coronation:

> We have at our heart in a very special manner our task as shepherd of the entire flock. All the other human qualities —learning, diplomatic perceptiveness and tact, organizing ability—can succeed in embellishing and complementing

the reign of a Pontiff, but they cannot in any way serve as substitute for this.

The central point is the zeal of the Good Shepherd, ready for every sacred undertaking, no matter how daring, straightforward, constant, even unto the supreme sacrifice. The Good Shepherd lays down his life for his sheep. (John X, 11) How beautiful is the Church of Christ, the sheepfold. The shepherd "goes before the flock," (John X, 4), and all follow him. If necessary, he engages in combat with the wolf in order to defend his sheep.

Then the horizon broadens: "And other sheep I have that are not of this fold; them also I must bring and they shall hear my voice and there shall be one fold and one shepherd." (John X, 16) Here is the missionary problem in all its vastness and beauty. This is the solicitude of the Roman Pontificate, the primary one, even though not the only one.

Directly connected with this primary burden is the one of keeping pure the deposit of faith received from the Master. The deposit is in Tradition and in the Sacred Scriptures, the latter posterior to the former and not closed until the death of the last Apostle, Saint John. He had assured: "Many other signs also Jesus worked in the sight of his disciples, which are not written in this book." (John XX, 30) Before the writing of the first Gospel by Saint Matthew in 42 A.D., the Church relied on Tradition, the spoken words of the Master treasured in the minds of the disciples, and this Tradition continues to be, with the Scriptures, the primary source of Christian doctrine. The preservation of pure doctrine is imperative if Christ's work is to continue on earth. If it is corrupted in the least it impugns his promise to be with the Church to the consummation of the world. Saint Paul strongly brought out the need of keeping the faith pure when he said: "Even if we or an angel from heaven should preach a gospel to you other than that which we have preached to you, let him be anathema." (Galatians I, 8)

In the face of the many in the Church who either in excessive piety or in the spirit of progressive liberalism forever want to amend, innovate, or improve on the teachings of the Master, the Pope has the difficult task of keeping the faith pure. Heresies and dangerous opinions have arisen in all ages, and they are present today, sometimes in a bold form, sometimes in an insidious one. The Pope has to be vigilant against them lest damage be done to the unwary. Pope Pius X gave a splendid example of this diligence when he condemned the teachings of Modernism, which, under the cloak of advanced scholarship, was beginning to undermine the very foundations of the revealed faith. Pius XII did the same when he pointed out in his encyclical, *Humani Generis* (1950), the dangers in the opinions of several Catholic scientists. If one were to look for a major source of worry and heartache to a Pope, it is this problem of keeping pure the teachings of Christ against all innovators whether of good or bad intent.

When defections have occurred, major as in the case of the recession of the Eastern Church and of Protestants from unity with Rome, or minor as in the case of the Old Catholics, of Father Feeney, and the like, then the heartache is real and the burden which saddens most the spirit of Christ's Vicar is very present.

Another burden is that of providing missioners and means for pagan lands. He has an efficient Congregation, that of the Propagation of the Faith, which handles the details of this work throughout the world, aided in turn by National Organizations, such as the one in the United States headed by Bishop Sheen, but the final responsibility is his. It may be said that he is receiving a good bit of consolation from the success which the missionary effort is achieving in Africa and in parts of Asia. The fields are indeed ripe for the harvest. It is his task to send the harvesters, who, as Saint Paul has reminded us, must plant and water before they can enjoy the increase which is only from God.

Christ left his Church the wealth of the Sacraments. It is his Vicar's responsibility to see that they are administered to the faithful. To this end he must erect dioceses and appoint bishops, who in turn erect parishes and appoint pastors and curates. As in the matter of faith, so in sacraments there is a possibility of strange innovations which must be constantly checked. He has to be vigilant, too, in seeing that circumstances of modern living impede not the approach of the faithful to the Sacraments. Hence, he must amend laws to make the Sacraments more available to people. *Sacramenta propter homines*—Sacraments are for men. Thus he permits afternoon or evening Masses when it is necessary, he relaxes the Eucharistic fast, and changes the old routine of the Holy Week services. He finds opposition to this from some of his counselors. He has the burden of making the decision that is practical, but that often offends the sensibilities of old friends.

One of his great joys, yet a burden as well, is the religious state of many of his subjects. Religious orders and congregations, made up of a vast number of men and women who have wanted to consecrate their lives under vows, are great helps to him in many of the spiritual, apostolic, educational and charitable works to be done in the Church. However, there are problems at times of their seeking privileges which encroach on the prerogatives of bishops, of their disputing among themselves on certain jurisdictional, theological or disciplinary matters, of their being adamant on a point of their rule, and of the need of dispensing petitioners from their vows.

The clergy is numerous, and while in its members the Pope has a host of dedicated, willing assistants in the shepherding of the flock, he is confronted with problems concerning them. Human nature being what it is, there are instances in which he will have to censure or rebuke a priest, deny certain concessions to human frailty asked of him from time to time on the part of some of them, individually or in groups, and recall them to more exemplary living. Nothing causes more sorrow to a priest than to have to correct another priest. While much of this burden falls on the immediate superiors, the bishops, a good part of it, and the most vexing aspect of it, falls on the Pope. In the case of Father Feeney, for example, the case went to Rome when it became apparent that the Archbishop of Boston could do nothing further in the matter.

Less vexatious, but still burdensome, is his duty of seeing to it that the ritual of ceremonies is kept uniform and decorous. There are many who want to bring all sorts of changes into the liturgy. If he were to listen to all of them we would have a confusion twice confounded in worship. The Pope tries to be as liberal as he can, respecting regional traditions and local needs, but he cannot avoid the task of maintaining, even in liturgy, a sort of unity throughout the whole Church.

His courts are a burden. Marriage case after marriage case comes to his court. Sometimes very intricate principles are involved which require the most patient and detailed study, and even when the right decision is reached, he runs the risk of being misunderstood and accused of having granted the annulment or divorce because of the prestige or the wealth of the petitioner.

Financial problems are a burden to all men, and the Pope is not free of them. His own personal needs are negligible, even if the expenses of maintaining the Vatican with its hosts of clerks and guards are included. The problem comes from the many pleas which come to him from distressed institutions, from hungry, destitute people, from war-ravaged lands. His fatherly heart cannot be insensible to the cries that pour out to him daily. It is one of the great glories of the papacy that it has always generously responded to these pleas.

Despite this, he has to bear the frequent criticism of those who claim that the Church is unduly wealthy and should unload her holdings in lands, in precious vessels and in museum pieces for the benefit of the poor, particularly the poor of Italy. It harks back to the discredited plea of Judas: "All this could have been sold for much and given to the poor." (Matthew XXVI, 9) Were it all to go for the poor, and it would be supplying for the need of only one day, then the world itself would be poorer. The Church keeps the world rich in guarding the priceless objects of art, the heritage of the genius of her gifted sons.

It is a burden to keep friendly relations with all governments, Catholic and non-Catholic. He has to be careful in his appointment of legates, nuncios and apostolic delegates. One incautious word by an envoy can create a crisis, which never helps the cause of religion. Careful, skillful diplomacy is not an easy thing to maintain, but its burden must be borne for the sake of spiritual gains. On the whole this burden has not been excessive, since his corps of diplomats has been careful in the main to avoid awkward situations. The apostolic delegation in the United States, for example, having the difficult task of operating in a country which officially does not recognize it and which is keenly sensitive to any violation of its principle of separation of Church and State, has an enviable record of harmonious relations with the American Government and people.

These burdens, very grave and always present, are the usual ones which beset any Pope. It is helpful to cite them. But far more helpful and more important it is to call attention to the very special burdens which this particular year of 1959 imposes on the happily broad shoulders of John XXIII.

First is that of a growing indifference to the essentials of religion on the part of large masses of people. The word doctrine or dogma is becoming unfashionable. The Church has her dogmas, asserts she will keep them, and thus dissatisfies many who want to shed the yoke of rigidity in faith for the fairer-looking pastures of freedom. There is a tendency to unite all religions under the one common banner of seeking the good of man, and if the character of Christ as a Divine Person impedes the union, he can be dispensed with as such, while retaining him as a wise, gentle teacher for the greater good of uniting all men in one organization which will include Jews, Hindus, Moslems, Eastern Catholics and Protestants. The Catholic Church, unyielding in doctrine, is charged as an enemy of this worth-while effort. The plan appeals to many as a solution to the senseless feuding among religions and as a rallying point for all who love the brotherhood of man.

The burden on him whose commission calls for dispelling this false plan is indeed heavy. The first Pope clearly enunciated the Christian doctrine: "There is no other name under heaven given to man by which we must be saved than . . . the name of Jesus of Nazareth." (Acts IV, 12)

In the wish to be all things to all men, in the wish to unite men under one common-denominator standard of basic religion, the dear character of the true Savior of men is being minimized or shunted aside. The pity is that it was he who laid down the sure, lofty principles around which men could rally into a true human unity based on the Fatherhood of God. "Holy Father, keep in thy name those whom thou hast given me, that they may be one even as we are." (John XVII, 11) "I am the way, the truth and the life. No one comes to the Father but through me." (John XIV, 6) After the missionary work of centuries, Christ still has to be preached to the world. It is very discouraging to realize that the answer to the main human problems has been given, has been accepted, and is now being rejected. That stone, which is Christ, was once rejected by the builders, only to become the cornerstone of the redeemed edifice. The Pope's task is to keep him the cornerstone of our civilization.

Another tremendous present burden, and certainly akin to the one above, is the moral situation of the world today. As man rejects dogma, he rejects precepts. There is a spirit abroad of rejecting the decalogue. It imposes restrictions, and the new-found psychology tends to do away with restrictions or suppressions, particularly in the matter of sex. Pornography has a wide market while obscene books are hailed as best sellers and made "musts" in courses of literature. Fornication and masturbation are not regarded as grave evils; adultery is often painted as a personal matter and even justified in some cases; homosexuality is regarded only as a sickness, not a crime against nature. The lie has become a warranted expedient in business and in international diplomacy. The Church has an uphill fight to maintain the Christian sense of morality. The age is becoming pagan. License to read what one wants, to see what theatrical performances one desires, to eat what one enjoys, and to use the Sunday for pleasure or shopping is demanded on the score that man needs emancipation from outmoded codes of conduct. Divorce is on the increase, even with Catholics; contraceptive practices are upheld as rightful personal decisions, and marriage is considered to be far more a man-made institution than a divinely instituted one. The burden to defend the morality of the Sermon on the Mount has become increasingly heavy in an era morally debilitated by major wars, by rumors of more wars, and by the acceptance of the humanly pleasing philosophy that man is his own lawmaker and his own destiny.

The greatest burden stems from the fact that atheism, no longer a mere talking danger in school and salon, is actually and powerfully entrenched in government. Communism governs the vast regions of Russia and Siberia and dominates its many satellite nations. It is warring with amazing forcefulness and ingenuity against Christianity. Its leaders have boasted that they will destroy the religion of Christ, and in the execution of their policy they have put to death, imprisoned and maltreated many of their Christian citizens and pressured and embarrassed others to make them abandon their belief in God.

Communism is a fearful menace. The Popes alone have realized it from the beginning and they alone have fought hard to rid the world of it. They have not succeeded. Communism is growing stronger, thanks to the weak and vacillating policies of the free world, and, accordingly, the danger it presents to the peace and liberty of the world is all the greater today. Its technique of posing as a peace-loving force and the only hope of the socially and economically oppressed peoples of the earth has been very successful. Communism is out to conquer the world, by intrigues in peace if it can, and by war if necessary.

The Communists have been gathering the implements of a successful hot war. They have the atom bomb, they have intercontinental missiles, they have sputniks in space. Only recently they launched a man-made planet, named simply No. 10 by us, but by them, first, *Lunik,* and later, *Mechta,* a dream. This dream of theirs is in orbit around the sun, having passed the moon, and has given them a tremendous propaganda advantage. The free world wonders if it can catch up with the Russians in the race for technological prowess. It is a crushing burden on the leaders of the free world to try to foil or balance these forces of destruction aimed at capitalism and their liberty. It is far more of a burden on the shoulders of the man in the Vatican to prevent this fearful power from destroying the spiritual life of his flock. It may be good to save capitalism and an occasional civilization. It is imperative to save for the children to come the story of the Christ Child, of the Crucified, and of the Chrism of the Holy Spirit which gives to man his spiritual life and verifies him as made in the image, not of a gorilla, but of God.

❁ 19 ❁

His Promise

WHAT promise does John XXIII make in his person and character to carry the heavy burdens of his high office?

The world, particularly the Catholic world, had witnessed the magnificent carrying of the load by the physically frail, intellectual, aristocratic Pius XII. Can this short, sturdy son of the soil, a man of plebeian origin, born in humble poverty, do as well? Pius was the polite, restrained type of person, always poised, always in control of self. John is not impolite, but there are no ultra-polished surfaces about him. He is obviously more at home in a gathering of gondoliers than in the salons of the smart.

Many observers felt that the first impression made on a world accustomed to the elegance of the Roman nobleman was one of disappointment. There appeared in the white papal soutane which for nineteen years had been filled with the tall, elegant frame of the nobleman, a short stubby figure. Some snobbishly-inclined Catholics were not impressed with the fact that the Church had a peasant for Pope, and these few expect little from him in the way of brilliant leadership. They are allowing a petty prejudice to cloud their view. They ignore the fact that blue blood has no monopoly on ability, and that the plain, red blood of the peasant has often surpassed the blue in quality of character and achievement. They ignore, too, the fact that the first apostles were all humble workers, and that nobility, as one of them expressed it, consists in serving the Lord. "To serve Him is to reign."

How will this new *Servus Servorum* serve? Let us weigh the evidence before us in this early period of his reign.

We have described his background and antecedents. He is a man of humble origin, a man of the soil, the son of a sharecropper born in a rude stone farmhouse. This fact is a great advantage to him because the need of the world today is actually to understand the plight of the poor. Communism is making the claim that Catholicism favors capitalism and the rich. John's call to the lofty eminence of the world's most honored throne deflates the force of that propaganda. Of course, Communism will minimize the election of a poor man of the soil, calling it a capitalistic feint and crying that for all his proletarian origin he is a tool of the rich, but the bald fact will stand out nevertheless: he is of the soil; he knows what it is to be hungry, to be in want; he knows what it is to work with his hands for his living; he knows what it is to go to market and find the prices unfair for honest work done. The poor of the world who are still harrowed by these problems can expect from this man who sits on Peter's throne a sympathetic understanding, and more than that, a sincere, practical attempt to remedy the ills. He is the People's Pope. Not all raised in a log cabin retain a love of their kind. John evidently does. All his acts and utterances from the time he rose to prominence as archbishop, nuncio and cardinal testify to it, and what he has said and done so far as Pope only serves to confirm his true attachment to the lowly of the world. He can be counted upon to champion in an effective way the cause of the poor, and this promise is a bright one because it will weaken the argument of Communism.

In body there is a fair measure of promise. His age is against him—he is now seventy-seven years of age, well beyond the retiring time of military men, business men, educators and others. Still some very old men have done excellent work in fields which require more brain than brawn. John's health is excellent and he takes fair care of himself. In appearance he is a short, heavy-set man, rather unprepossessing and plain. Some persons in describing him have included the comment that he has no sex appeal. This may seem an irreverent comment, but since modern psychology has accentuated this feature as impelling from the fair sex a greater interest which proceeds to acts of loyalty and service, it is not out of place to mention it. Candidates for the American presidency or governorships have had to take this factor into consideration. John can be expected to survive this handicap. Indeed, he has one superior advantage: a kindly face which wins the confidence of men and women.

Have you noticed the hands in the pictures? They are quite capable still of milking a cow, pitching hay, and saddling a horse. Those hands can very firmly carry a crook and apply it with dexterity to keep an erring sheep in line or bash in the head of a wolf.

He has been described as "earthy." This is generally meant as a compliment. It definitely is. A shepherd has to be a very practical man, down to earth, whence problems arise, where brambles are found to ensnare the sheep and where wolves prowl. He may raise his eyes to the stars to give his aesthetic needs some mode of satisfaction, and he may go beyond the stars to contemplate the majesty of God in his glorious heaven, but he must not forget the earth, the ciborium from which his physical parts and his flock must be nourished. Unless the body is fed the soul departs. While spiritual needs are the more important, they often depend, by reason of the interdependence of the elements which compose man, on the material for their thriving.

John will nourish the souls of men, but he will not forget the needs of their bodies, and we can expect positive, down-to-earth measures to be taken toward that end.

Pope John has shown a warm humanity in many things. Some may have pretended to be shocked upon learning that he smokes cigarettes and drinks an occasional cocktail, but the vast numbers of smokers and of temperate drinkers will find in these indulgences a drawing kinship. Too, ordinary people have warmed to the news item which appeared concerning the action of his seventy-two year old sister Assunta in bringing a box of home-made sausages "because his stomach has always been delicate, and God knows what kind of food they give him here (at the Vatican)."

The Vatican service men and women, so long accustomed in their conversations to say Papa Pio, had difficulty in adding his number, *Vigesimoterzo.* He smiled at their difficulty in calling him properly and assured them that he would be content with Papa Gio'ani and not to bother with *ventitresimo* or the more correct *vigesimoterzo.* They expressed their feelings promptly among themselves: *lo vogliamo gia bene,* we already like him. Out of the mouth of babes in their humility often comes the truth. These servants—and who is a hero to his own servants?—have likely sounded the keynote that will become the consolation of many: he likes us.

So much for the body and things physical. Intellectually, the new Pontiff is quite promising. He is an avid reader, storing up both practical and classical knowledge. He has written books and he can be very articulate in conversation. His scholarship is sound; he has a deep appreciation of learning although he has not been rated to be as brilliant as his predecessor. At best that is an arbitrary judgment. Brilliancy is not essential. He may have it or not. It is certain he has a good brain and a logical mind, fast-thinking and wide in scope.

He is a good linguist. He speaks, besides his native Italian and his required Latin, French, Spanish, German, Bulgarian, and Greek. He can read English, German, and even Russian. American tourists may be disappointed in not hearing his greeting in fluent English, but they should be consoled in that he can read Russian and pierce the intricate mind of the Masters of the Kremlin. He is trying to learn English.

He is quite businesslike in all his dealings.

He goes to the heart of things quickly and makes prompt decisions. He has given abundant evidence of this virtue. The Roman tradition is one of painful slowness. An American Prelate once described it this way: Rome is very wise to delay decisions; time often makes the decisions for her. John has more of the American approach. He is impatient to clear his desk.

He has displayed a pleasing wit. Jovial and friendly, he will joke about things and keep his company pleasantly entertained. On one occasion he quipped about his own humble origin. "In Italy, there are three ways of losing one's money: women, gambling, and farming. My father chose the most boring way of the three. He became a farmer." Shortly after he became a cardinal he invited some prominent Frenchmen to a party. Attending were ex-Premiers Faure, Pinay, Gouin, Mayer, and Pleven, all divergent in political affiliations. The cardinal commented: "Only under my roof could French politicians from such diversified horizons gather peacefully together." When the plaza of St. Mark was flooded one day, he walked through a café, the Birreria Leoncini, the Little Lions Beer-Hall, to get to his destination. The bar-keeper looked up in a surprise. "Wanting to wet your throat?" "No," replied the cardinal, "just want to keep my feet from getting wet."

They say that ridicule is the most effective technique to

demolish an adversary. John may not be inclined to ridicule, but he has wit, and wit is even a better form to show the absurdity of the Communist position.

Pascal sagely said: "The heart has its reasons which the head knows not." Effective as the head is to solve the world's problems, the heart must definitely have its place. Unless one puts his heart in a thing, all his mental brilliance will be diminished. John is definitely a man of heart—warm, sympathetic, gentle, affable. He feels for people. Doctors and diplomats may have to learn to suppress their personal feelings, but a priest need not. A priest without a heart is an anomaly. "Learn of me for I am meek and humble of heart," said the Priest of Priests. (Matthew XI, 29) A Pope, for all his brilliance of mind, must possess the qualities of heart which will make him one with his flock. He must love them with a genuine affection. The Apostle John had written: "Let us love one another, for love is from God. And everyone who loves is born of God, and knows God. He who does not love does not know God, for God is love." (I John, IV, 7-8) The Pope gives ample evidence of possessing this supernal virtue of charity. Charity not only covers a multitude of sins but accomplishes what hate or severity never can. St. Francis de Sales has said that you can catch more flies with a spoonful of honey than with a tub of vinegar. John's warm, loving nature is calculated to achieve with the indifferent, the sneering, the rebellious, and even with the Communists, far more than the most careful planning can do.

This human warmth which he radiates is not to be confused with weakness. John is affable but firm. He will uphold principle but he would rather smile while doing it than growl. He is the same sort of happy warrior in the spiritual contest that Al Smith was in the political arena.

All talents of head and heart will not achieve their best objective if they are not based on a supernatural motive or implemented by spiritual insight. One who has to rule in spiritual matters had best be spiritual-minded himself. John is deeply spiritual. His faith in God and the supernatural, inbred from infancy by his pious peasant parents, rivals the proverbial faith of the Breton peasant. He has warm devotion to the Blessed Sacrament, the fountain of all holiness. He says his Mass devoutly, he reads his breviary, he recites his rosary. He is genuinely pious. It may seem odd to cite these things concerning a Pope, but de facto a Pope is not automatically pious. Some priests are not pious. They are good priests in fulfilling the letter of the law, but at times there is lacking that personal sense of warmth in worship. Some characters are cold or know not how to display affection, thus cheating themselves and those dependent on their affection of the finer joys of their state. Pope John is plainly pious, relishing the spiritual and setting a fine personal example of the man and priest who takes joy in performing the sacred functions. He nourishes the spiritual constantly with his meditations, readings, and prayers. He thus acquires that strength of soul that serves far more than talents of head or heart the welfare of the world.

He is paternal and priestly, true to the best tradition of a *papa.* He had a good father who made his childhood joyous by his attentiveness, consideration and affection. What he acquired from his father he now passes on to his own spiritual children, and with his fine sense of priesthood which was developed in him by his association with good parish priests, seminary professors and his bishop, he promises to be that most successful type of Pope which his predecessor, Pope Pius X, with the same characteristics, was.

Thus heritage and environment are on his side to make him successful. There remains experience to be considered. He has had formal experience as a bishop's secretary, as a seminary teacher, and for twenty-seven years as an envoy. He was excellent in all three roles. He has not had too much experience in actual priestly ministering, yet he always desired this as his first choice, and he performed the sacerdotal functions in parishes whenever he could. No one need fear that this lack of abundant experience in administering the Sacraments will blunt his perceptiveness in planning for an increase in sacramental reception. It has been his declared policy to be a pastoral Pope, and he will move with all the powers in him to accomplish this sacred objective.

The Church has in him a dedicated man. He will stand for peace but without that appeasement which makes it dishonorable. He will convey clear, forceful thoughts to his bishops and to the heads of government. He will rule, not just gloriously reign. He has already shown a firm hand in government for all his amiability, and he will attend to details as well as to top-level policies. He will push the missionary effort with all the vim of his enthusiastic nature, since he wants the Kingdom of Christ expanded, for the spiritual good of the heathens and to offset the gains of Communism.

As for Communism, he is going to attack it hard because he is thoroughly convinced that it is a threat to all that is sacred and right in the world, but he will do it, probably, in a surprising way. He astonished the Vatican itself when as Patriarch of Venice he granted an audience to that city's Communists. He does not mind treating with them directly. When Nuncio in Paris, he often chatted amiably at dinner with Alexander Bogmolov, the Soviet ambassador. Before his election, the Communists had hoped for a "neutral" sort of Pope. Since his election they have labelled him a "paternalistic conservative." He will be more of a woodshed father as far as they are concerned. He does recognize that some of the economic reforms they preach must be effected in Italy, but he knows all about their Trojan Horse tricks and is ready to thwart them.

All together, he gives a fair promise of being an exceptional Pope. The critics have said that he is too old; that he was elected as a compromise, a stop-gap Pope who will reign for a few years colorlessly and inconspicuously. Critics have been wrong before in matters affecting the papacy.

What he has done to date is most colorful. Editors do not assign expensive newsmen to cover the happenings of a pale politico. The Vatican swarms with top-flight reporters because they sense in John a very newsworthy person.

It is a conservative estimate to say that he will prove to be a very strong Pope. He has, for all his years, an abundance of health, exceptional talents of heart and mind, a deep spirituality, a fine priestly sense, an amiable nature, and a firm will to pursue what he thinks right. He captivated France in a difficult period by his urbanity and charm. It may well be a presage of his power to captivate the world.

Those who know him intimately have remarked that he can wrap around his little finger any personage he interviews. He listens quietly and even smilingly to the most vehement protest or objection, his fertile mind racing all the while to find that proper phrase that will disarm the critic. He finds that phrase and the visitor leaves happily agreeing with him. This is a rare ability which can serve the Church to great advantage. The same "voices" mentioned in Chapter 13 assert that were he to face Khrushchev or any other enemy of the Church he would easily best him. The Pope has keen, perceptive eyes, and his conversation is like lacework, passing from one subject to another with skillful grace, while keeping true to the beautiful pattern before him of a serene Church at work for the greater glory of God.

The fertile soil of Lombardy from which he sprang is one which promises a goodly harvest if the land is well tilled, watered and weeded, and if the weather is right. His own person promises more for the Church and for the world—if he pursues industriously as he has started to do the implanting of the word of God, its watering, its weeding; and, of course, if God gives the increase.

❁ 20 ❁

The Outlook of His Reign

HOW will John XXIII fare as a Pope? What can be expected to happen? Will he be as good as Pius XII, or better, or fall far short? Will he advance the papacy or harm it, or just keep it in a sort of status quo? Will he succeed or fail? Will he do much tilling, much watering, much weeding, and will the conditions of the world and plans of national leaders conspire to aid him or thwart him in his endeavor to be a good Pope? These are interesting questions and quite naturally present in the minds of many; hence the outlook must be considered.

In the old days a soothsayer quartered an animal and by studying the entrails of the beast he presumed to be able to foretell the future. This method was far from satisfactory. Quite likely the plan we adopt, namely, to quarter the world and examine the political, social, economic and spiritual situation on our planet today will prove as ineffective. However, it is a fair sport and might possibly afford some atom of light in the nebula which surrounds the days to come.

Politically, the world is divided into two camps, freedom and subjugation. The two camps are gargantuan in size and power, and at present are engaged in what is termed a cold war. The titans are like boxers in a ring coolly appraising each other, wondering if it is expedient to strike, feinting a blow, watching for an opening, and, for the time, content not to risk an open assault.

Each of the two titans, the free world headed by our own nation, the United States, and the subjugated world, dominated by the Soviet Union, is bending every effort to win mastery over the other without resort to a hot war. A hot war, bringing into play the devastating destructive power of atomic missiles, might very well spell the suicide of the world; hence it is not sensible for either to inaugurate such a conflict unless one side is assured that it will survive while the opponent will perish. The ingenuity to devise more and more destructive engines of war is happily matched by an equal ingenuity in devising protections against them. Hence the titans are in a stalemate on the point of power. As long as a fair balance exists between them in possession of implements of war, the shooting war will not start. But the situation is a precarious one. The recurring crises, the brink-of-war affairs, may not always be resolved by a calm and adroit diplomacy.

In all this the Church holds a perilous position. She is abetting all efforts for peace, and her Pope can be expected to continue the manful try of his predecessor to ensure a peace, but as Pius X failed and Pius XI with Pius XII failed, he is likely to fail. The world leaders pay little attention to the Pope. Communism derides him and can be counted on to do the opposite of what he suggests. The free world may listen politely but it is worried more about its own concern. The altruism or spirituality which he enunciates runs counter to the cold facts of politics and business. Experience teaches that when nations engage in a race of armament, the point is finally reached when one is ready for war, or thinks it is ready, and the cataclysm starts. Russia is playing a shrewd game of dependence on propaganda rather than on bullets, and it may be that this strategy will save the world from war, but if the world is spared the war, the strategy might accomplish bloodlessly what the world wants to avert, namely, subjugation under the Hammer and Sickle. It is at best a miserable situation.

Religio depopulata, religion depopulated, was the dire prophecy of Malachy for Benedict XV, who ruled during World War I, which lost so many Christian lives and saw the rise of Atheistic Communism in Russia. World War III might possibly start in John's reign, and if it does the Church will suffer greatly. Italy is within easy reach of the striking power of the Bear and Rome's destruction is something the beast contemplates with relish. The Popes have been Communism's greatest moral obstacle in its quest of world power, as the United States has been its greatest military obstacle. John is logically the first victim it intends to liquidate. He hinted at this in his coronation homily. "The Good Shepherd lays down his life for his sheep." (John X, 11) It is precisely the outlook he faces. Many have thought they might be able to do business with the Kremlin, as others had thought they might do business with Hitler. Many deceive themselves with the hope that Communism will soften and go civilized. The fact is that Communism is a cold, ruthless, amoral power bent on the destruction of religion. Far from weakening it, the years, aided by the inept diplomacy of the West, are making it stronger and more arrogant. The only force that can stop it now is the divine one.

The social problem in the world presents a forbidding outlook. At one time races in Africa and Asia, and the Americas as well, lived in meek subjection, simply because they were friendless and powerless. They are no longer friendless and powerless. In our own country we witness a very articulate and powerful National Association for the Advancement of Colored People adroitly using its legal skill and political power to force integration. The Supreme Court had no newer principle on which to base its recent historic decision to integrate than it had in 1868 when the Fourteenth Amendment was adopted. It was the pressure from the NAACP that made it see at last the justice of the matter. The decision, just as it is, is causing turmoil in the country because old racial prejudices will not automatically die with court orders to do so. Our country is in for an awkward period because of the existing prejudice, and the Church in America is herself gravely concerned. The bishops at their annual meeting in November bravely and wisely issued a statement supporting the integration decision, but they counselled moderation in enforcing it.

The same problem, and worse, faces the total Church in the world-wide scope of the question. The South American and Central American Indian strains are no longer content to accept the position of inferior citizens; the vast hordes in India, China, Malay, Oceana, and Africa are becoming conscious of their equality and are proceeding to demand it. The Church is in the unfortunate position of being classed as an abettor of the oppressor simply because in many cases the oppressor is a Catholic nation. Catholic missioners, whose primary objective it was to bring the faith to pagan lands, have been accused of bringing their flag with their cross. All this was taken somewhat complacently once, but it is no longer true. People long under the domination of a foreign power now want freedom or at least equality of civil rights. They want the Church to champion these rights, not only by the expedient of literary, beautifully-sounding encyclicals but by forceful action. Unless that is done, the harm already accomplished in the suspicious attitude of oppressed peoples towards the Church will become greater and well-nigh irreparable.

Sleeping giants are awakening. In a sense, Communism has awakened the giants. Some say that they have been awakened by the World Wars and the spirit of the times, for the spirit of democracy is riding high, but it is still true that Communism has taken advantage of the situation and has heralded itself as the champion of the oppressed. Its motives are not altruistic, yet quite naturally inferiorly-treated peoples are not going to question too closely the voice that is raised rather vociferously in their behalf. True, the United Nations program has been one of steady liberation of the oppressed and the recognition of human rights, but the Communists have been able to take much of the credit. This outlook as well is not too bright for the Church. Like the embarrassment our own State Department felt in the Algerian situation—it was in theory favorable to Algerian freedom but was constrained by ties with France to withhold support—the Church is embarrassed in the situation. She has wanted civil rights and political liberty accorded to all peoples ready for it, but has felt a constraint in pushing it forcefully lest she seriously offend her own daughter nations and bring on a greater harm to her own freedom and well-being.

Pope John will have to be a Solomon to decide on the better course. Is a bird in the hand worth two in the bush? The hordes in Asia and Africa are the potential Catholic peoples of the future. They must have assurance that the Church is their friend by her pushing ardently for their civil rights. Otherwise they would rather listen to the siren voice of the Soviets. The Church offers them the true faith, the greater good, but humanly they like the antipasto before the main dish of a bit of rice or the appetizing cocktail of civil rights.

In reviewing the economic situation in the world, the picture is not brighter. A good one-third of humanity is ill-housed, ill-clothed, and ill-fed. Many are jobless or working for wretched wages. When President Roosevelt in 1937 employed these phrases to describe the economic condition of America, he startled the country by the facts and galvanized it into some action. Pope Leo in 1891 had spoken eloquently about a living wage, unions, and the general condition of the laborer. He too had galvanized the world into some action, but while that great encyclical, *Rerum Novarum,* will stand as a magna carta of labor's rights and dignity, the fact is that it was not pushed too vigorously by some churchmen and capitalists.

The gains which the working people in America and Europe have made is not credited to the Church but to organized labor which has had to fight tooth and nail for the position it now enjoys. In the fight, it has received help from the Church in America, but it is not as acknowledged as is the help which it received from elements like the Socialists more or less linked with the Communist movement. Labor in America should be made to realize more than it does that the Church is its friend; otherwise its outlook here is not as favorable as it should be. Labor throughout the world should be equally assured that the Church is its friend and champion. The impression has been implanted that the Church is largely on the side of capital and management, just as in the older days she was labeled as the supporter of monarchy. Unless the laboring classes get to feel that the Church is definitely on their side, the Church will lose more and more of the workers she has and will not get a response from the workers not yet in her communion. She has lost many in Italy and France. Her churches are not filled to overflowing with men on Sunday. That has to be corrected. To be corrected, as well, is the situation of so many Italians, Frenchmen and Spaniards in the Communist party. The main reason for their membership is economic misery. They want jobs and bread. The Communists at least talk about helping them and they grasp at the straw of that promise which an existing Christian government does not hold out to them. Excommunication by the Church has not deterred too many from trying out Communism. A hungry man, unless he is heroic, will make his league with a devil offering porridge for himself and his children rather than with an angel offering grace.

The election of a worker Pope should help. A Pope of the People can have a powerful appeal to the people provided he has not lost his touch with them. Pope John has not lost this touch; he is of the people and will battle as he always has for their welfare. From this standpoint the outlook is bright. If only he could prevail upon governments and industrialists to provide work at a living wage for those who are forced to stand all the day idle, half the battle would be won. The Popes have tried. A better publicity concerning their honest efforts to help the poor of the world will avert the catastrophe of the Church losing the loyalty of the lowly.

The spiritual situation is alarming. The moral one connected with it has been discussed already in the Chapter on burdens. After a big war or similar catastrophe, people have a spiritual rebirth, but when things go along smoothly they forget the spiritual to turn to the fleshpots. More and more the old age of faith is waning. Science vies with religion for the adoration of the world. Materialism, creature comfort, and pleasure are found to be more attractive than the welfare of one's soul. The possession of a soul, at least of a spiritual, immortal one, is more and more doubted. Darwinism has taken its toll. Bible stories are openly discredited, the supernatural order entices much less than does the law of nature, and men are listening more to the old Epicureanism that we should eat, drink and be merry today, for tomorrow we die.

Unless this tendency is checked, the Church's magnificent victory over paganism in her early centuries will suffer a reversal. It is the tremendous challenge to her prowess, her true battle. The flesh lusts against the spirit, and the spirit must enter the lists with the flesh. Unless she fights this battle hard and unrelentingly, the world will go along the way of the flesh, and so to its degradation whose end, as St. Paul assures us, is destruction. (Philippians III, 19). Will she win? She will because of the divine promise of Christ to be with his Church, but the measure and the speed of her victory will depend on the zeal with which she continues the battle.

In summary, we may say that the outlook of the Reign of Pope John XXIII is not too bright if we look at it only from the human standpoint. The problems are huge, with little solution in sight. It is difficult to see, granted all his talents of heart, mind and soul, that he can correct in any major way the ills of the world. Still, no sensible man should expect him to do that. If he can only make a beginning of a definite correction in one field, it will be an outstanding achievement. On this the outlook is much brighter. The farmer's boy will make a dent in the stubborn glebe of human problems by the strength of his priestly heart and by the power which will flow to him from the Eternal Priest. This divine help can be said to be manifest in the support which the Church, his pride, has already promised to her visible head in the contest.

❁ 21 ❁

The Church Behind Him

CHRIST is in His Church, wherefore the universal action of the Church is reflective of the will of Christ. The Church has clearly performed a universal action in expressing throughout her far-flung dioceses and by mouth of her members, great and small, a joyous satisfaction in the election of John XXIII; and she has indicated that she stands behind him. He is her elected Captain. She will follow as he leads.

The deep sorrow that came to the heart of the Church in the passing of the great Pontiff Pius XII, was turned into joy when his successor was chosen. The newspapers were full of reports of the crowds that assembled in the plaza of St. Peter during the conclave. When the whiff of white smoke curled upward from the chimney of the Sistine Chapel telling the world that an election had taken place, greater crowds began assembling to hear the name of the new Pope. When Cardinal Canali intoned the ritualistic words: "I announce to you a great joy; we have a Pope, the Most eminent and Most Reverend Lord Cardinal Angelo Joseph Roncalli," the vast assembly broke out into long and resounding cheers. It was a most impressive demonstration, spontaneous and genuine, unpoliced, unrehearsed, and unrestrained.

Unless one has heard a Roman crowd, he will not appreciate the special character of its cheering. It is voluble, exuberant, irrepressible. The Italian is emotional and he is not one to hide his emotions. What that crowd of two hundred thousand Italians shouted on that clear night when the news broke of the election of the Patriarch of Venice was a rousing paean of relief, pride, and cheer, wild revelry, the power of whose message of merriment echoed to every other piazza in Italy and was taken up in equal volume and emotion by thousands more who swelled into millions. "Viva! Viva Il Papa! Viva Roncalli!" they shouted in wave upon wave of crescendoing enthusiasm. This vivid demonstration of popular approval became a positive frenzy of cheering, clapping, and waving of handkerchiefs when the Pope appeared on the balcony and imparted to them his first blessing. As he heard those cheers for his name, he modestly observed that they should shout instead, "Viva La Chiesa," "Long Live the Church;" but the crowd was the Church and it sang out her exultation for the person of John, her new visible head. The many American, English, German, French and Spanish tourists or workers in Rome at the time caught the contagion of the crowd and shouted themselves hoarse as well. It was a thrilling sight to see and music to hear.

The crowd maintained its enthusiasm in another and even more convincing form when on the day after, as the cardinals emerged from the conclave, it thanked the prelates for having given to the Church so "fine a Pope."

On November 4, when the Pope was crowned, the enthusiastic demonstration was repeated with even greater numbers participating. It was all the more remarkable because it was a very inclement day.

Immense crowds throughout the world followed with

great interest the ample newspaper, radio and television coverage given to the election and the coronation. Some non-Catholics simply took the accounts as ordinary news items, with a few grunts of disapproval for the extensiveness of the coverage, while a fair number seemed genuinely intent on learning the procedure of the Roman Church in electing her head. Most had no opinion one way or another, while a few, having heard of the diplomatic achievements of the new Pope, expressed satisfaction. We shall see later some official and complimentary expressions of Protestant leaders on the election of Pope John.

The shouts of the crowds and the interest of millions in the news stories and pictures, however, were insignificant when compared to the more substantial spiritual forms of approval shown to the new Pope. Catholicism en masse gathered in cathedral and parish church, in university shrine and convent chapel, to offer to God Almighty through the supreme act of Catholic worship, which is the Mass, its thanks for the divine favor of granting—so quickly, so peacefully—so good a Pope. The joyous strains of the Te Deum, that magnificent thanksgiving anthem of Saints Ambrose and Augustine, rose in moving melody to heaven from thousands of choirs and congregations. Bishops and pastors everywhere gathered their flocks to pray for their new chief shepherd and to express both through liturgical orations and private pleas, their loyalty.

In audience on May 8, 1896, Pope Leo XIII granted an indulgence of five hundred days once a day for the reciting of the following prayer for the Pontiff. It beautifully expresses the mind of the Church towards her Visible head:

> O Lord, we are the millions of believers, humbly kneeling at Thy feet and begging Thee to preserve, defend and save the Sovereign Pontiff for many years. He is the Father of the great fellowship of souls and our Father as well. On

this day, as on every other day, he is praying for us also, and is offering unto Thee with holy fervor the sacred Victim of love and peace.

Wherefore, O Lord, turn Thyself toward us with eyes of pity; for we are now, as it were, forgetful of ourselves and are praying above all for him. Do Thou unite our prayers with his and receive them into the bosom of Thine infinite mercy, as a sweet savor of active and fruitful charity, whereby the children are united in the Church to their Father. All that he asks of Thee this day, we too ask it of Thee in union with him.

Whether he weeps or rejoices, whether he hopes or offers himself as a victim of charity for his people, we desire to be united with him; nay, more, we desire that the cry of our hearts should be made one with his. Of Thy great mercy, grant, O Lord, that not one of us may be far from his mind and his heart in the hour that he prays and offers unto Thee the Sacrifice of Thy Son. At the moment when our venerable High Priest, holding in his hands the very Body of Jesus Christ, shall say to the people over the chalice of benediction, these words: "The peace of the Lord be with you always," grant, O Lord, that Thy sweet peace may come down upon our hearts and upon all the nations with new and manifest power. (Raccolta, Prayer 608)

All Rome, his See, voiced enthusiastic support for its new bishop. The bells of its many churches pealed gladly their song of loyalty. This must have been his greatest consolation. The major pastors of Rome, the cardinals, had voted for him; the other prelates accepted him, and, above all, the people took him to their hearts.

Throughout the rest of Italy the story was the same. In his own home town there was intense jubilation. The humble villagers of Sotto il Monte gathered in the parish church said prayers of thanksgiving for him; and then in a civic demonstration, the greatest, naturally, in the history of that hamlet, they showed their pride and delight that a son of their town had mounted Peter's throne. There were fireworks, bonfires, parades, speeches and prolonged feasting.

In Venice, whose archbishop-patriarch was now Pope, the celebration reached a height typical of the fervor and culture of that lovely city. Flags and bunting appeared on every building, gondolas were gayly decorated, and gay singing kept filling the air. St. Mark's plaza and basilica were jammed with people who shouted their joy and swore their fealty.

Throughout the whole Veneto—Padua, Verona, Vicenza, Udine, Treviso—the celebrations went on, and beyond, to Trent and Trieste. In adjacent Lombardy, Bergamo, the diocese of his origin, went wild with delight, while its other towns, Como, Brescia, Mantua, Pavia, Cremona, and, principally, Milan, conducted impressive church and civic programs to show him their attachment. To the West in the Piedmont, with Turin leading, the demonstration went on in Aosta, Cuneo, Alessandria, Vercelli, and Novara, and continued in the strip of Liguria to the South in its metropolis of Genoa and her satellites of Porto Maurizio, Noli, Savona, Chiarvari, and Spezia. In Emilia, the famed cities of Parma, Modena, Ravenna, Ferrara, Rimini and Bologna took up the promise of fealty with the cities of the Marches to the South, Pesara, Ancona, Macerata, Ascoli and Urbino; while the little sovereign state of San Marino in between the two let out its own pledge of obedience. Tuscany would not be denied its desire to stand with him, and so in Lucca, Pisa, Siena, Orbetello, Cortona, and, particularly in Florence, splendid demonstrations of loyalty took place. Towards the central Adriatic, Abruzzi and Molise in their big towns of Chieti, Teramo, Bojano, Gioia, and Aquila, swelled the paean, while further down in Puglia, the towns of Foggia, Bari, Monopoli, Brindisi, Lecce, Gargano, Sasano and Taranto contributed their pledge.

These demonstrations were rivalled in Calabria at Cassano, Rossano, Catanzaro, Monteleone and Reggio; in the Basilicata at Potenza; in Sicily at Messina, Syracuse, Trapani, Girgenti, and Catania; in Sardinia at Sassari, Ozieri, and Cagliari, and surpassed in the exuberant Campania where the towns of Pontecorvo, Caserta, Capua, Benevento, Avellino, Pompei, Salerno, Amalfi, and, above all, Naples the beautiful, put on their best festive display. The whole peninsula with its adjacent islands pronounced gladly its oath of obedience to the new Pontiff, its son. Likely, the high sentiments of its soul were best expressed by Archbishop Florit, coadjutor to Cardinal Della Costa of Florence, during the Solemn Mass of thanksgiving on November 5 in the Cathedral of Santa Maria del Fiore:

> The new Pontiff has placed himself entirely in the service of peace. We trust that his relations with the heads of government and with all those responsible for the public welfare will inspire and effect that harmony without which international peace and social justice can never be realized. . . . He is now the Captain whom we obey without question or hesitation; he is now the Shepherd whom we follow into the pastures that lead to divine grace; He is now the Father whom we love and whom we will defend with the ardor and generous impulse of filial sons.

In other parts of Europe, there was equally solid evidence of a deep joy and a promise of fidelity although it might not have matched the external fervor of Italy. With Paris giving the cue, France responded to the election with remarkable warmth, due to the popularity which the Pope had gained in that country while he was nuncio. The bells of Notre Dame pealed forth their joy and their music was caught up by the carillons in the great cathedrals of Chartres, Orleans, Bordeaux, Marseilles, Lyons, Cherbourg, Brest, Rheims, and the rest; in the town of great basilicas like Lourdes, Lisieux, Paray-Le-Monial; in historic old towns such as Rouen, Calais, Toulon, Grenoble, Strasbourg, Metz, Vichy, Dieppe, Sedan,

Toulouse, Carcassone, Nice, Dijon, Bourges, Avignon, Arles, Verdun, Versailles, and many others. The independent principality of Monaco, with our own Grace Kelly, its princess, participating, joined the anthem, together with all the colonies or territories of France throughout the world.

The Iberian peninsula added its own Latin exuberance to the demonstration. There were services in Madrid, Barcelona, Cordoba, Seville, Salamanca, Valladolid, Palencia, Granada, Burgos, Cadiz, Toledo, Segovia, Santander and elsewhere, with the refrain continued in Portugal's Lisbon, Coimbra, Oporto, Leiria, Braga, Gaviarra, Guarda, Covilha, Portalegre, Castello Branco, and, of course, in Fatima.

In Ireland, the exultation was very evident. Archbishop McQuade of Dublin led his countrymen in their traditional and persevering homage to the Vicar of Christ. Scotland paid her tribute, and England did as well. These two countries, long victims of animosity against the papacy, are slowly softening in their attitude. The Catholics that are there are good ones. They, and their fathers, particularly, have suffered, as Ireland suffered, for their defence of "popery." This spirit of loyalty to the Holy Father is quite intense and is very gratifying to John XXIII.

The Scandinavian countries are overwhelmingly non-Catholic so there wasn't much of a flurry there. In Germany, however, with Switzerland and Austria, the large Catholic population was prompt and clear in its protestations of fidelity.

In the Balkan peninsula, largely Orthodox, there was more than a polite interest since the new Pope had worked for many years in the region and had left with much prestige.

In the Soviet satellite or subjugated states, such as Poland, Hungary, Czechoslovakia, Jugoslavia, the demonstrations were externally subdued, while in the hearts of the faithful Catholics there burned a brighter hope as they reiterated their old faith that the new Pope would somehow help them become free. Cardinal Stepinac, unable to attend the conclave on account of illness and house-arrest, wept with joy at the news and led his stricken people in imploring help for the new Pontiff. Cardinal Mindszenty of Hungary, refused permission to attend the conclave, was nevertheless able to lead his country's pledge of loyalty under his protection in the American embassy. In those countries, the radio and TV air-waves were jammed frequently during the period of the election and coronation, an old Communist technique, so that the news reaching them was skimpy and fraught with doubt.

In Russia herself the English-language service reported the papal election without comment. In its domestic broadcasts, there was no reference made to it. The Voice of America carried it, but with what success is not known. The Iron Curtain stifles information.

In Asia, there was a fair demonstration here and there depending on the Catholic population and influence in the region. In Jerusalem, there was a formal ceremony. In Armenia, from which region the popular Cardinal Agagianian hails, there was a demonstration. There were some ceremonies in India, Pakistan, Malaya, Oceana and Formosa. China, with many Catholics, but all groaning under the Red heel, had no great manifestation; but it was made up by the fervor in the Philippines and in South Korea. Japan was fairly demonstrative.

Australia, having a Cardinal and growing steadily in Catholicism, gave its sign of favor to the new Pontiff. Services were held principally in Sydney, Melbourne, Canberra, and Brisbane. The Catholics in New Zealand gave their evidence of approval.

In Africa, lustily growing in the faith, the dark continent's voice rang with enthusiasm in every one of its Catholic centers, or wherever there was a good segment of Catholics. Cairo had a demonstration as also did Alexandria, Tripoli,

Tunis, Gambia, Sierra Leone, Uganda, Nairobi, the Congo, Angola, Mozambique, the Gold Coast and the Transvaal.

In South America the typical Latin fervor came to the fore. Great demonstrations were held in Buenos Aires, Rosario, Rio de Janiero, Sao Paulo, Montevideo, La Paz, Santiago, Asuncion, Sucre, Lima, Valparaiso, Arauco, Quito, Caracas and Bogota, while commensurate ones were held in the smaller towns.

Going up to North America, typical Latin celebrations occurred in Panama, Costa Rica, Nicaragua, San Salvador, the Honduras, Guatemala, Mexico, Cuba, Haiti and San Domingo, with all the other islands of the Caribbean. In Canada, particularly where the French culture predominates, huge and voluble manifestations took place. The whole St. Lawrence region and the Hudson Bay area celebrated the election, while the Great Lakes portion and the far West section up to the Yukon, although more moderate on account of smaller numbers of Catholics, were none the less sincere.

In our own United States the jubilation was quite marked. In every cathedral, in every parish church, in every college, in every motherhouse of religious, services were held which rendered thanks to God and warmly protested affection for the new Pontiff.

In New York, for example, as soon as the word flashed at 11 A.M. that a new Pope had been elected, Bishop Flannelly, administrator of the Cathedral, assembled his staff and that of the chancery; and the fifty of them sang the Te Deum. At 12:10, the ordinary noonday Mass, celebrated by Father Oscar Lynch, became an official one of thanksgiving. Later, more solemn services were held. After Cardinal Spellman returned to his See from the conclave, he voiced his people's sentiments thus:

> In the name of the priests, religious and laity of the Archdiocese of New York, I have pledged to his holiness the

> loyalty of constant prayer that God may direct, protect and console him in the tremendous responsibilities of his office during these trying times.

In Washington, Archbishop O'Boyle led his flock promptly in a formal celebration, which later was made more solemn and official. The diplomatic corps in Washington and the Catholic University participated in the ceremonies.

Similar demonstrations took place in the great archdioceses of Philadelphia, Boston, Chicago, New Orleans, St. Louis, St. Paul, Dubuque, San Francisco, Los Angeles. Archbishop Boland of Newark, in whose diocese this book has been prepared, said:

> Looking back, it's hard to see where a more capable choice could have been made. He has a certain combination of qualities rarely found in one figure, and any one of which would make him an excellent choice.

Sentiments of like nature were expressed by other archbishops and prelates. The forty million Catholics of America showed themselves to be happy in accepting their new leader.

Besides the acclaim of Catholics, the election of Pope John was hailed by many secular personages of note. Our own President sent the following message:

> Your Holiness, it is with great pleasure that I have learned of your election as Supreme Pontiff of the Roman Catholic Church. I join with other Americans in extending my congratulations on your elevation to this high office. My best wishes for the success of your endeavor, are, I am certain, shared by men of good will everywhere.

The Italian parliament adjourned out of respect; and President Gronchi, Prime Minister Fanfani, with the leaders of both houses sent warm greetings. The French Premier, General de Gaulle, conveyed "the homage of filial respect" from his nation. Queen Elizabeth of England cabled her "best wishes for your health and welfare in the discharge of the exalted duties to which you have been called." And so with all heads of state in friendly relations with the Holy See.

A fine touch was added by Dr. Isaac Halevy Herzog, chief rabbi of the Holy Land, who sent a warm message of congratulations in thanks for the help he had received from the Pope when he was apostolic delegate in Istanbul during World War II.

American tourists had become familiar with Pope Pius XII, and many who never travelled to Europe had the happiness of seeing that stately man when he visited America shortly before he mounted the throne of Peter. They are not as familiar with John, and with the contrast of appearance and background some of them are a trifle reserved in expressing enthusiasm. But loyalty they have. The American Church has a good record of fidelity to the Holy See and to the Pontiff. It will continue its generous financial support, and, more than that, its great moral support and its affection. The United States has been a great source of comfort to the recent Popes; and the present Holy Father can count on the known attachment of the American people to his office, while they will grow more and more to appreciate and love his person.

It can be said with conviction that the Church is behind John XXIII. In days past, many elections were fraught with feuds and dissensions, many segments of the Church proving hostile to the elected one. The extensive coverage of the election revealed no discordant note. A good number of reporters were non-Catholic. They, certainly, and even the Catholic ones, would be honest enough to report any dissatisfaction. None has appeared, and so thankfully, proudly, and most hopefully we witness the happy spectacle of a Church solidly united in accepting and pledging its loyalty to the new Vicar of Christ, her visible head. With such sincere and overwhelming support, John XXIII faces the future with utmost confidence. "I know Mine and Mine know Me," said the Good Shepherd. (John X, 14) John knows his flock, and his flock now knows him. Between shepherd and sheepfold there is understanding and mutual affection.

❁ 22 ❁

Peter Renewed in Him

THE Introit of the Mass and the chapter of the Office of St. Peter are taken from the Acts of the Apostles, twelfth chapter, verse five, which reads:

> Peter therefore was kept in prison. But prayer was made without ceasing by the Church unto God for him.

The Church was behind Peter. We have shown that the Church is behind John. Prayer is made for him every day without ceasing in the very canon of the Mass. We would like to show further that John is *Petrus redivivus,* Peter renewed. The office that Peter held is the same which John holds today, and the life which Peter led is remarkably the life which John has already led and which he will be asked to lead from now on.

It is the faith of all religious men that God in His Providence plans the welfare of men. God is the Creator of the universe, and he fixes its destiny in general and in detail. He is the first cause of all things and the primary cause in all happenings except sin. Without his decree or consent nothing happens; without the influx of his power nothing can move from potency to act.

From all eternity the universe was planned. For God there

are no surprises, not even the surprise of sin, the only field into which he does not enter as primary cause, because he knows whether one is going to sin or not through his perfect understanding of the ways of the will of a free agent. God gives sufficient grace or power to the agent to choose the good; he leaves him free to make the choice, yet he knows what the choice is going to be. We do not fully understand how he does it. For Catholics, it is of faith that man has free will and that God knows beforehand how man will act. The free will of man is denied by some. However, without it, man is not the creature made in God's image, not a person truly, not one responsible for his actions, and so the whole drama of humanity is reduced simply to a show of marionettes acting as the strings are pulled. Normal man is conscious of a personal responsibility, which can stem only from his freedom. He is not a marionette. He has the dignity of personal choice, for good or ill.

God planned the Church, and he planned Peter in the Church. Peter, freely, was to exercise a particular ministry. That ministry was never to die, even though Peter the man was to die. The Church for whom the ministry was planned was to continue to the end of time, and so was the ministry of Peter to continue to the end of time. It was to be assumed successively for stated periods by men whom the divine dispensation selected while employing the human medium of an election to it by other men.

This man, Peter, first chosen for that particular ministry, lived a life replete with incidents which first prepared him for the ministry and which later referred to the manner in which he accomplished his ministry. These incidents formed a precedent for all his successors. More than that, they are a remarkable synopsis of all things that have ever happened to his successors. What happened to him was a presage of what was to happen to his followers.

It should be interesting, then, to study the incidents in

Peter's life to see how truly they apply to his present successor.

Peter was a poor, humble, unlearned fisherman of Galilee. He had to toil hard to earn a living. Some of his successors were not poor, nor humble, nor unlearned. But their charge was to toil hard to provide for the spiritual living of men. "Hereafter you shall be fishers of men." (Mark I, 17) John XXIII is closer to Peter than were his rich, aristocratic, learned successors, for he was as poor as Peter, he is as humble as Peter, and he was as unlearned as Peter.

Peter came from a race and nation that was intensely devoted to God. It was the chosen people, beloved of God, fierce in its patriotism, and unyielding in its determinations to the point of being tenaciously stubborn. Its own Sacred Scriptures characterize it as stiff-neckedness. (Exodus XXXII, 9; XXXIII, 3; Deuteronomy IX, 13; II Chronicle XXX, 8).

John comes of a race and nation that is inclined to piety. In a way, it is a chosen people, since by God's Providence its capital became the central see of Christendom, and while there is no law that dictates a Pope to be Italian, the custom of the past four hundred years and long experience has well-nigh made the papacy the monopoly of the Italian race. The Italian loves his fatherland, his *patria,* his family, and his blood, sincerely and warmly. Soft and yielding on many points of law, he is nevertheless rigid in many ideals, such as manly honor, feminine purity, social protocol and politeness. John responds to these national traits. He is devoted to religion, intensely patriotic, sentimental for family and friends; and, while willing to go along with the times on relaxation of unessential discipline, he rigidly maintains it in principle and in its essential forms.

Peter worked in harmony with his fellows. Commercial fishing required teamwork and he manifested this good trait in labor even when he was in his own boat. Later, this same trait is seen in his consulting his fellow apostles on all important matters, calling them into council, and discussing with them the pros and cons of a proposition before making a decision. So democratic were the sessions that, as the Scriptures record, the apostle "born out of due season," St. Paul, resisted him to his face and won on his point of releasing Christians from the yoke of circumcision. John is so inclined. Farm-work required cooperation and he gave it. Now that his farm is the world, he is anxious to work with his cardinals and bishops, consulting them, (he extended the conclave for this very purpose), holding a prompt consistory, and in other ways. While never surrendering his position of commander-in-chief, he makes the Church understand that he is more of a colleague than an autocrat.

Peter was lovable despite his several faults. He was quick-tempered, testy, impulsive and protested too much at times, but he was firm in faith and intensely devoted to the Lord. He denied knowing the Master in the courtyard of the high priest, not out of cowardice, but likely as his way of wanting to stay close to him in his hour of trial. There is no record to the effect that he was under the cross, as St. John was, and this argument of his absence at the crucial moment, though only of silence, is truly inexplicable. If he were there, St. John would surely have mentioned him, for he took pains to mention persons of less importance. Though inexplicable, and most likely a grave failing, there is no record of the Lord's rebuking him for it. The record clearly shows that he retained his favor with the Master. The resurrected Savior appeared to him.

We are not aware of what particular faults John has. That he has some may be admitted, but we would not include as faults his moderate smoking or indulging in an occasional cocktail. Happily, he does not seem to have the historic one of nepotism. His brothers and sisters are still poor, and his many nephews and nieces have not been given any special preferment. Peter left his wife and home. John never had a wife to leave, but he did leave his home; and he has not let his family interfere in his ministerial work. Everyone speaks of him as lovable, paternal and kindly. He has not betrayed a trust. His faith in the Master, like Peter's, is unshakable; and as Peter did, set on this rock of utter conviction, he confirms it in others.

Has there been, or will there be a *Quo Vadis* story in John's life as there was in Peter's? The legend has it that in the face of severe harassment at the hands of Nero, Peter entertained the idea of quitting the wicked city of Rome for some other place that would afford him a better chance of advancing the Gospel. As he was leaving the city by its southern gate, the Appian Way, he met the Master. Astonished at the appearance, Peter asked: "Quo vadis, Domine? Where art thou going, Lord?" The Master gently replied: "I am going back to be crucified by the Romans." Peter blushed with shame at his retreating under fire, and with new-found courage he returned to Rome. Shortly after, he was crucified by the Romans on Vatican Hill. Everyone knows the story that he begged his crucifiers to have him hang head down from the cross because he felt unworthy to hang upright as his Master had.

We do not think there has been a *Quo Vadis* incident in John's life, and still it would never be too surprising, for the pressures on a man in high office are fearful. He is of flesh, as we all are, and there are dark moments of discouragement and futility in every man's life. Some succumb to the pressures and seek an escape. Some survive the brief escaping to return to their duties with chastened fervor, as Peter did, while others never return but sink lower and lower in dereliction of a trust, as Judas did. We do not mean the good, normal escaping by way of a vacation or change of routine and environment. It is wise so to relieve oneself of the constant pounding of the pressure.

We mean, of course, the definite retreat from responsibilities. It is said that some of the Popes thus retreated, even as some presidents and kings have done. It is not likely that John will. He is a buoyant man, sanguine and even jolly. He is seventy-seven years of age, has been under terrible strains, and has never exhibited any sign of cracking. He knows how to take in a bit of play and conviviality. He is conscientious without becoming a slave to routine, and he will see the bright side of a problem no matter how dark it is when presented to him. True faith generates good hope. John has the faith, wherefore he has hope; and this virtue of hope, resting on the divine assurance of help in any crisis, is the best medicine against the sickness of the manic depressive.

Peter showed, despite his lack of formal learning, a remarkable administrative ability. The Holy Spirit had come upon him on Pentecost day to supply the deficiency of any formal training. The records may not be ample but the conclusion is validly drawn from the harmony that existed within the Church in his day that it was his skill in handling difficult situations and strong personalities with tact that enabled the Church to present a united front in those critical, initial days and operate smoothly and efficiently. His directives were good, his appointments were wise, his disposal of problems was decisive. When we remember that travel and communications were not then as they are now, his feat is all the more praiseworthy.

John has shown an equal ability. He has the advantage of immediate communication through telephone and radio. He can even project his form by way of television, through which he can almost appear in one's living room, talking person to person. His record in the important administrative posts of legate, nuncio, and diocesan leader is an excellent one. He knows how to give good orders, he is careful in appointments and he is prompt in decisions. He attends to his work, he is fair in the distribution of work and favor, he absorbs reports, plans ahead, and is assiduous in seeing that regulations are carried out. That is being the good executive.

Peter was an inspiring leader. He preached effectively; he wrote beautifully and solidly. His two Epistles are short but full of sublime, encouraging thoughts. His many recorded words in Gospels and Acts, besides his own Epistles, convey a clear sense of the lofty leadership that was in him to give to the Church.

John has been a good leader in Venice, and he is certain to be a good leader of the whole Church. He speaks clearly and forcibly. In his few papal pronouncements to date he has conveyed his message clearly and briefly, garnished with many apt scriptural quotations. His allocutions and encyclicals are likely to take their place with the immortal documents of some of his literary predecessors.

Peter faced his own race's leaders in an important dispute. They asked him coldly: "By what authority or in what name have you done this?" (Acts IV, 7) Facing a foreign enemy is often easier than the facing of one's own indignant neighbor. Peter acquitted himself well. His answer was a marvel of logic, theology and eloquence, and won for him plaudits instead of punishment.

John found himself in a somewhat similar situation when he was hurriedly dispatched to France to face an indignant de Gaulle. The Catholic leader was demanding the dismissal of thirty-three French bishops for their supposed collaboration with Vichy. It was a touchy situation. John stood up to de Gaulle and by his logic and eloquence, all done with the charm of simplicity, he won his point and saved the Church from a grave setback.

Peter travelled extensively, mostly on foot. He broke Jewish precedent by fixing his residence in the chief city of the Gentiles. John has travelled extensively using every modern means of transportation. He went to dedicate the lower basilica of Lourdes last spring, travelling by jet plane. Although it was first said that he would break the precedent of a century and a half by leaving Italy to close the Marian year in Lourdes, the latest report is that he will content himself with closing it by radio address from Rome. The last time a Pope was in France, he became a prisoner of Napoleon at Fontainebleau for four years. Pius VII had gone to Paris in 1804 to crown Napoleon as Emperor. Napoleon crowned himself and later made this gentle Pope his prisoner, 1809 to 1813.

Peter made good friends. In Jerusalem he drew many to him personally, among them Cornelius, his first Gentile convert, and principally, young John Mark, who became his secretary, whom later he sent to Alexandria as that city's first bishop, and who has preserved so much of Peter in his Gospel. Incidentally, at this point, it may be advisable to correct an impression given by some concerning the years of Peter's tenure as Pope. It is claimed that Pius IX had the longest reign of all the Popes, 1846 to 1878, thirty-two years, and he is often hailed as one who "surpassed the years of Peter." This is only true if we restrict the years to Peter's occupancy of the See of Rome, which is dated 42 or 43 A.D. But he was Pope from 29 A.D. to his death in 67 A.D., hence no one up to date has surpassed the years of Peter as Pope. He made good friends in Antioch, his second see; and when finally he went to Rome, he won the friendship of the few Jews living there and soon even of some of the patricians of the city, who aided him greatly in establishing his diocese.

John has made many friends, Catholic and non-Catholic. His liberal attitude, urbanity, and ingrained charity draw souls to him. This is an invaluable quality redounding to the great advantage of the Church.

Peter had many problems of expanding the faith through persecution from without and some dissatisfaction from within. To solve them, he brought into play the fine resources of his character. He was alert and practical. However, his real strength stemmed from his firm faith. He was the steady rock against which storms lashed but never crushed. Inclined though he was to impulsive action, he nevertheless skillfully organized the infant Church. The Acts tell us, for example, of the astounding social experiment of community ownership and of the distribution of goods to each according as one had need, the ordaining of deacons to serve the poor at table, and the establishment of deaconesses to assist in various social services. St. Peter's stinging rebuke to Ananias and Sapphira, the wretched pair who lied in confession about the price they had received for selling their land, reveals a tone of authority he was not afraid to use when the occasion required it. He knew how to utilize the fine talents of his fellow apostles, of the disciples, and of the gifted converts who had come to him. He dispersed the apostles sending them to preach the Gospel in far-flung regions. He assigned the new deacons, Stephen, Philip, Prochorus, Nicanor, Timon, Parmenas, and Nicholas to local ministry; and he approved the missionary journeys of Paul and Barnabas. He respected highly the first of these, and there ensued between them a friendship that has been perpetuated in liturgy throughout the ages, for the martyrdom of Saints Peter and Paul, occurring on the same day, June 29, 67 A.D., is celebrated by the Church jointly on that day, and she orders that whenever the name of one is to be mentioned in prayers, the name of the other is to be included.

John rests the hope of his reign on his own firm faith and practical skill. He is already organizing better the offices of the Holy See and the services it renders in behalf of the potential converts and the needy. He uses his authority when there is need, but hopes to entice better obedience by a brotherly approach. He is assigning his talented men to key posts and he is inspiring a sense of glad cooperation in his subjects.

Among the problems that Peter faced was the one of handling the ambitious Simon Magus. This charlatan wanted to buy spiritual power and dignity with money. The evil of it has taken its specific name from him, and is known as simony. The Popes have been steadily plagued with this problem and John need not be expected to escape it even though its spirit has now largely waned. His record to date gives assurance that he will be as alert and as forceful as Peter in suppressing it, should it ever seriously arise.

The spirit of Peter speaks to John in the words of his First Epistle:

> Lay aside therefore all malice, and all deceit and pretense, and envy and all slander. Crave, as newborn babes, pure spiritual milk, that by it you may grow to salvation . . . The Lord is sweet. Draw near to him, a living stone, rejected indeed by men, but chosen and honored by God. Be you yourselves as living stones, built thereon into a spiritual house, a holy priesthood. (II, 1-5)
>
> Finally, be all like-minded, compassionate, lovers of the brethren, merciful, humble, not rendering evil for evil or abuse for abuse, but contrariwise, blessing, for unto this were you called. (III, 8-10)
>
> And who is there to harm you, if you are zealous for what is good? (13)
>
> Be prudent, therefore, and watchful in prayer, but above all things have a constant, mutual charity. (IV, 7-8)
>
> Your adversary, the devil, as a roaring lion, goes about seeking someone to devour. Resist him, steadfast in the faith. (V, 8-9)

Peter, the Rock, communicates his strength to John. His spirit abides in him who now holds the keys originally given to himself. It was part of his office to feed the sheep. John is his own special sheep, as all the Popes that succeeded Peter have been; and as he enjoys now the glory of God's vision following his own faithful stewardship, he prays for the man on whose shoulders the mantle he dropped has fallen, imploring God that John, too, will prove a good steward of the tremendous wealth left in his care by his possession of the keys of the Kingdom of Heaven.

23

The Previous Popes Named John

THE world was surprised by the choice of John as the title by which the new Pope wished to be called. We have explained the reason why he chose the name. The Church had grown accustomed to the name, Pius. John was a new name to the public. It had not been heard in the Church since 1410, and then only illegitimately. The last legitimate Pope named John died in 1334.

New as the sound of the name John may be to us, it happens to be the most popular of the papal names. As we well know now, the number XXIII follows the name of the new Pope. No other name reaches this high number.

We have considered that it might be useful and interesting to give a brief history of all the Popes named John. John XXIII himself, in declaring the name by which he wanted to be known, referred to the fact that all the Johns before him had had a brief reign, and that none of them had achieved any great fame. However, the accumulated experiences of these particular predecessors might furnish an interesting clue to what the new John can expect to face, and how he will face the problems that come to him.

John I

It was not till the sixth century that the Church had a Pope named John. On August 13, 523, John of Tuscany was elected to succeed Pope Hormisdas. In this early period of the papacy, a Pope did not choose an official name but retained his baptismal one. This first John encountered great trouble with the Ostrogothic King Theodoric, who was supporting the Arian heresy in Italy. In an effort to avert persecution in Italy, John journeyed to Constantinople, the first Pope to do so, to seek the aid of the Eastern Emperor, Justinian. The great Justinian received him with filial respect and promised his aid. The news infuriated Theodoric; and though the Pope in a spirit of conciliation went to report to him at Ravenna, he found the King more vindictive than ever. The cruel King had the Pope imprisoned and in prison John died on May 18, 526, after a reign of two years, nine months and five days. He is a Saint and Martyr, a splendid beginning of Popes with so beautiful a name.

John II

The second John was a Roman of the family of Conti, who by reason of his eloquence was surnamed Mercurius. He was elected in 532 to succeed Boniface II. Simony had become a scourge in the Church and he fought against it. The phrase, "One of the Trinity has been crucified," was being used to reconcile the Catholic and the Arian viewpoints on Christ. It had been condemned before, but was becoming popular. John II condemned it anew. The West suffered from much feuding among its barbaric conquerors, and from their cruelty in treating those who disagreed with them. The Emperor Justinian sent his great general, Belisarius, to subdue them; but it helped little. John died in 535 after a reign of two years, four months and twenty-five days.

John III

He was also a Roman. He had the surname of Catelinus and was elected in 560 to succeed Pelagius I. Although his reign was fairly long, only a few details survive, due to the troubled times of the wars in Italy between the barbarians and the forces of the Eastern Emperor. It seems that he was a magnanimous person, kindly and zealous for the welfare of his flock. He defended Narses, the new general of the East, when he fell into disgrace with his Emperor, but was ill repaid for it. Narses, angered at being replaced by Longinus, invited the Arian Lombards to invade the Roman provinces. They did it under their King Alboin rather thoroughly, sacking and pillaging. Pope John had to seek refuge in the catacombs.

During his reign, in 571, Mohammed, who was to prove a greater scourge of the Church, was born.

John died in 573 after a reign of twelve years, eleven months and twenty-six days.

John IV

He was born in Salona, Dalmatia, and elected to the papacy in 640 following the two-month reign of Pope Severinus. He rebuked the Catholics of Scotland for not observing the Christian ritual for paschal ceremonies, he warned them against the Pelagian heresy, and he condemned the Monothelite heresy of Sergius. He defended his predecessor, Pope Honorius I, against the charge of having voiced the main tenet of the heresy, namely, that there is only one will in Christ. He sent huge sums for the relief of captives in his native Dalmatia, and he sought to convert the Slavs who were invading from Russia to the upper Balkan Peninsula.

He died in 642 at the end of a reign of one year, nine months and eighteen days.

John V

He was a Syrian, born in Antioch, and elected Pope in 685, succeeding Benedict II. When a cardinal deacon, he had represented Pope Agatho at the Sixth Ecumenical Council, the III Constantinople, commonly called In Trullo, held in 680. He had tremendous energy, deep learning and was moderate in his actions. He showed vigor in resisting the usurping by Citonatus of the papal right to consecrate the bishop-elect of Turris in Sardinia, and he showed his generosity in advancing large sums for the relief of the poor.

He was, despite his drive, a chronic invalid, finally dying in 686 after a rule of one year and eleven days.

John VI

On October 30, 701, the vacancy left by the death of Saint Sergius I was filled by the election of a Greek, John VI. The Eastern Emperor, seeking to secure a firmer hold in Italy, sent thither Theophylactus as exarch. The people of Italy rose to oppose him. John tried to pacify them with arguments and with gifts of money. Taking advantage of the turmoil around Rome, the Lombards under their Duke Gisulf advanced and reached the fifth milestone on the Via Latina out of Rome. John hurriedly sought to pacify them with grants of gold to save his people from further distress. He succeeded in persuading Gisulf to retreat. St. Wilfrid of York begged him for the peace of England to confirm his appointment as bishop, an action which had been delayed. John did confirm it and sent him back with letters to King Ethelred and others. He also confirmed Brithwald as Archbishop of Canterbury and sent him the pallium.

On January 11, 705, John died, after having reigned three years, two months, and eleven days.

John VII

He succeeded his namesake immediately, March 1, 705. He was a Greek, although born in Rossano, the son of Plato and Blatta, to whom he was exceptionally attached. His father had made various restorations in the Palatine Palace of Rome and had lived in a small house near the Church of Santa Maria Antiqua, nearby. Out of affection, John had this enlarged to the size of a palace so that he could live where once his parents had lived. He also erected a memorial in 687 to them, dedicating it to a "most loving and incomparable mother, and to the kindest of fathers." In the church his mother had attended, Santa Maria Antiqua, he caused several frescoes of the Madonna to be painted. In 1900, when excavations brought to light this ancient church, the legend, "Servant of Mary," was discovered at the base of the ambo which John had built. This Pope also erected a chapel to Our Lady in St. Peter's.

Filial and personally pious though he was, he proved timid in his relations with the Greek Emperor Justinian II. This monarch sent him the minutes of the Quinisext Council in which were several criticisms of the Roman Church, and asked him to indicate which ones he approved. John returned the minutes without comment, creating the impression that there was nothing in the minutes to be corrected. He showed more spirit with King Aripert II of the Longobardi and he insisted that the clergy of England, in England and residing in Rome, discard its secular garb in favor of the clerical.

Upon his death, January 11, 707, after a reign of two years, seven months and seventeen days, he was buried in the Lady Chapel he had built in St. Peter's.

John VIII

One hundred and sixty-seven years passed before another John came. He was a Roman, elected on December 14, 872, succeeding Adrian II. His election was opposed by Formosus, who later succeeded him after three other pontificates. His seemed to be a personality that was a curious mixture of greatness and smallness, of ability with ruthlessness, of the sharp executive with vindictiveness, of the zealous priest with worldliness. He did great things in his reign and some petty ones. We cannot give a complete history here, but a few highlights should be afforded.

He supported St. Methodius, against opposition, as missioner of the Slavs; he vacillated with the sons of Charlemagne; he made the mistake of confirming Photius as Patriarch of Constantinople, but happily revoked it; he marshalled forces to resist the Saracens sparing not his person, his time, nor his private funds to save Christendom from the scourge, and he assumed personal command as general in the defense of Rome. Further, he became an admiral and with his fleet defeated the Saracen navy off Circe. Grave moral disorders beset Rome. He sought to correct them, although some historians assert that he was involved in them and opposed only those perpetrated by his foes. It was a horrible period, as any would be which could give rise to the story of a Popess Joan which seems to have been inspired by events in the reign of John VIII, and of annals in the monastery of Fulda to the effect that he was first poisoned by one of his relations who wanted to seize the papal treasures, and that when the poison failed, he was beaten to death with a hammer.

He died December 16, 882 having reigned ten years and one day.

John IX

He was a Benedictine, a native of Tivoli, elected in 898 following Theodore II, and known as intelligent and moderate. He sought to bring peace to the warring factions in Rome, to which end he revoked the ghastly action of those who had exhumed the body of Pope Stephen VII (885-891) so that it could stand trial before their court. He created for the Moravians a hierarchy independent of the German one and he sought to effect a reconciliation with the Greek Church.

He died in 900 after a reign of two years and fifteen days.

JOHN X

He was born in the Romagna at Tossignano, and after the death of Pope Lando in 914 he was elected to succeed him. His election was likely due to the influence of the Roman noblewoman Theodora, a kinswoman, and the mother of the notorious Marozia. It seems that the Roman clergy did not accept him till the following year. He tried to keep the factions within bounds, and to resist the Saracens. He crowned Berengarius as King of Italy, and after he died the Pope supported Hugh of Burgundy. This led to John's death since Marozia, having risen to power in Rome and knowing that Hugh's rise would spell her defeat, had the Pope arrested, and, according to some historians, had him murdered in prison by suffocation in bed.

He died in 928 following a reign of fourteen years, two months and three days.

JOHN XI

His is the saddest story of them all. His mother, for certain, was the wicked Marozia, while it is reputed that he was the natural son of Pope Sergius III. Through her domination in Roman affairs, Marozia had her son, at the age of twenty-one, succeed to the papacy upon the death of Stephen VIII in 931. The young man was first the pawn of his mother, and later, when she was deposed, of his brother Alberic II, who denied him any power of administration except the purely spiritual. He was a virtual prisoner in the Lateran. The papacy had reached its lowest level of degradation. Curiously, the only act recorded was his grant of great privileges to the monastery of Cluny in France. This monastery became vastly instrumental in bringing back to the papacy its honor and power.

John died in 936 having been four years and ten months in office.

John XII

He was the son of the above Alberic II, whom he succeeded as Patrician of Rome at the age of sixteen. His name was Octavian at birth, and upon his election to the papacy in 956 at the age of eighteen, he changed it to the apostolic one of John, an action which was continued thereafter by all his successors. His reign was one of intrigue to consolidate the position of his family in Rome. Lest Berengarius II dominate in Italy, John made an alliance with the German Emperor, Otto, then conspired against him. The wrathful Emperor, after defeating Berengarius, went to Rome. Summoning a council, he had John deposed on the charge of immorality, and named one in his stead as Leo VIII. The crafty Emperor secured from this spurious pope a declaration of the supremacy of the Emperor of the Holy Roman Empire over the papacy and of the requirement that an elected pope should be confirmed by the Emperor after a pledge of fealty to the secular crown. To his credit, John resisted both the anti-Pope and the Emperor and repudiated the declaration. An insurrection in his favor made Leo flee from Rome. John returned to open power, the Emperor prepared to oust him anew by force, but before there was more bloodshed, John died on May 14, 964. It was rumored that he was struck dead by the devil who had enticed him to sin. It was an unhappy reign of seven years and nine months.

John XIII

He was a Roman related to the above and succeeded in 965 to Peter's troubled throne. The Emperor Otto, now that Leo was dead, confirmed him in office but the Roman populace, angered at German interference, imprisoned John. He escaped and sought refuge with Pandolf, Prince of Capua. When the populace heard that Otto was coming in force to restore John, they invited him back of their own accord. He remained subservient to the German power to his death on September 6, 972, after reigning six years, eleven months and five days.

John XIV

Twelve years later, Peter of Pavia, who changed his name to John, was elected Pope. His reign was a miserable one. The Roman factions under Crescentius had created an anti-Pope, known as Boniface VII, in protest against the German influence. When Otto II died unexpectedly, John was imprisoned, where he soon died, August 20, 984, some say of starvation and misery, others by assassination ordered by Boniface. He was in office eight months and ten days.

John XV

Some chroniclers placed after Boniface VII, the anti-Pope whom they illegally listed as the successor of John XIV, a four-month reign of a certain John XV. This is spurious, but it has caused confusion in the numbering of the Johns. The true John XV, sometimes styled in books, thanks to those chroniclers, as John XVI, was a Roman who came into power in 985. He was severely hampered by the Roman faction, yet he accomplished a good deal. In his reign, a formal process of canonization was adopted. On January 31, 993, the first saint so proclaimed being Ulrich, Bishop of Augsburg. His influence brought peace between England and Normandy, while many monasteries were helped by his generosity. He died in 996, after ruling for ten years, four months and twelve days, and while waiting to crown Otto III in Rome.

John XVI

The next Pope to succeed him was John XVI, likewise a Roman. He crowned Otto as planned by his predecessor, but suffered the animosity of the Romans after the Emperor left. The mob led by a new Crescentius drove John out of the City and named John Philagathus as Pope illegally. John died after being in office four months and twelve days.

John XVII

He was a native of Rapagnano, of the Sicco or Secchi family, who had gone to Rome to live. There he married and joined the Roman faction. Upon the death of the philosopher-pope, Sylvester II (Gerbert) on May 12, 1003, there was no authority in Rome, thus permitting the mob under John Crescentius to seize power. On June 13, Secchi was named Pope by the faction taking the name of John XVII. He died on November 6 of the same year, thus reigning but a brief four months and twenty-five days, not leaving a single record.

John XVIII

On Christmas Day of that year, 1003, another John, baptized Phasianus, was appointed Pope through the influence of the Roman faction. He tried his hand at reconciliation with the East, he crowned Henry II at Pavia, he called the disobedient Bishops of Lens and Orleans to his tribunal, and in other matters showed energy. The Greeks recognized him as Bishop of Rome.

He died in June, 1007, after sitting for five years, seven months and twenty-eight days.

John XIX

He succeeded his brother, Benedict VIII, in 1024. He was a layman, so he had to be given holy orders in canonical stages. He sought to win over the Roman people by lavish gifts. In turn Basil II, Eastern Emperor, sought to bribe John into recognizing the Archbishop of Constantinople as Ecumenical Patriarch, a false and dangerous title to which we have already alluded. The rich gifts almost persuaded John to agree; but the people of Rome violently protested, and he finally denied the petition. He vacillated in many other matters as well. He seems to be the first Pope to grant indulgences for almsgiving. It was he who encouraged Guido of Arezzo to produce his beautiful music.

He died in November, 1033 after a reign of nine years, eight months and eight days. His immediate successor was a nephew, a boy of twelve, known as Benedict IX.

John XX

In the new lists of Popes, there is no John XX. This was done to correct the mistake of the chroniclers who had falsely intruded into the lists of John Philagathus, the anti-Pope during the reign of John XVI, as John XVII.

John XXI

The next John redeemed the ill-savor of many of his name. He was Peter the Spaniard, born in Lisbon. He became a brilliant scholar, excelling in philosophy and medicine. He was a practising physician, and a master of theology. He rose fast in the Church, culminating in his election as Pope on September 13, 1276. He was crowned as John XXI. He sought to prevent war between Philip the Strong and Alphonse of Castile, asking them rather to use their militia in a crusade against infidels, but he was unsuccessful. He originated the names of the nineteen legitimate modes of the syllogism. His death was a sad one. He had, for quiet study, made a room for himself in the papal palace at Viterbo. While alone there, May 20, 1277, the roof caved in upon him crushing him to death. He was Pope for eight months and five days.

John XXII

This last lawfully named predecessor of John XXIII (since there was an anti-Pope in 1410, one Baldassar Cossa who took the name of John XXIII) was a Frenchman born in Cahors in 1249. His name was Jacques d'Euse; he was the son of a shoemaker, and so ugly that no historian fails to mention it. It was redeemed by the good education he had from the Dominicans, by his personal austerity and by his marked administrative ability. Elected to the papacy in Lyons on August 7, 1316, following Clement V who had moved the papal residence to Avignon, he proved to be the most energetic of the Popes in this so-called Babylonian Exile. He issued sixty thousand official documents. He was very French-minded and tried to ensure both the continuance of the Popes in France and their French origin by creating seven French cardinals. He canonized, meritoriously, indeed, the pious Louis IX who had been King of France. He hoped, as this great King had done, to initiate a new crusade, but it came to naught.

He had entertained the opinion and preached it in sermons that the beatific vision was not enjoyed by a just soul immediately after death but only at the general judgment. He was told that this was not the doctrine of the Church. He asked the masters of theology at Paris and elsewhere to study the question thoroughly; upon their finding for the traditional doctrine, he retracted his private view. He had never advanced his opinion as official teaching, hence the critics of papal infallibility have no case.

He died, December 4, 1334, with a record of eighteen years, three months and twenty-eight days. He was a good Pope, but his excessive love of France created the impression that the Church had become national and no longer catholic.

So ends the record of the Popes John before the record which the present John is writing. It is his opportunity to bring that beautiful name to better renown.

24

The Gates of Hell Against Him

JOHN XXIII can bring renown to his name, to the papacy, and to the Church in only one way. He must oppose the gates of hell which have constantly rattled against righteousness. The "gates of hell" is the poetic expression of a raw realism in human life. The Master Himself coined the phrase on the occasion of his promise to confer the primacy on Peter. At Caesarea Philippi, Peter had just made his grand, prompt confession upon the Lord's pointed question: "Whom do men say that the Son of Man is?" His brother apostles were uncertain; Peter was not. "Thou art the Christ, the Son of the Living God." The Master then spoke those magnificent words which are the constitution and mission of the papacy: "Blessed art thou, Simon Bar Jona, for flesh and blood have not revealed this to thee, but My Father in heaven. And I say to thee; Thou art Peter, and upon this rock, I will build My Church, and the gates of hell shall not prevail against it." (Matthew XVI, 13-18)

What did he mean by the gates of hell? In the chapter on burdens, we tried to point out the many duties and responsibilities resting on a Pope. Did he mean these? No. By that strong phrase he meant something beyond the ordinary duties and problems of the office. He was indicating something more important in the whole philosophy of that special ministry which is the papacy. He was telling Peter that he must enter into the same essential work for which he had become incarnate, namely, to redeem man from the satanic forces of sin.

St. Paul caught this depth of meaning when in writing to the Ephesians, VI, 12, he mentioned:

> For our wrestling is not against flesh and blood, but against the Principalities and Powers, against the world-rulers of this darkness, against the spiritual forces of wickedness on high.

St. Peter knew that the Master meant that all-important warfare, for he re-echoed it in the injunction he gave to Christians, and which we have already quoted in Chapter XXII: "Your adversary the devil, as a roaring lion, goes about seeking someone to devour." (II Peter, V, 8)

The Master alluded to it again shortly before his Passion, when, after a contention among the apostles as to who should be reputed the greatest, he spoke to Peter saying: "Simon, Simon, behold, Satan has desired to have you, that he may sift you as wheat. But I have prayed for thee, that thy faith may not fail; and do thou, when once thou hast turned again, strengthen thy brethren." (Luke, XXII, 31-32)

By his lies, Satan succeeded in inducing the first man to sin. By that sin, we became children of wrath, lost our heavenly heritage, and were worthy of hell. "Through one man sin entered into the world, and through sin, death, and thus death has passed unto all men because all have sinned." (Romans V, 12) The gates of hell had prevailed.

In his mercy, God gave man another chance through faith in his Son who was to come, and faith in him after he came. His mission in coming was to free man from the gates of hell. He accomplished this sublime purpose by his death on the cross wherein he entered the lists with Satan and defeated him. Satan had once tempted him to dereliction of ideals by the offer of bread, of prestige, and of power. He failed. He loosed against him every wickedness hoping to break him. The story of the Passion is incredible if we attribute its cause only to the envy of the Jewish leaders and the ambitions of the Roman Procurator. It was spawned of hell, which in its fury against this Just Man who could not be convicted of sin, vented upon him every cruelty its wickedness could devise.

Satan knows his Master as a result of that encounter on the cross. Christ's victory over death, sin, and hell by his resurrection is the glorious story of the universe. Hereafter, if man wills it and accompanies his will with appropriate actions, he is free of the old dominion of Satan over him. "This is the victory that overcomes the world, our faith." (I John, V, 4)

Satan, defeated as he has been by Christ in securing the damnation of all men which would have been inevitable following the sin of Adam, still has his envy and his malicious desire to have the gates of his kingdom open to receive the individual man. Christ's death made it possible for man to avoid hell, but it is up to the individual man to apply unto himself the merits of Christ's Passion so as to escape the damnation. Christ's death did not automatically assure salvation for each man. This would not be consonant with man's character as a free agent. He must by an act of his will choose to be saved, which had been lost through Adam's sin, and ask for graces to help him take advantage of his chance of salvation.

This, in itself, gives Satan a chance of winning individual souls for his black kingdom. If he can turn men's minds away from Christ and his grace, if he can get them to prefer the bread, the prestige and the power of earthly things to the spiritual benefits of virtue, he will salvage in part the ruin caused him by Christ. This, then, is the satanic plan following the intrusion of Christ into his dealings with man. He will entice the individual man to the gates of his kingdom.

Against this diabolical plot Christ continues his saving work for all men in general and in particular. The only obstacle is man's own free will. He will not force it; he wants it to choose him in love and freedom, the only proper way of entrance into heaven. So the battle continues between Christ and Satan for the winning of the will of man.

The generals have their lieutenants. Christ has constituted his own mother as first adjutant and the Pope as his personal aid in the field. "Behold thy mother" (John XIX, 27), he had said to his beloved disciple and through him to his entire Church as he was dying on the cross. The Church has thereafter called her the Virgin Most Powerful, Help of Christians, and very Gate of Heaven. To the Vicar he gave the keys of the kingdom of heaven.

Leaving aside the tremendous help which the Mother of Christ affords in the battle, we should study at this point the part which Pope John is to play in the warfare.

Once the Church had to fight on the front of an ancient superstition which acknowledged the reality of the devil in such an abominable way as to reverence him either as an actual co-god or as the spirit to be most feared and placated. This somehow survives today in voodooism among very backward tribes and in isolated instances of quiet devil worship among degenerate intellectuals. Today, the Church has to fight on another front. The modern mind claims to have liberated itself from the old, medieval superstition concerning the devil. The idea of the devil's being real is ridiculed. There is no devil, the liberals say, except as a fancy of the pious mind or as a creation of theologians to bring out God's goodness in bold relief through contrast.

The Evil One was flattered by the reverence he received from the ancients, but he is far more pleased with this new attitude of denial, because he is able thereby to do more mischief. An invisible man in a room can do more damage than one who is visible. The devil is no longer feared; he is no longer a reality in the mind of the modern man. Perhaps as one reads this chapter there may be a wonderment as to why the point of the gates of hell is stressed. This very wonderment is an achievement of the evil spirit. The more he can lessen fear of himself in the hearts of men, the easier is his work on their souls.

The new front is more difficult to fight on than the old one, but it must be fought on. The gates of hell swing too easily when there is no belief that they exist. Steadily, by its growing denial of the existence of the devil, the modern mind is coming to believe that there is no hell. Hell is here on earth, they say, and, admittedly, judging from what one sees on earth, they have a point. Many Christians, even Christians who are quite pious, tend more and more to deny that there could be an eternal hell. How can a good God, an all-just and merciful God, inflict with eternal torment a soul which in a moment of weakness committed a fault which theologians glibly call a mortal sin? Thus, while continuing in their devotions, they refuse assent to a cardinal doctrine of Christianity. That the Lord whom they worship spoke so often and so clearly on hell and the devil, on eternal torments and on unclean spirits that can enter into a man, disturbs them in no way. It is only metaphor, they say, the oriental hyperbole, the poetic license. Psychiatrists have shown that insanity is not due to possession by a devil. It is only a mental disorder due to organic debility or to psychic pressures easily determined in cause.

This trend to discard the old notions of hell and devil is a severe rattling of the gates of hell against the Church. With the discarding of hell comes the discarding of the notion of sin. This is Satan's cleverest idea to date. When he can get people to pretend that there is no sin, then sins are multiplied under respectable guise. Pope John has to contend with it as the greatest, extant evil.

The Church has suffered many physical persecutions. So cruel were many of them that the devil's work was quite evident in them. Satan has tried the crude, physical approach, with some success, since in all persecutions some fall by the wayside to save their skins. He is trying now the cruelest form of persecution known to man. When we read of the ingenious, psychological torments inflicted on a cardinal of the Church which renders him willing to confess to many crimes, are we not permitted to wonder if Satan's own evil genius has not permeated the spirit of the Communist leaders? Whence so much skill and know-how in obtaining their objectives? Whence such astuteness in propaganda and diplomacy as to bewilder the best brains of the West? Is brainwashing today so vitally different from the biblical account of possession by the devil?

The Church has survived physical persecutions and will continue to survive them. She has suffered from and will continue to triumph over the more subtle, insidious persecutions of secret societies, of bigotry, of sophistication, and of the so-called intellectual. She was warned to expect these things by her Master. "If the world hates you, know that it has hated Me before you. If you were of the world, the world would love what is its own. But because you are not of the world, but I have chosen you out of the world, therefore the world hates you." (John XV, 18-19) And further: "These things I have spoken to you that you may not be scandalized. They will expel you from the synagogues. Yes, the hour is coming for everyone who kills you to think that he is offering worship to God." (John XVI, 1-2)

The devil knows how to get his lieutenants to do his nefarious work. If it is not a Nero, a Caligula, a Julian, it is a Hitler or a Stalin or a Khrushchev. Above all, he likes to employ the corruption of the mind through heresy and the corruption of the heart through vice. There have arisen many false christs and many false prophets to lead men astray. The gates of hell swing invitingly open to receive the unwary.

Pope John has to wage the battle for Christ lest Satan win the mastery. There are at present some severe physical persecutions against the Church. He must fortify the spirit of those caught in the maw of madmen who out of hatred for Christ want to liquidate anyone who honors his Name. He must be patient with those who are not showing the brand of Christian fortitude their heritage requires of them. The spirit is often willing but the flesh is weak; and he must in priestly kindliness still reach out to them to revive in them the courage of their ancestors.

He must be alert lest in high seats of learning, through a desire to win the esteem of the elite and to go along with liberalizing trends, Catholic teachers compromise on doctrine, water-down truths or otherwise weaken the strong gospel message. Many universities in America which started as Protestant religious colleges have lost all connection with religion and are seminaries of agnosticism and atheism. Some grand Catholic universities in Europe, like the Sorbonne, have lost their religious affiliation becoming instead deriders of the supernatural. Universities do influence public attitudes. People look to them for guidance and even one famous professor's word carries great weight. Much mischief stems from universities which have lost their spiritual horizons.

As has been noted, Pope John's predecessor, Pius X, was alert to stop the trend in some Catholic intellectual circles to Modernism. His action saved the Church from much damage within. So did the action of Pius XII through his encyclical *Humani Generis.* The gates of hell seek to win the battle through the vanity of intellectualism. It is an ever-present menace particularly in this age which vaunts the value of high secular learning over the merits of the simple catechism.

An insidious philosophy is abroad. It would have men believe, and it is fair to behold, like the apple of Eden, that man is his own lawmaker and destiny. The serpent lies anew: "You shall be as gods knowing good and evil." (Genesis III, 5) Men are fascinated by the thought that they can determine for themselves what is right and wrong. They are delighted with the prospect of possessing in their being all the dignity and power there is in the universe. Have they not penetrated space, and what is to stop them from conquering the planets? It is their universe, to do with as they please.

Christ's message to the world was not only one of rebuke against the sensuality of the ancients but more importantly one of warning against false teachings. St. Paul has told us: "The wrath of God is revealed from heaven against all ungodliness and wickedness of those men who in wickedness hold back the truth of God. . . . And so they are without excuse, seeing that, although they knew God, they did not glorify him as God or give thanks, but became vain in their own reasonings, and their senseless minds have been darkened. For while professing to be wise, they have become fools and they have changed the glory of the incorruptible God for an image made like to corruptible man." (Romans I 18-23)

Such a philosophy does more damage to the souls of men than does a persecution. It corrupts the heart, whereas the latter only mangles a body. Against the insidiousness of this evil teaching the Pope must remain forever vigilant. He is the constituted teacher who is to instruct the school of the world in the positive truths of God's kingdom and warn it against the negating statements of a worldly philosophy.

The Church has a commendable attitude on this very serious problem. In her liturgical praying she implores:

From the Gates of Hell
Deliver us, O Lord.

After each low Mass, she enjoins the priest to lead the people in reciting this prayer:

> Holy Michael, the Archangel, defend us in battle. Be our protection against the malice and the snares of the devil. Restrain him, O God, we humbly beseech Thee, and do Thou, O Prince of the Heavenly Host, by the divine power, thrust into hell Satan and all the evil spirits who prowl about the world seeking the ruin of souls.

"The nations rage and the people devise vain things. The kings of the earth rise up and the princes conspire against the Lord and against His Christ (Psalm II, 1-2)." The gates of hell shake and open enticingly wide to gather in the spoil of souls; the devil is still going about seeking whom he can devour.

That is the battle still facing the Savior of men, and it is the battle of his Vicar, his first lieutenant.

❁ 25 ❁

The Christ Behind Him

THERE is a law in physics that a force can be counteracted only by an equal force or a superior one. We have shown that arrayed against the Church is the very powerful force and enmity of Satan, the prince of the world of darkness. Satan is a fallen angel of the highest order, and he retains, despite his consignment to hell, all the natural powers of his angelic being. These are vast and utterly superior to any human ingenuity whether we consider it singly or collectively.

Were it possible for Satan to have his way with men, he would win easily. He is too clever, too intelligent, too ingenious for man to withstand his blandishments for long.

Happily, he has not a clear field with men. He can only work on them as God permits. God is the sole power in the universe. All who exercise power exercise it under this permission and control. This situation saves man from being an immediate victim of the devil's envy.

God allows man to be tempted by the devil. "The Lord said to Satan: Behold, all that he hath is in thy hand; only put not forth thy hand upon his person." (Job I, 12) When this permission is granted, God gives to the tempted sufficient grace to resist the temptation. This he must do in justice. Armed with this grace and using it, man can triumph in the test. If he does not use it, he will fall. The decision is his. We need not enter here into the reasons why God permits the tempting. Sufficient it is to say that they are always good and intended to have man earn the glory held out to him.

Over and above this grant of sufficient grace, the Lord in his mercy can grant a superabundant amount of grace. Grace is a divine force. It is this force, both of sufficient and of abundant grace, which counteracts the power of Satan.

The Pope has many trials both as an individual and as official head of the Church. If he were left to his own devices in the suffering of them he would be defeated. Happily, he is not left to his own devices. He has the divine assurance of constant and abundant help.

This was explicitly promised. "All power in heaven and on earth has been given to me. Go, therefore, and make disciples of all nations, baptizing them in the name of the Father, and of the Son, and of the Holy Spirit, teaching them to observe all that I have commanded you; and behold, I am with you all days, even unto the consummation of the world." (Matthew XXVIII, 18-20)

Christ is in his Church personally and through the person of the Holy Spirit whom he sends. Personally, he directs. It is his Church; he is the head and as head he is always in command. He is the one who transmits to the body its impulses to actions, he is the one who unifies the operations and sanctifies the whole. As St. Paul put it, we "grow up in all things in him who is the head, Christ. For from him the whole body (being closely joined and knit together through every joint of the system according to the functioning in due measure of each single part) derives its increase to the building up of itself in love." (Ephesians IV, 15-16)

Personally, too, he is present, not only as God who is everywhere by his essence, his presence and his power, but physically as the God-Man through the Sacrament of His Love, the Eucharist. In this Blessed Sacrament he is present in body and blood, soul and divinity. In this great and sweet Mystery of Faith he gives himself utterly as sacrificial victim for a renewed calvary, as meat and drink for the soul, and as a pledge of our future glory. He had said: "I am the bread of life. He who comes to me shall not hunger, and he who believes in me shall never thirst. I am the bread of life. Your fathers ate the manna in the desert and have died. This is the bread that comes down from heaven, so that if anyone eat of it, he will not die. I am the living bread that has come down from heaven. If anyone eat of this bread he shall live forever, and the bread that I will give is my flesh for the life of the world." (John VI, 35 and 48-52)

Could he be closer to the Church than by this device of his love eternally planned and definitely executed on the night before his death? "I will not leave you orphans," he had promised. (John XIV, 18). The Church is his own mystical body and in her is his precious blood which, coursing through her frame, keeps her alive, energetic and holy.

He is present too by the person of the Holy Spirit. "When he, the Spirit of Truth, has come, he will teach you all the truth. For he will not speak on his own authority, but whatever he will hear he will speak, and the things that are to come he will declare to you." (John XVI, 13)

The Holy Spirit keeps the Church from error and inspires all her holy resolves. To him is entrusted the actual sanctification of her members, from him proceed all her right counsels and just works.

The Vicar of the Savior as the chief member of the Church receives all these general benefits of the divine dispensing, and some special ones as sole visible head.

Having received the commission from Christ to feed his lambs and sheep, to be their rock of unity, and to hold the keys of the kingdom, it was natural for the Lord to confer on him personally a special strength. Again we quote: "I have prayed for thee (Peter), that thy faith may not fail." (Luke XXII, 32) This special strength is called in theology, sacramental grace, which is a particular grace given to one so that he can properly perform the office to which he has been called. The measure of this grace is given according to need. Because he has the most vital and exacting office on earth, he is given a superabundant amount of it. When Christ confers an office or power, he wants it to be exercised not only properly but perfectly. He grants his grace accordingly, and by correspondence to this grace the Pope can be perfect in the discharge of his office.

No matter then the burdens, the menaces, or the temptations of the devil. Christ is behind his Vicar with more than sufficient grace to have him succeed.

Christ has a special love for his priests. They are his by the eternal bond of the Order of Melchisedec; they are his *alter egos* performing his own saving functions; they are his anointed. For the high priest among them he must have a particular predilection. "Every high priest taken from among men is appointed for men in the things pertaining to God, that he may offer gifts and sacrifices for sins. He is able to have compassion on the ignorant and erring, because he himself is beset with weakness, and by reason thereof is obliged to offer sins as on behalf of the people, so also for himself. And no man takes this honor to himself; he takes it who is called by God, as Aaron was." (Hebrews V, 1-4)

Did he not show this special love for his priests by insisting on washing their feet before they sat down to that eucharistic supper with him? And did he not show a particular regard for Peter when he directly insisted, despite Peter's protest, on washing his feet? "If I do not wash thee, thou shalt have no part with me." (John XIII, 8)

Christ so much wanted part with Peter, and he wants part with Peter's successor. It is proper to think that as a father who sends a boy on an important errand watches him closely so that he can be on hand if a danger arises, so does Christ watch closely his Vicar and is ready to help him if difficulties arise. And as a mother hen might hover over her chicks, (Our Lord's own example: Matthew XXIII, 37), Christ's spirit hovers over his Vicar lovingly, protectively, and helpfully. For all their own weaknesses and even occasional derelictions of duty, the record of his Vicars remains incomparably grand. It is grand because Christ has been with them. It is miserable in spots, not because Christ was not with them, but because they, in their exercise of free will, chose not to utilize the strength he offered them.

Pope John is not one who will ignore this proffered strength. All his life he has abided in the love of Christ. As a farmer he knows how a branch receives its life—from the vine. He knows he is a branch and must abide in the vine, which is Christ.

He repeats what his first predecessor voiced when on Mount Tabor he saw the transfigured glory of the Savior: "Lord, it is good for us to be here." (Matthew XVII, 4) He is conscious of the trust reposed in him, and he has shown by his acts so far that he intends to be faithful to the trust.

Christ loves fidelity. It was one of the reasons why he chose Peter. Peter was firm in faith, and despite that exceptional incident in the courtyard of the high priest, Christ loved him for his fidelity. Peter had boasted: "Even if I should have to die with thee, I will not deny thee!" (Matthew XXVI, 35) He denied him that same night. "At that moment a cock crowed. And Peter remembered the word that Jesus had said, 'Before a cock crows, thou wilt deny me three times.' And Peter went out and wept bitterly." (Matthew XXVI, 74-75) This bitter weeping, and his constant fidelity thereafter, redeemed the fault and retained Christ's affection for him.

Pope John has been the recipient of Christ's special regard.

Is it not Christ's doing that he, a poor farmer's son, should now be Pope, the Rector of the World? Is it not Christ's doing that this boy raised in a rude hamlet should know how to talk with diplomatic finesse with the elite of the world? With us men it is often a practice to promote one to a higher post so as to get rid of him in a lower post wherein he is proving obnoxious. Christ does not do that. When he promotes, it is because he trusts one to serve well in a higher post as a reward for having done well in a lower. "Well done, good and faithful servant; because thou hast been faithful over a few things, I will set thee over many." (Matthew XXV, 21)

Christ loves simplicity. "Behold, I am sending you forth like sheep in the midst of wolves. Be therefore wise as serpents and guileless as doves." (Matthew X, 16) John is direct and simple. For all his training in diplomacy which fosters intrigue, he retains the simplicity of a man of the soil. Christ loved Peter for his simplicity, and he must love John as well since this virtue is apparent in the new Pope.

Christ loves chastity. A farmer's boy sees nature in the raw and the desire to mate sweeps early and strongly in him. Angelo, true to his name, however, determined to enter the Catholic priesthood which demands of one chaste and celibate living. "O how beautiful is the chaste generation with glory; for the memory thereof is immortal, because it is known both with God and with men. When it is present, they imitate it, and they desire it when it has withdrawn itself, and it triumpheth crowned forever, winning the reward of undefiled conflicts." (Wisdom IV, 1-2) On the Mount, the Master had spoken this beatitude: "Blessed are the clean of heart, for they shall see God." (Matthew V, 8) The Apostle John, beloved above all his brethren for this virtue, wrote later: "These (the pure) follow the Lamb wherever he goes. These were purchased from among men, first-fruits unto God and unto the Lamb." (Apocalypse XIV, 4)

Christ loves obedience. He himself was obedient unto death. Joseph, the foster-father of the Lord, was magnificent in obedience. Angelo Joseph shines in this virtue. He has been a model of obedience from the time he was a boy. On his heraldic shield is the legend: *Obedientia et Pax*, Obedience and Peace. He obeyed his father, his seminary rectors, his bishops, Pope Pius XI, Pope Pius XII, and finally the mandate of the College of Cardinals in conclave assembled. Thus he has been obedient to God, and because he has in this manner confessed the Christ before men, Christ confesses him before his Father in heaven.

In the beautiful Litany of the Sacred Heart, there is found this petition: "Heart of Jesus, from whose fullness we have all received, have mercy on us." If we ordinary members of his mystical body have received a fullness, what shall we say of him who is the chief member of the mystical body?

Is Christ ever indifferent to his own? The Good Shepherd has a care for his sheep. "I pray for them; not for the world do I pray, but for those whom thou hast given me, because they are thine, and all things that are mine are thine, and thine are mine, and I am glorified in them. And I am no longer in the world, but these are in the world, and I am coming to thee. Holy Father, keep in thy name those whom thou hast given me, that they may be one even as we are. While I was with them, I kept them in thy name. Those whom thou hast given me, I guarded; and not one of them perished, except the son of perdition." (John XVII, 9-12)

If he has this care of his sheep, even of the lost ones for whom he goes seeking in brambles and wilderness, has he not a tender solicitude for his chief assistant?

Is not the beautiful story of the walking of Peter on the

sea significant of this solicitude for his Vicar? Let us quote it as St. Matthew reports it in XIV, 25-33:

> In the fourth watch of the night, he came to them walking on the sea. And they seeing him walking upon the sea, were greatly alarmed, and exclaimed, "It is a ghost!" And they cried out for fear. Then Jesus immediately spoke to them, saying, "Take courage; It is I; do not be afraid."
>
> But Peter answered him and said, "Lord, if it is thou, bid me come to thee over the water." And he said, "Come." Then Peter got out of the boat and walked on the water to come to Jesus. But seeing the wind was strong, he was afraid; and as he began to sink, he cried out saying, "Lord save me!" And Jesus at once stretched forth his hand, and took hold of him, saying to him, "O thou of little faith, why didst thou doubt?

Conscious of the great mission consigned to him and of the protection promised to him, the Vicar becomes bold to attempt a great thing, and the Lord encourages him in it. But the work becomes too big for the man, and he is about to fail. Again and again, Christ stretches forth his hand to save his Vicar. And this, in short, is the simple story of the papacy. Christ is always behind his chief steward lest he perish. The steward's work is Christ's own work, and he will see to it that despite any human frailty it will not fail.

Before he entered into his passion, he gave to his chosen ones the inspiration and the norm of victory in their own passion. "Peace I leave with you, my peace I give to you; not as the world gives do I give to you. Do not let your heart be troubled, or be afraid." (John XIV, 27)

Pope John XXIII has accepted his great burden protesting that he is in fear and trembling. The fear of the Lord is the beginning of wisdom, and this very wisdom takes out of John the fear of himself as the Master bade him to do. Christ, the Shepherd of this visible shepherd of his Church, the Master Fisherman of this fisher of men, is the Emmanuel of

Earth; he is God with us. He is the divine power behind his Vicar always stretching out his strong, right hand to uphold him lest he sink through his own weakness or by reason of the furious storms which the gates of hell hurl against him.

With God with him, he will not fail. The Bark of Peter has weathered every sort of tempest, and it shall weather this present one. John is at the helm, a John beloved of the sweet Star of the Sea, who is Mary, and of her divine Son, the Master Mariner, who unerringly guides the Vessel of Honor, which is his Church, to the harbor of grace and of salvation.

Date Due

NOV 27 '63			
JAN 6 '64			
JAN 20 '64			
3/12/68			
5/20/68			
DEC 19